Best Hikes Near
Denver and Boulder

SECOND EDITION
SANDY HEISE AND MARYANN GAUG

FALCONGUIDES

GUILFORD, CONNECTICUT

FALCONGUIDES®

An imprint of Globe Pequot
Falcon and FalconGuides are registered trademarks and Make Adventure Your Story is a trademark of Rowman & Littlefield.

Distributed by NATIONAL BOOK NETWORK

Copyright © 2017 by Rowman & Littlefield

A previous edition of this book was published by Falcon Publishing, Inc., in 2010.

Maps by Melissa Baker © Rowman & Littlefield

All photos by Sandy Heise unless otherwise noted

British Library Cataloguing-in-Publication Information available

Library of Congress Cataloging-in-Publication Data available
ISBN 978-1-4930-2481-0 (paperback)
ISBN 978-1-4930-2482-7 (e-book)

∞™ The paper used in this publication meets the minimum requirements of American National Standard for Information Sciences—Permanence of Paper for Printed Library Materials, ANSI/NISO Z39.48-1992.

Contents

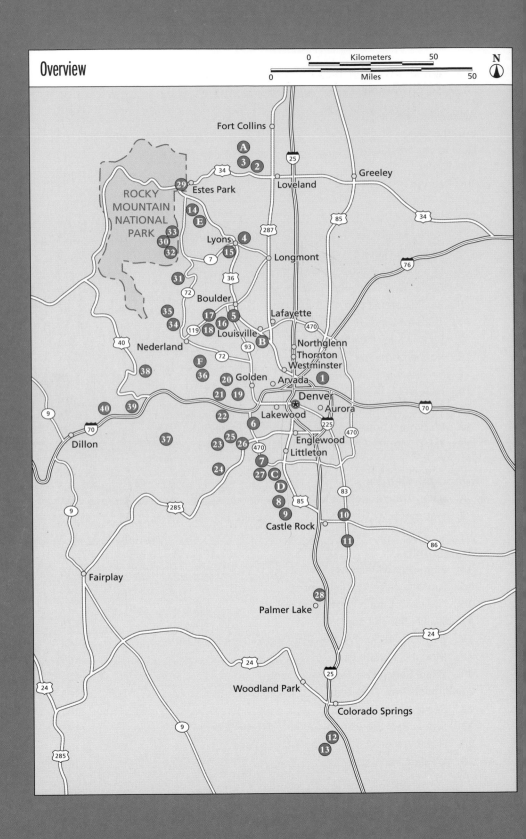

Honorable Mentions

The Mountains 216

Honorable Mentions

Acknowledgments

My great appreciation to those who joined me on these hikes: Beth Utton, Kitty Turner, Patty Tweed, Chris Klotz, and Dotty Fox. I couldn't ask for better friends and hiking partners. Much gratitude to Maryann Gaug for creating another wonderful hiking guide and then passing it on to me. Updating this book has been a joyful journey! Thanks to the whole team at Falcon.

Maryann and I would like to thank all of the contacts in the many different agencies responsible for the lands and the trails in this book. These wonderful people work for City and County open space departments, City mountain parks, Colorado State Parks, USDA Forest Service, National Park Service, and US Fish and Wildlife Service. They took time from busy schedules to answer questions, review chapters and provide feedback.

We would especially like to thank all those who not only saw the need to preserve open spaces and wildlands, but who followed through on their visions. Over the years, many people have continued working to create the wonderful collection of parks and open space properties, along with the national forests, parks, and wildlife refuges that we enjoy today in Colorado's Front Range. Thanks also go to the citizens in the various cities and counties for consistently voting to tax themselves to purchase and preserve more lands, not only for recreation and urban buffers, but also to protect wildlife habitat. We all owe a great debt to these people and to the people who continue the work of maintaining existing properties and procuring new ones.

Thanks to all the individuals in the many volunteer groups who help the land management agencies with everything from trail maintenance and construction to fund-raising to keep these places so very special. Please consider joining one of these groups to add your talents to help in whatever way is needed.

To all of those I met on the trails, thanks for your good cheer and fun stories. I truly enjoy the diversity and enthusiasm of people that I get to chat with while spending time in my favorite places.

Many thanks to you readers and fellow hikers for buying *Best Hikes Near Denver and Boulder*. We hope you find it useful and interesting, and that you enjoy many hours exploring and appreciating the trails described between these covers.

—Sandy Heise

"I could walk forever with beauty. Our steps are not measured in miles but in the amount of time we are pulled forward by awe." —Terry Tempest Williams

Introduction

Hikers in the Denver and Boulder area, rejoice! Within about an hour's drive, you can experience every facet of hiking in Colorado except western canyon country. From open prairies to old ranches preserved as parks in the foothills, to crystal clear mountain streams and lakes, you can select a terrain and hike length to suit you on any given day. With such beautiful public lands so close, you have no excuse to stay at home. Time to take a hike!

The spine of mountains that lie easternmost in Colorado from the Wyoming border to about Castle Rock is known as the Front Range. To confuse everyone, the cities just east of this mountain range are also called the "Front Range."

Since 1912, people living in the Front Range have seen value in preserving land and in wandering about in natural areas to recreate and replenish their spirits. As mentioned in the acknowledgments, we're so grateful to many people over the last hundred-plus years for having the foresight to obtain, preserve, and maintain precious lands for the enjoyment of all, now and for the indefinite future. While hiking across these beautiful areas, we've often said "thanks" when a trail would suddenly wind past a subdivision or when a new, huge house appeared in the backdrop of a familiar area. If these lands had not been preserved, they would probably be covered with hundreds of houses by now. A healthy balance between development and preservation serves everyone in these communities.

Colorado blue columbine, the state flower.

Because the Denver metro area is roughly 30 by 40 miles, we used the metro-area beltways as the "starting" places for the hour drive.

Cities, Counties, the State of Colorado, USDA Forest Service, National Park Service, and US Fish and Wildlife Service have all designated lands for both recreation and wildlife preservation, from the eastern edge of Denver west to the Continental Divide. Whether you enjoy wildlife, geology, or history, or just want to get away from the hustle and bustle of the city, you can't go wrong living in the Denver–Boulder area. Many people move to this thriving metropolis because so many outdoor amenities are available within relatively short distances.

For this book, we chose a variety of newer trails and some of our favorite hikes that have been around for a while, like those in Boulder's Open Space & Mountain Parks (OSMP) and Rocky Mountain National Park (RMNP). Many open space parks with excellent trails have been established since the early 1990s, and we enjoyed exploring new terrain for this book. We chose a number of hiker-only or hiker/equestrian-only trails to highlight those opportunities.

This book is divided into three sections: Plains, Foothills, and Mountains. This division creates three north–south strips, each higher in elevation than the one to the east. In each strip, we started with hikes closer to Boulder, and ordered them by which highway you take from Boulder, Golden, or Denver. The strips are useful in determining hiking seasons and winter snow depth. You can hike many of the plains trails year-round except after a major snowstorm. Some shady areas may harbor snow or ice, so be aware and prepare for that. Most of the mountain trails are not snow-free until late June.

Plains hikes include those in "flatter" areas to the east of the foothills. Some hikes climb mesas towering over surrounding lowlands. Wildflowers, grasses, and wonderful views—not to mention some spectacular geology and remains of plants and dinosaurs from millions of years ago—reward hikers. These trails can be easier to get to when the weather is less than optimal or if your time is limited.

Foothills are the lower mountains that rise abruptly from the plains. Mostly covered in ponderosa pine and Douglas fir, these trails offer a variety of steepness and usually provide good viewpoints along the way. Many include historical features, from old railroads to the remains of mansions. Others explore former ranch lands with interesting rock formations. Roughly speaking, this strip is east of the north/south sections of State Highway (SH) 119, SH 72, and SH 7, and west of the "flat" plains.

The mountain hikes take you to beautiful lakes, wonderful wildflowers, and scenic vistas. Roughly speaking, this strip is west of the north/south line drawn by SH 119, SH 72, and SH 7.

You may wonder why some popular parks or areas are not included in this book. Occasionally, a land management agency requested that we not include certain areas due to overuse or user conflicts. With so many options from which to choose, eliminating these areas just made room for other wonderful hikes.

Because of the varied elevations of the three sections in the book, here are some guidelines for approximate times when trails dry out (from the USDA Forest Service Dillon Ranger District). Check with the listed land management agency for current trail information.

- Below 9,500 feet—mid-May
- Between 9,500 and 10,000 feet—end of May
- Between 10,000 and 10,500 feet—mid-June
- Between 10,500 and 11,500 feet—July 1
- 11,500 feet and above—mid-July

A word about the details in this book: Featured trails were all rehiked during 2015 and spring/summer 2016. The information is as accurate as possible from that timeframe.

A golden-mantled ground squirrel near Gem Lake.

A bristlecone pine with male cones and dots of resin on its needles.

Determining trail mileage is as much an art as a science, even for land managers. We used Global Positioning Systems (GPS) to obtain these mileages. In some areas, poor satellite reception may have provided less-than-accurate information. Please realize that trail locations and conditions, roads, and signage are subject to change over time. Even trailheads can move, and some trails are rerouted to prevent environmental damage, or as a result of fire or flood damage. Finding accurate historical information was sometimes interesting when different books contained conflicting information! We tried to find appropriate websites, only to discover that URLs change rapidly or sites don't get updated.

Henry David Thoreau said, "In wildness is the preservation of the world." Aldo Leopold added, years later: "When we see land as a community to which we belong, we may begin to use it with love and respect." Our wish for you is to enjoy hiking and learning about yourself and the world around you, to which we all belong. Remember, only *we* can preserve wildlands for ourselves and future generations.

As you hike these trails, which are all easily accessible from the Denver–Boulder area, capture part of nature's spirit and hold it close to your own so that, no matter where you travel or live, the peace and beauty of this wild country will remain with you always.

Front Range Weather
An interpretive display at the Moraine Park Museum in Rocky Mountain National Park explains: "Climate is what you expect. Weather is what you get."

Difficult to forecast and prone to change quickly, Colorado's weather is a wonder in itself. A temperature drop of 10°F to 20°F in one hour is not unheard of. Along the Front Range, March and April are the snowiest months, and September often has the most sunshine. Snow sometimes buries Denver and the foothills in either late September or October and also in mid-May, killing newly planted gardens and damaging trees. The majority of precipitation along the Front Range falls from April through September. The average annual precipitation in Denver is about 17 inches.

A low-pressure system sitting in Colorado's southeastern corner often produces the state's worst weather. The counterclockwise circulation pushes storms up against the mountains, where they may sit for a few days. Another weather event, typically occurring from November through March, is the chinook wind. These warm "snow-eater" winds blow over the Continental Divide, picking up speed like a waterfall descending the east slope. With hurricane force, they blast the area between Colorado Springs and Fort Collins. In the autumn of 1986, 131-mile-per-hour winds were recorded in Boulder.

Normal high springtime temperatures in Denver range from 52°F in March to 71°F in May, making hiking pleasant on the plains. During spring, the foothills—rising up to 4,000 feet higher than the plains—can be snowy in places and dry in others. You'll need skis or snowshoes in the mountains.

A yellow-bellied marmot foraging near the Chasm Lake Trail. Marmots are the largest of the ground-dwelling squirrels.

Summer brings temperatures in the 80s, 90s, and even 100s to the Denver metro area. This is a great time to escape to the high mountains, where snow usually melts by July 4, and flowers peak in mid-July to early August. Colorado experiences a monsoon starting about mid-July and ending in early September. Moist air combines with the forces that produce thunderstorms, making the afternoon event more a certainty than a rarity. Three problems can result from thunderstorms: One is lightning, a killer from above; the second is a flash flood, which can roar out of nowhere, destroying everyone and everything in its path; the third is more subtle—rain in Colorado tends to be cold, and unprepared hikers can become hypothermic very quickly, even in the middle of summer.

Autumns can be beautiful, with normal high temperatures in Denver ranging from 77°F in September to 53°F in November, and are a great time to hike and enjoy gorgeous fall colors!

An interesting rule of thumb: For every 1,000 feet of elevation gained, the temperature drops about 4°F. When it's 80°F in Denver at 5,280 feet, it may be only 49°F at the top of 13,132-foot Mount Flora, the highest point in this book.

Flora and Fauna

The hikes in this book range in elevation from 5,080 feet to 13,132 feet, across about 60 miles "as the crow flies." In the rain shadow of the Rocky Mountains,

Larkspur.

Orange paintbrush.

the plains are high and dry with about 17 inches of precipitation per year. As you travel west and up in elevation, moisture increases, especially with winter snows. Summer high temperatures at these higher altitudes may only reach 50°F. With such extremes in a short distance, a wide variety of flora and fauna call Colorado home.

In the high plains around Denver, shortgrass, midgrass, and tallgrass prairie dominates the landscape, depending on elevation and moisture. As the land rises, you pass through mountain shrublands, juniper, ponderosa pine, Douglas fir, mountain grasslands and meadows, mountain wetlands, lodgepole pine, aspen, spruce fir, limber and bristlecone pine, and alpine tundra ecosystems. Some of these communities favor shady, cooler areas while others prefer hot and dry ones.

As you hike through different ecosystems, notice what plants and animals live among which trees and the different soil types. For example, aspens grow in moist, protected areas. Bushes such as chokecherry, gooseberry, serviceberry, and snowberry provide browse (vegetation eaten by animals) for mule deer. Grasses and other plants offer good eats for elk, who also scrape the bark off of aspens in winter. Black bears often leave claw marks while climbing their favorite aspen trees. The pink Woods' rose, blue and white columbine (the Colorado state flower), mariposa lily, white geranium, strawberry, and blue lupine are a few of the flowers you'll see. Keep an ear open for the chick-a-dee-dee-dee call of the mountain or black-capped chickadee.

Prairie dogs, mule and white-tailed deer, coyotes, and pronghorns rule the plains. Little critters provide food for coyotes, foxes, eagles, hawks, and even the great horned owl. Elk, mule deer, and black bears live in forested areas, while mountain lions prowl the rocky slopes. On cliffs and rocky steeps, mountain goats and Rocky Mountain bighorn sheep somehow survive and thrive. Long gone are grizzly bears and wolves. Canada lynx were recently reintroduced in the mountains amid much controversy. You can still see bison at Rocky Mountain Arsenal National Wildlife Refuge (RMANWR), Daniels Park, and Genesee Park.

The plains are mainly grasslands, with cottonwood trees along watercourses. Several types of cactus and yucca can make for painful experiences. Watch out for rattlesnakes, too.

As you gain elevation, animals and plants show their adaptations to shorter summers, less oxygen, colder temperatures, and high winds. Above treeline, you can't miss the cute little pikas scurrying around with mouths full of grasses, or the lazy marmots sunning themselves on rocks. Chipmunks, ground squirrels, and marmots might approach you aggressively, expecting a handout. Please don't feed wild animals! Handouts from humans could cause them to stop foraging for themselves. Several species of birds are easy to spot: crows, magpies, blue Steller's jays with their black crowns, and pesky Clark's nutcrackers and gray jays (nicknamed "camp robbers").

Fishing in Colorado can be superb. Native cutthroat trout are making a recovery after introduced sport fishes, such as rainbow and brown trout, almost outcompeted them.

If summer has experienced normal or greater precipitation, mushrooms pop out in August and early September. Many mushrooms are poisonous, while others are edible and incredibly delicious. Don't pick any unless you know what you're doing!

Bristlecone pines grow in Colorado, most commonly south of I-70. These incredible trees live 1,500 to 2,000 years in our state. Between the alpine tundra and spruce-fir or limber pine ecosystems, you'll find *krummholz* (German for "crooked wood"). These stunted trees, usually Engelmann spruce, subalpine fir, or limber pine form shorter tree "islands" with a few flag trees sticking up. The deadwood on the windward side of these islands protects the rest of the tree organism, so please don't use it for firewood.

The most incredible plants grow above treeline: alpine forget-me-nots, sky pilot, moss campion, old-man-of-the-mountain, alpine avens, Parry's clover, and more. Each flower has its own particular niche, whether on wind-blown slopes or next to sheltering rocks. If you have a chance, learn about this incredible land above the trees and what you can do to protect it.

Leave No Trace

Everyone needs to pitch in to keep our Earth clean, beautiful, and healthy. Please follow Leave No Trace (LNT) practices whenever you're outdoors. Visit LNT.org for more information.

Leave No Trace Principles (from LNT.org)

Please understand and practice these principles whenever you spend time outdoors:

- Plan ahead and prepare
- Travel and camp on durable surfaces
- Dispose of waste properly (including dog poop bags and food scraps)
- Leave what you find
- Minimize campfire impacts
- Respect wildlife
- Be considerate of other visitors

The Leave No Trace program establishes a widely accepted code of outdoor ethics to help ensure a sustainable future for parks and wildlands. Originating in the 1970s with the USDA Forest Service, Leave No Trace was developed to help recreationists minimize their impacts on the natural environment while enjoying the outdoors. In the early 1990s, the Forest Service teamed with the National Outdoor Leadership School (NOLS) and the Bureau of Land Management as partners in the Leave No Trace program "to develop hands-on, science-based minimum-impact education training for recreational activities."

The Leave No Trace Center for Outdoor Ethics incorporated as a nonprofit organization in 1994 with the mission "to protect the outdoors by teaching and inspiring people to enjoy it responsibly." The Center unites federal land management agencies—the USDA Forest Service, National Park Service, Bureau of Land Management, and US Fish and Wildlife Service—with manufacturers, outdoor retailers, user groups, educators, and individuals who share a commitment to maintaining and protecting our natural lands for sustainable enjoyment. The LNT program now reaches millions of people around the world with direct training and educational tools.

"In its simplest form, LNT is about making good decisions to protect the world around us—the world we all enjoy." For more information, call the Center for Outdoor Ethics at 800-332-4100, 303-442-8222, or visit LNT.org

Leave No Weeds

Noxious weeds can be harmful to wildlife and entire ecosystems. These weeds tend to crowd out our native flora, which in turn affects animals and birds that depend on them for food. Yes, just like birds and furry critters, we humans can carry weed seed from one place to another. To minimize the spread of noxious weeds:

- Learn to identify noxious weeds and exotic species. The Colorado Weed Management Association is a good source of information; check them out at cwma.org
- Regularly clean your boots, tents, packs, hiking poles, and vehicles of mud and seeds. Brush your dog, horse, goat, or llama to remove any weed seed.
- Avoid camping and traveling in weed-infested areas.

Trail Etiquette

The American Hiking Society (AmericanHiking.org) has compiled an excellent list of guidelines that we can all follow to increase our enjoyment (and the enjoyment of our fellow hikers) of time out on the trails. In addition to the Leave No Trace principles, please:

- Yield to uphill hikers when you're heading downhill.
- Move off the trail when you're taking a break so that others can easily pass by you.
- Don't take up the whole width of the trail when hiking in a group; allow others to pass.
- Hike quietly. Turn your cell phone down, if not off. Leave the music at home and enjoy the sounds of nature, while letting others do the same.
- Take everything out with you that you brought in, including bags of dog poop, banana/orange peels, apple cores, and any other food scraps. Food peels and cores might be "natural" but they are still garbage.
- If you need to relieve yourself but a facility is not nearby, go 200 feet away from the trail and any source of water.

Thanks for being a courteous hiker!

Getting Around

Public transportation in Denver and Boulder is mostly via Regional Transportation District (RTD) buses or light rail. While you can take a bus throughout both cities and even up to Nederland, Lyons, Parker, Evergreen, and Conifer, getting to the trailheads in this book unfortunately requires a vehicle. For information on RTD routes and fares, take a look at rtd-denver.com; new stops and routes are occasionally developed. You can also call them at 303-299-6000.

Area Codes

The Front Range area of Colorado is split into three telephone area codes. The Denver metro area and towns roughly up to the Continental Divide use 303 and 720. This includes the area from Castle Rock on the south to Longmont on the north. For Colorado Springs and points south and east and somewhat west, the area code is 719. For the rest of the state, including Loveland and Fort Collins, the area code is 970.

> 🍂 **Green Tip:**
> *Keep your dog on a leash unless you are certain it can follow your voice commands. Even then, keep the leash handy and your dog in sight. Do not let it approach other people and their pets unless invited to do so. Some people are afraid of all dogs. Even if your dog is usually well-behaved, it may suddenly act differently around strangers. Never allow your dog to chase wildlife.*

Dog waste has become a problem on some trails. Please deposit waste bags in a trash container, not along the trail.

Sugar Bowl.

Cell Phones and GPS Units

A word of caution: Cell phone coverage is lacking on many of the trails and even some of the state highways mentioned in this book. On a few hikes, drainages are narrow and GPS units have trouble connecting with enough satellites for good readings.

Road Information

Call the Colorado Department of Transportation (CDOT) at 303-639-1111. Or visit them at cotrip.org for road conditions, closures, construction status, and maps or webcams.

How to Use This Guide

Take a close enough look and you'll find that this guide contains just about everything you'll ever need to choose, plan for, enjoy, and survive a hike near Denver and Boulder. Stuffed with over 300 pages of useful Denver/Boulder-specific information, *Best Hikes Near Denver and Boulder* features forty mapped and cued hikes, along with six honorable mentions. Here's an outline of the book's major components:

Each section begins with an **introduction to the region,** in which you're given a sweeping look at the lay of the land. Each hike then starts with a short **summary** of the hike's highlights. These quick overviews give you a taste of the hiking adventures to follow. You'll learn about the trail terrain and what surprises each route has to offer.

Following the overview, you'll find the **hike specs:** quick, nitty-gritty details of the hike. Most are self-explanatory, but here are some details on others:

Distance: The total distance in miles of the recommended route—one-way for loop hikes, the round-trip on an out-and-back or lollipop hike, point-to-point for a shuttle. Options add additional mileage.

Hiking time: The average time it will take to cover the route. It is based on the total distance, elevation gain, and condition and difficulty of the trail. Your fitness level will also affect your time.

Difficulty: Each hike has been assigned a level of difficulty. The rating system was developed from several sources and personal experience. These levels are meant to be a guideline only and may prove easier or harder for different people, depending on ability and physical fitness.

Easy—4 miles or less total trip distance in one day, and/or elevation gain less than 600 feet, and/or paved or smooth-surfaced dirt trail, and/or with less than a 6 percent average grade.

Moderate—Up to 8 miles total trip distance in one day, and/or elevation gain of 600 to 1,200 feet, and/or with a 6 to 8 percent average grade.

Difficult—Up to 12 miles total trip distance in one day, and/or elevation gain of 1,200 to 2,500 feet, and/or trail with an 8 to 10 percent average grade.

Most-Difficult—Up to 16 miles total trip distance in one day, and/or elevation gain of 2,500 to 3,500 feet, and/or trail that may not be well-defined in places, and/or a trail with a 10 to 15 percent average grade.

Strenuous—Mainly reserved for peak climbs. Trails are greater than 15 percent grade on average.

Elevation gain: From the GPS track on the topo maps, we calculated the elevation at the lowest

and highest points, rounding to the nearest 20 feet. If the trail undulated a lot, we calculated elevation gain for the various undulations and added it on.

Trail surface: General information about what to expect underfoot.

Seasons: General information on the best time of year to hike.

Other trail users: Such as horseback riders, mountain bikers, inline skaters, and others.

Canine compatibility: Know the trail regulations before you take your dog hiking with you. Dogs are not allowed on several trails in this book, or they must be kept on leash. Failing to follow these regulations can result in fines.

Land status: National forest, county or city open space, national park, wilderness, etc.

Fees and permits: Whether you need to carry any money with you for park entrance fees and permits.

Maps: This is a list of other maps to supplement the maps in this book. Be aware that the USGS maps are often out-of-date and do not show many of the trails in this book or the trails that were rerouted since the map was last revised.

Trail contact: This is the address, website URL, and direct phone number for the local land manager(s) in charge of all the trails within the selected hike. Before you head out, get trail access information, or contact the land manager after your visit if you see problems with trail erosion, damage, or misuse.

Other: Other information that will enhance your hike.

Special considerations: This section calls your attention to specific trail hazards, like a lack of water, hunting seasons, or potentially dangerous flora and fauna.

The **Finding the trailhead** section gives you dependable driving directions from Boulder, Golden, I-25 or I-70 right to where you'll want to park. **The Hike** is the meat of the chapter. Detailed and honest, it's a carefully researched impression of the trail. It also often includes lots of area history, both natural and human. Under **Miles and Directions**, mileage cues identify all turns and trail name changes, as well as points of interest. **Options** are also given for many hikes to make your journey shorter or longer depending on the amount of time and energy you have. The **Hike Information** section provides information on local events and attractions, hiking tours, and hiking organizations.

Each regional section ends with **Honorable Mentions,** detailing some of the hikes that didn't make the cut, for whatever reason—in many cases it's not because they aren't great hikes, but because they're overcrowded or environmentally sensitive to heavy traffic. Be sure to read through these. A jewel might be lurking among them.

Don't feel restricted to the routes and trails that are mapped here. Be adventurous and use this guide as a platform to dive into the Front Range backcountry and high plains, and discover new routes for yourself. One of the simplest ways to begin this is to just turn the map upside down and hike a route in reverse. The change in perspective is often fantastic, and the hike should feel quite different. With this in mind, it'll be like getting two distinctly different hikes on each map. For your own purposes, you may wish to copy the route directions onto a small sheet of paper to help you while hiking, or photocopy the map and cue sheet to take with you. Otherwise, just slip the whole book in your backpack and take it with you. Enjoy your time in the outdoors and remember to pack out what you bring in. NEVER leave used toilet paper on the ground; bring a zip-lock bag to put it in, and bring it out with you for proper disposal.

How to Use the Maps

Overview map: This map (see page iv) shows the location of each hike in the area by hike number (or in the case of honorable mentions, by letter).

Route map: This is your primary guide to each hike. It shows all of the accessible roads and trails, points of interest, water, landmarks, and geographical features. It also distinguishes trails from roads, and paved roads from unpaved roads. The selected route is highlighted, and directional arrows point the way.

Soaring along the Devil's Backbone.

Trail Finder

Hike No.	Hike Name	Best Hikes for Back-packers	Best Hikes for Waterfalls	Best Hikes for Geology Lovers	Best Hikes for Dinosaur Lovers	Best Hikes for Children	Best Hikes for Dogs	Best Hikes for Peak Baggers	Best Hikes for Great Views	Best Hikes for Lake Lovers	Best Hikes for Canyons	Best Hikes for Nature Lovers	Best Hikes for History Lovers
1	Rocky Mountain Arsenal National Wildlife Refuge Loop					●						●	●
2	Devil's Backbone Loops												
3	D. R. Trail to Mahoney Park												
4	Eagle Wind Trail—Rabbit Mountain						●		●				
5	Big Bluestem Loop												
6	Trails for Dinosaur Lovers												
7	South Valley Park Loop												●
8	Roxborough State Park Loops												
9	Swallowtail Trail												

Hike No.	Hike Name	Best Hikes for Backpackers	Best Hikes for Waterfalls	Best Hikes for Geology Lovers	Best Hikes for Dinosaur Lovers	Best Hikes for Children	Best Hikes for Dogs	Best Hikes for Peak Baggers	Best Hikes for Great Views	Best Hikes for Lake Lovers	Best Hikes for Canyons	Best Hikes for Nature Lovers	Best Hikes for History Lovers
10	Hidden Mesa Trail												
11	Castlewood Canyon State Park Loops			●							●		
12	Blackmer Loop—Cheyenne Mountain State Park											●	
13	Talon Loops—Cheyenne Mountain State Park			●								●	
14	Homestead Meadows	●					●						●
15	Nighthawk Trail—Hall Ranch												●
16	Green Mountain West Ridge Trail							●	●				
17	Walker Ranch Loop								●			●	●
18	Rattlesnake Gulch Trail—Eldorado Canyon State Park			●					●		●	●	●

Hike No.	Hike Name	Best Hikes for Backpackers	Best Hikes for Waterfalls	Best Hikes for Geology Lovers	Best Hikes for Dinosaur Lovers	Best Hikes for Children	Best Hikes for Dogs	Best Hikes for Peak Baggers	Best Hikes for Great Views	Best Hikes for Lake Lovers	Best Hikes for Canyons	Best Hikes for Nature Lovers	Best Hikes for History Lovers
19	Mount Galbraith Park												
20	White Ranch Park Northwest Loop	●							●				
21	Travois Trail—Centennial Cone Park						●						
22	Beaver Brook Trail												
23	Sisters/Bearberry Loop—Alderfer/Three Sisters Park								●				
24	Shadow Pine Loop—Flying J Ranch Park					●	●						
25	O'Fallon Park Loop						●						
26	Mount Falcon Park Upper Loop												●
27	Bill Couch Mountain—Deer Creek Canyon Park							●					
28	Spruce Mountain Loop						●		●				

Hike No.	Hike Name	Best Hikes for Backpackers	Best Hikes for Waterfalls	Best Hikes for Geology Lovers	Best Hikes for Dinosaur Lovers	Best Hikes for Children	Best Hikes for Dogs	Best Hikes for Peak Baggers	Best Hikes for Great Views	Best Hikes for Lake Lovers	Best Hikes for Canyons	Best Hikes for Nature Lovers	Best Hikes for History Lovers
29	Gem Lake								●	●			
30	Sandbeach Lake								●	●		●	
31	Buchanan Pass Trail 910	●							●				
32	Ouzel Falls and Lake	●	●						●	●			
33	Chasm Lake		●	●					●	●			
34	Caribou Ranch Loop					●							●
35	Arapaho Glacier Trail 905			●					●				
36	Black Bear/Horseshoe Loop—Golden Gate Canyon State Park	●											●
37	M. Walter Pesman Trail—Mount Goliath Natural Area					●		●	●				
38	Mount Flora Trail						●		●			●	
39	Griffin Monument												●
40	Herman Lake						●			●			

Map Legend

Transportation

═╤70╤═	Freeway/Interstate
═85═	U.S. Highway
═83═	State Highway
═1431═	Other Road
═ ═ ═ ═	Unpaved Road
= = = = =	4WD Road
⊢—⊢—⊢	Railroad

Trails

▬▬▬▬	Featured Trail
- - - - -	Trail or Fire Road
→	Direction of Travel

Water Features

⬭	Body of Water
▥	Glacier
⸖	Swamp
〜	River or Creek
⸏⸱⸏	Intermittent Stream
≋	Waterfall

Symbols

⏝	Bridge
■	Building/Point of Interest
▲	Campground
⸾	Gate
❓	Information/Visitor Center
⛫	Lookout Tower
▲	Mountain/Peak
P	Parking
⊞	Picnic Area
⛊	Ranger Station
⚐	Restroom
⮜	Scenic View
○	Town/City
20	Trailhead
⊢—⊣	Tunnel
⬛	Water

Land Management

▭	State/Local Park
⬚	Open Space/ Conservation Area
▢	National Park/Forest/ Wildlife Refuge

Trail Ratings

Easy

Moderate

Difficult

The Plains

The Big Bluestem Loop in Boulder.

These thirteen hikes explore a geological wonderland of tilted rocks rising like spear points and hogback ridges that provide homes for raptors and other birds. One hike takes you to fascinating outdoor dinosaur and ancient-life exhibits, while another offers great wildlife viewing opportunities.

The plains are those "flatter" areas east of the foothills and include mesas that rise from the plains. Hikes start as low as 5,000 feet and rise to 6,860 feet. They vary in length from 0.85 to 8.4 miles. With temperatures reaching over 90°F in the summer, hiking these trails is best done either during early summer mornings or in the spring and fall. Most trails are hikeable year-round except after a big snowstorm.

To understand the plains today, let's head back in time. About 355 million years ago, Colorado sat near the equator. The Ancestral Rockies were uplifted from the seas and formed part of the supercontinent Pangaea. As time progressed, the mountains eroded. The present Rocky Mountains were uplifted starting 70 million years ago. As they rose, the bordering land arched, creating hogback ridges. Erosion wore away softer materials, leaving some interesting tilted rock formations like the flatirons near Boulder and the freestanding rocks in Roxborough State Park and South Valley Park. Volcanic activity 25 million years ago created plateaus and several mountain ranges. As the mountains eroded, the debris pretty much buried

Explore a geological wonderland of tilted rocks rising like spear points and hogback ridges that provide homes for raptors and other birds.

them. Then 25 to 5 million years ago, the entire region began to rise 5,000 feet to its present high elevation. Streams washed away the accumulated debris.

Prehistoric Native Americans wintered among these interesting rock formations and hogbacks starting about 12,000 years ago. Stone hunting blinds in the alpine tundra date back 7,500 years. By AD 100, these people made pottery and hunted with bows and arrows. Each summer they crossed the Continental Divide to hunting grounds in North Park, Middle Park, and South Park. After AD 1300, other Native American groups like the Cheyenne and Arapaho moved into the eastern plains. Later, ranchers and farmers tried to tame the land to produce food for hungry miners and city-bound entrepreneurs. Today's parks were mostly obtained from private landowners.

Signs are posted at many trailheads that warn of rattlesnakes and caution hikers to stay on trails. The snakes are easier to see on trails than off in the grasses and bushes. The signs explain that snakes will usually slither away as you approach, but keep an eye open, especially if you're hiking with a dog. Some rattlesnakes will just look at you and not move. They react to motion and any perceived threat, so keep your distance and don't panic.

Enjoy hiking in these special areas. They provide habitat for a variety of wildlife and birds, so look around while hiking. You may spot a deer in the bushes, prairie dogs yapping their warnings, or a raptor soaring overhead.

Rocky Mountain Arsenal National Wildlife Refuge Loop

Established by Congress in 1992, Rocky Mountain Arsenal National Wildlife Refuge (RMANWR) is a work in progress. Over the years, the 1- to 2-mile-wide buffer around the old chemical weapons plant provided a refuge for prairie animals and birds as the Denver metro area expanded. White-tailed deer, mule deer, eagles, prairie dogs, hawks, waterfowl, burrowing owls, and bison thrive on the refuge. Black-footed ferrets, the most endangered mammal species in North America, were reintroduced to this Refuge in October 2015. This gem is close to Denver, yet so serene. Enjoy watching wildlife on your hike through shortgrass prairie, woodlands, and wetlands rich in farming and military history. RMANWR offers many different wildlife-viewing tours and nature programs.

Start: Trailhead by interpretive signs southwest of Visitor Center
Distance: 5.9-mile loop
Hiking time: 1.75 to 2.75 hours
Difficulty: Moderate due to distance; an easier loop is available.
Elevation gain: 40 feet
Trail surface: Natural surface trail, crusher fines, dirt road, and some paved roads
Seasons: Best Mar through Nov. Avoid hot summer days—visit in early morning.
Other trail users: Hikers only; anglers around Lakes Mary and Ladora (Apr through Oct)
Canine compatibility: Only assistance animals allowed
Land status: National wildlife refuge
Fees and permits: None required
Schedule: Open year-round sunrise to sunset seven days a week (closed federal holidays). Check website or call Visitor Center (9 a.m. to 4 p.m. Wed through Sun, closed on all federal holidays) before heading out to hike.
Maps: USGS Montbello
Trail contact: US Fish and Wildlife Service, Rocky Mountain Arsenal National Wildlife Refuge, 6550 Gateway Road, Building 121, Commerce City; 303-289-0930; www.fws.gov/refuge/rocky_mountain_arsenal
Other: Please stay on designated trails and roadways. Obey all posted signs. Alcohol and controlled substances are prohibited.
Special considerations: Bring water with you, as no drinking water is available on trails.

Finding the trailhead: From I-70 in Commerce City, take exit 278, Northfield/Quebec Street; head north on Quebec 2.6 miles to Prairie Parkway/64th Avenue. Turn right onto Prairie Parkway; drive 0.6 mile to Gateway Road. Turn left onto Gateway Road; continue 1.1 miles to the Visitor Center. Check in at Visitor Center, where water, restrooms, exhibits, and a bookstore are available. Then drive 1.7 miles to the Contact Station and park by the trailhead. Or, walk 1 mile on the Legacy Trail from the Visitor Center to the Lake Mary Trail near the Contact Station. You can also ask for directions at the Visitor Center.

THE HIKE

Originally shortgrass prairie, RMANWR was home to antelope, deer, gray wolf, and bison. Arapaho and Cheyenne tribes made their living here before homesteaders arrived in the late 1800s. The bombing of Pearl Harbor in 1941 changed the fate of these 27 square miles (17,000 acres) of land. The US Army bought land from farmers and built a chemical weapons manufacturing complex, the Rocky Mountain Arsenal.

After World War II, the army leased some facilities to private companies to offset operational costs and maintain the complex for national security. One company manufactured agricultural pesticides. Although waste generated during production years was disposed of according to accepted practices in those days, part of the Arsenal became contaminated. It was declared a Superfund site in 1987. The entire cleanup program was completed in 2010.

Looking across Lake Ladora at the snow-capped Rockies in springtime.

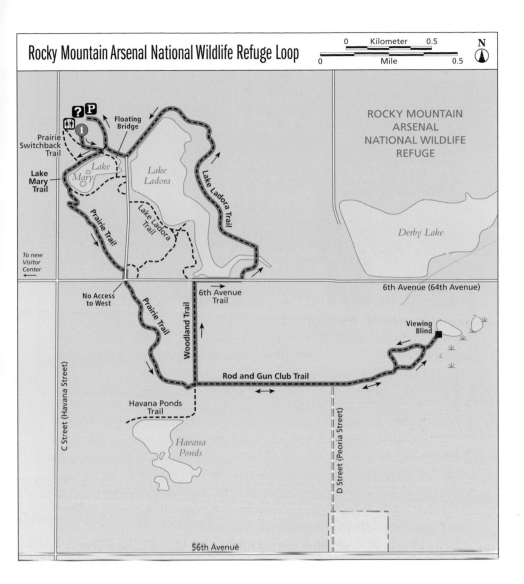

Rocky Mountain Arsenal National Wildlife Refuge Loop

As a result of the buffer zone established around the manufacturing facilities, over the years a large animal population began to thrive in the Arsenal. With the discovery of a communal roost of bald eagles, the US Fish and Wildlife Service (the Service) became involved in the area. In 1992, Congress designated the Rocky Mountain Arsenal National Wildlife Refuge, which at 15,000 acres is one of the largest urban wildlife refuges in the country. Exhibits in the Visitor Center and interpretive signs at several trail junctions relate more historic and natural history details.

During your first visit, take a free, guided, nature program or a wildlife-viewing tour (available by phone reservation). Then take a hike! The Service also offers numerous environmental education classes to schoolchildren.

A floating bridge snakes along the east side of Lake Mary.

This featured loop takes you on a tour of the various facets of RMANWR. Swallows and songbirds fly around Lake Mary, while ducks and geese enjoy the water. The Prairie Trail takes you past several prairie dog colonies, whose members yip and yap warnings when you walk by. The Woodland Trail proceeds through an old homestead area. Cottonwoods line abandoned lanes, and elms, fruit trees, white poplars, New Mexico locusts, and even a ponderosa pine reveal a human touch. White-tailed deer, a woodland species, roam freely here. They bound away as you approach, white tails held high. RMANWR staff revegetated the old lanes and fields to restore the native shortgrass prairie. Native grass seed is collected and planted.

A viewing blind, down a spur trail off the Rod and Gun Club Trail, overlooks a wetland area where the vegetation is very different than along the Prairie Trail. Red-winged blackbirds sing a symphony, with other birds joining the chorus. The Lake Ladora Loop Trail presents opportunities to watch ducks, great blue herons, various shorebirds, and other waterfowl enjoying the lake. Watch for cormorants with their outspread wings. Deer wander around, browsing the grasses, casting a glance toward hikers.

RMANWR is an oasis in a bustling urban area. Check the website frequently for new interpretive programs and tours. Visit often when you have a little time. Watch the seasons change and take advantage of the many nature programs, kids programs, and tours that are offered throughout the year.

MILES AND DIRECTIONS

0.0 Start at the trailhead by the interpretive signs southwest of the Contact Station. Elevation: 5,210 feet. After 500 feet, reach a T-intersection with the Prairie Switchback Trail. Turn left and head to Lake Mary.

0.15 Come to a Y-intersection near more interpretive signs. Turn right (west) onto the Lake Mary Trail and soon cross a bridge.

0.2 Reach a junction with the Prairie Switchback Trail. Continue straight ahead.

0.4 Junction with the Prairie Trail. Turn right. At the top of the switchbacks, enjoy the antics of the prairie dogs.

0.9 Reach a junction with a road. Turn right and continue down this road until it reaches another road. Turn right.

1.0 At this junction with the 6th Avenue Trail (intersection of 64th Avenue and Joliet Street), go across the road to the continuation of the Prairie Trail. GPS: N39 48.78' / W104 51.67'.

1.6 Reach the four-way junction with the Woodland Trail, the Rod and Gun Club Trail, and Havana Ponds Trail. Go straight to continue the hike, heading east on the Rod and Gun Club Trail.

2.4 Arrive at the start/end of the Rod and Gun Club Trail loop. Turn right. There's a bench here.

2.5 Spur trail to the Rod and Gun Club viewing blind. Turn right onto the spur.

2.6 Viewing blind with interpretive signs and views of the wetland. GPS: N39 48.60' / W104 50.38'. Return on the spur.

2.7 Arrive back at the Rod and Gun Club Trail. Turn right to complete the loop.

2.9 Arrive back at the start/end of the Rod and Gun Club Trail loop. Turn right.

3.1 Continue west on the Rod and Gun Club Trail.

3.9 Return to the junction of Havana Ponds Trail and Woodland Trail. Turn right onto the Woodland Trail and continue north.

4.3   Turn right onto the 6th Avenue Trail.

4.5   Arrive at the Lake Ladora Loop Trail and turn left. Cross the arm of the lake on a floating boardwalk. Continue to the west and north roughly following the shore of Lake Ladora.

5.4   The trail curves over the Lake Ladora dam.

5.7   Turn right to return to the Contact Station. GPS: N39 49.18' / W104 51.66'.

5.8   Head to the left and walk through the picnic area to the Contact Station.

5.9   Arrive back at the Contact Station.

Options
1. For a very short and easy hike, walk the 0.9-mile lollipop from the Contact Station around Lake Mary and back.
2. For a 1.9-mile loop, start as in the featured hike, but at mile 0.9 turn left and look for a trail to the right that heads east. Turn and walk 0.25 mile to Lake Ladora Trail; turn left. At the paved road turn right, then in about 200 feet turn left on the trail that switchbacks down to Lake Mary. Turn left at the next junction, then right to walk on the floating bridge on the east side of Lake Mary. Follow the instructions from mile 0.15 above, in reverse, back to the Contact Station.
3. A number of different loops of varying lengths can be created by looking at the trail map.

HIKE INFORMATION

Local Information: Metro North Chamber of Commerce, Westminster; 303-288-1000; metronorthchamber.com
VISIT DENVER, The Convention & Visitors Bureau; 800-233-6837, 303-892-1112; denver.org
Aurora Chamber of Commerce; 303-344-1500; aurorachamber.org
Local Events/Attractions: Various nature programs and tours, fishing, and a self-guided Wildlife Drive; Refuge Roundup celebrating National Wildlife Refuge Week; RMANWR Visitor Center, Commerce City; 303-289-0930; www.fws.gov/refuge/rocky_mountain_arsenal
Denver Museum of Nature and Science; 303-370-6000; dmns.org
Denver Zoo; 720-337-1400; denverzoo.org
Hike Tours: RMANWR Visitor Center, Commerce City; 303-289-0930; www.fws.gov/refuge/rocky_mountain_arsenal
Organizations: Fish and Wildlife Volunteers at RMANWR; 303-289-0931; www.fws.gov/refuge/rocky_mountain_arsenal/what_we_do/get_involved
Friends of the Front Range Wildlife Refuges, RMANWR, Commerce City; 303-287-0210; ffrwr.org

🍃 Green Tip:

Carry a reusable water container that you can refill at the tap. Bottled water is expensive; lots of petroleum is used to make the plastic bottles; and they're a disposal nightmare. It's best to pre-cycle by not buying plastic items to begin with, even if you can recycle them.

Bison Reintroduced to the Plains near Denver

March 17, 2007, was a very special day at Rocky Mountain Arsenal National Wildlife Refuge (RMANWR). Sixteen bison from the National Bison Range (NBR) in Montana arrived at their new home. The US Fish and Wildlife Service ("the Service") will allow the herd to expand to approximately 210 animals over time. As of spring 2016, there are 74. Bison once roamed the shortgrass prairie where the Denver metro area now lies. This small herd helped the Service evaluate the bison's impact on RMANWR's native shortgrass eco-system. The Service operates a bison conservation program that includes the NBR, established in 1908 to save the American bison.

Some bison have been crossbred with domestic cattle. The DNA of the bison chosen for RMANWR was tested, and the results showed no cattle genes in their ancestry. By moving pure bison to different appropriate wildlife refuges in at least five states, the Service hopes to assure the long-term con-servation of the species.

The Service plans to double the size of the RMANWR bison habitat to 6,373 acres by the end of 2016, and their long-range plan is to increase this area to 12,000 acres—a majority of the Refuge!

The bison live in an enclosed area behind 8-foot-high steel fences, away from the trails. You can take a tour (by reservation only) to see these original natives of Colorado's eastern plains.

Devil's Backbone Loops

Hike up and down hogbacks and along the distinctive Devil's Backbone rock formation, experiencing the interesting geology firsthand. The area's human history is explained on several interpretive signs and in a trail guide available at the trailhead. Red-tailed hawks, ravens, swallows, and a great horned owl nest in the niches of the Backbone formation. The views are great, too! From prairie to rocky ridges to a lush little gully, the trail constantly changes. With three possible loops, you can find a short or long hike to suit your fancy. The trail system winds for over fifteen miles through Devil's Backbone Open Space, up to Horsetooth Mountain Open Space and Lory State Park. About midway, it connects with Coyote Ridge Natural Area to the east.

Start: Devil's Backbone Trailhead

Distance: 4.4 miles out and back, including two loops

Hiking time: 1.5 to 2.5 hours

Difficulty: Moderate due to length and some steep sections

Elevation gain: 480 feet, with two climbs

Trail surface: Natural surface trail

Seasons: Best Mar through Nov

Other trail users: Equestrians and mountain bikers on some sections; other sections are hikers-only

Canine compatibility: Dogs must be on leash

Land status: Larimer County Parks and Open Space

Fees and permits: None required

Schedule: Open year-round from sunrise to sunset

Maps: USGS Masonville

Trail contact: Devil's Backbone Open Space, Larimer County Department of Natural Resources, 1800 South County Road 31, Loveland; 970-619-4570; larimer.org/naturalresources

Other: These trails might be closed due to muddy conditions or other situations. Check current conditions before you go, at larimer.org/naturalresources/conditions.cfm

Special considerations: Beware of rattlesnakes. Bring water, as none is available along the trail.

Finding the trailhead: From I-25 exit 257-B, Loveland/US 34 West, drive west on US 34 (also known as Eisenhower Avenue) for 8.5 miles through town to Hidden Valley Drive. Turn right onto Hidden Valley Drive and head north for 0.3 mile to the Devil's Backbone, Larimer County Open Space sign. Turn left into the parking lot.

If the parking lot is full, please return another time. Vault toilets and water are available at the trailhead. Loveland can also be reached via US 287.

THE HIKE

Devil's Backbone Open Space (OS) has been assembled in pieces and, with the opening of the Blue Sky Trail, preserved lands extend from US 34 west of Loveland to Lory State Park west of Fort Collins. It all started in 1998, when Steven Wild sold a mile-long section of the Devil's Backbone to Larimer County Parks and Open Space Department. The grandson of Alfred Wild, who grew hops and apple trees, and started Colorado's first plaster industry with gypsum mined nearby, wanted the area "to remain as it always has." Fire clay found on Alfred's property was transformed into bricks in a kiln west of the formation and north of US 34. He built the "Buckhorn Northern," an unusual 2-foot-gauge railroad, which traveled under the Devil's Backbone through a tunnel. The tunnel was later blown apart.

Other large purchases creating today's Devil's Backbone OS include the Hunter parcel in 1999, followed by Hidden Valley and Indian Creek in 2003. Carl Fink owned the Hunter property from 1937 to 1947, raising cherry trees and silver foxes.

An outstanding feature of the Devil's Backbone is the Keyhole, a large window created by erosion. Many years ago, local historian Harold Dunning proposed the creation of an impressive entrance to the Rockies by enlarging the Keyhole down to road-level so cars could drive through it. Fortunately, that never happened.

Today, a pair of ravens nests near the Keyhole. This black bird has a thick beak and a scruffy, unkempt head with long shaggy feathers. Larger by about

The upper part of the Wild Loop Trail runs along the Devil's Backbone.

6 inches than its cousin, the crow, the raven sports a wedge-shaped tail, while the crow's tail is more rectangular or slightly rounded. Ravens build bulky nests of twigs, branches, dirt, moss, and other materials, typically on cliffs. They lay three to eight eggs, which incubate in about twenty-one days. Males attract females with flight maneuvers such as tumbles and barrel rolls. Their diet includes carrion, rodents, insects, seeds, and bird eggs.

Red-tailed hawks live along the Backbone. These raptors range over most of North America. Their upper tails are red with brown-gray banding on the lower edge. While hunting they hover and glide, looking for a tasty morsel of a small mammal, bird, or reptile. Devil's Backbone OS's population of black-tailed prairie dogs and rattlesnakes is like a food market for these birds.

A community of cliff swallows builds their nest on Devil's Backbone. These little birds (6 inches long) zoom and dive after insects. They mix mud with grass to build and attach their gourd-shaped homes to the cliffs. Breeding in North America in spring and summer, they fly to South America in the fall.

A great horned owl also nests in the Backbone. This impressive, daunting hunter has tufted ears and big yellow eyes. Mainly a nocturnal hunter, the owl typically perches while waiting for an unsuspecting meal to wander by. Its large menu includes insects, rabbits, domestic cats, skunks, mice, birds, reptiles, fish, geese, crows, great blue herons, and even red-tailed hawks. These owls live in the old stick nests of other raptors or niches in cliffs. On the plains in winter, you can often find a nest in leafless cottonwood trees, complete with an owl scanning the countryside.

Looking through the Keyhole in the Devil's Backbone, at snow-covered Mount Meeker and Longs Peak.

Wild Loop is an interpretive trail, and its west side traverses below the Backbone formation. A spur trail off of it heads west up to the Keyhole. Hunter Loop crosses a low, open grassland with a lone cottonwood tree, and then climbs up a gully with trees and bushes to a ridge with nice views south and east. You get a bird's-eye view of the Devil's Backbone from here.

MILES AND DIRECTIONS

0.0 Start from the Devil's Backbone OS Trailhead. Elevation: 5,120 feet. GPS: N40 24.71'/W105 09.16'. Pick up a Wild Loop Interpretive Guide at the bulletin boards near the restrooms if you'd like to read about points of interest along the first part of the hike. Please return this Guide at the end of your hike. Walk down the trail that starts in between the bulletin boards and the restrooms.

0.4 Junction with Wild Loop. There's a bench and signpost 2 (Pioneer Industrialist). Turn left to head up to a closer view of the Devil's Backbone formation. This section is hikers-only.

0.75 Spur trail goes to the left. Hike up to read about the history of the area and enjoy nice views of peaks in Rocky Mountain National Park (RMNP). Return back to Wild Loop, and turn left onto it.

1.0 Junction with Keyhole Loop. If the trail is open, head to the left and walk 0.1 mile to the Keyhole. If it's closed, continue straight ahead on Wild Loop.

1.2 Junction with Keyhole Loop from either trail. If you went to the Keyhole, turn left onto Wild Loop. If you didn't, continue straight ahead on Wild Loop.

1.3 Junction with Hunter Loop trail. Turn left. This section is multiuse (hikers, mountain bikers, and equestrians).

1.5 A short trail to the right leads to a cottonwood tree and cabin remains. Continue straight ahead on Hunter Loop trail, which heads somewhat steeply up a little gully.

1.9 Start/end of Hunter Loop. Turn right and climb up the little hogback. Reach a high point at 5,520 feet.

2.3 Junction with Laughing Horse Loop trail. GPS: N40 26.05'/W105 09.47'. Turn left to continue on Hunter Loop. This section is hikers and equestrians only.

2.6 Junction with Hunter Loop trail. Head right and go down the gully you came up earlier. This section is multiuse.

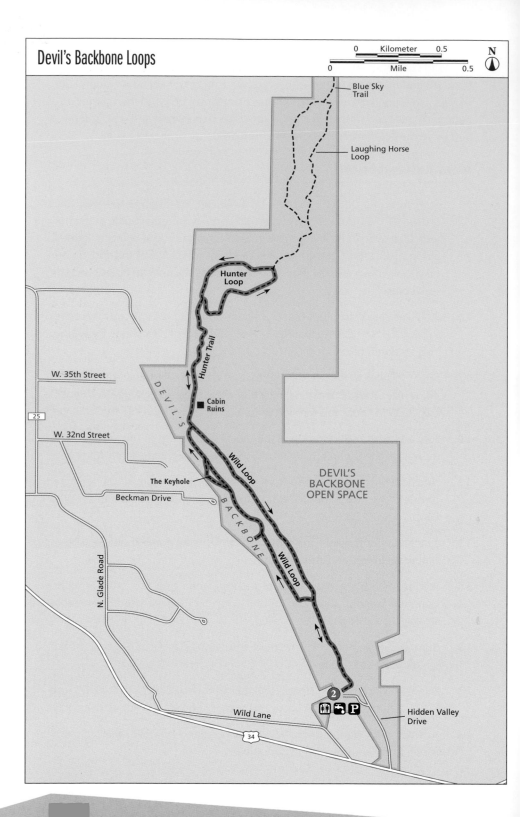

Devil's Backbone Loops

0 — Kilometer — 0.5

0 — Mile — 0.5

N

Blue Sky Trail

Laughing Horse Loop

Hunter Loop

Hunter Trail

W. 35th Street

25

Cabin Ruins

W. 32nd Street

D E V I L ' S

The Keyhole

Wild Loop

Beckman Drive

B A C K B O N E

DEVIL'S
BACKBONE
OPEN SPACE

N. Glade Road

Wild Loop

2

Wild Lane

Hidden Valley Drive

34

3.2 Junction with Wild Loop. For an easier and slightly shorter hike back to the trailhead, continue straight ahead on the east side of Wild Loop. This section is multiuse. (**Option:** To take a look at Devil's Backbone from the other direction, turn right and return the way you came. This section is hikers-only.)

4.4 Arrive back at the trailhead. If you took the west side of Wild Loop, the total is 4.5 miles at the trailhead.

Options

1. For a longer, 6.3-mile hike, at mile 2.3 above, turn right onto Laughing Horse Loop trail. This trail becomes quite rocky, with mini-flatirons in places. At 2.6 miles, turn right onto Laughing Horse Loop. At 3.2 miles continue straight ahead on Laughing Horse Loop. The Blue Sky Trail starts to the right. GPS: N40 26.59′ / W105 09.24′. At 3.4 miles is a little viewpoint to the right. Elevation: 5,520 feet. GPS: N40 26.50′ / W105 09.38′. Continue along Laughing Horse Loop to its end, turn right, and return the way you came, taking the west side of Hunter Loop for variety (mile 2.3 above).

2. For a 5.6-mile hike, at mile 2.3 above, turn right onto Laughing Horse Loop trail. This trail is quite rocky, with mini-flatirons in places. At 2.6 miles, turn left onto Laughing Horse Loop. Hike to the high point, which is a nice viewpoint off to the left. Elevation: 5,520 feet. GPS: N40 26.50′ / W105 09.38′. Return the way you came, or take the west side of Hunter Loop for variety.

HIKE INFORMATION

Local Information: Loveland Chamber of Commerce; 970-667-6311; loveland.org

Local Events/Attractions: Old Fashioned Corn Roast Festival; 970-667-6311; loveland.org

Loveland Loves Barbecue; 970-222-7772, lovelandlovesbbq.com

Loveland Stone Age Fair, Loveland Archaeological Society; 970-667-6311; stoneagefair.com

> 🐾 **Green Tip:**
> *When hiking in a group, walk single file on established trails to avoid widening them. If you come upon a sensitive area, spread out so you don't cut one path through the landscape, especially on the tundra. Don't create new trails where there were none before.*

Hike Tours: Larimer County Department of Natural Resources Education Program, Loveland; 970-619-4489; larimer.org/naturalresources/registration

Organizations: Friends of Larimer County Parks and Open Lands, Loveland; 970-619-4570; larimer.org/naturalresources/friends

Volunteers in Larimer County Parks and Open Lands, Loveland; 970-619-4552; larimer.org/naturalresources/volunteer

Friends of Larimer County Parks and Open Lands is a 501(c)(3) nonprofit organization that helps Larimer County protect and improve the relevance of public lands in people's lives, in local communities, and for future generations. The group holds yearly fundraisers to benefit improvements in a chosen park or two and even to help purchase new parks.

Loveland, the Sweetheart City

Loveland has long been known as the "Sweetheart City." A Valentine card remailing program was created in the 1930s when the Loveland Stamp Club decided that a hand-stamped Valentine cancellation on envelopes would be an interesting item for stamp collectors. The Chamber of Commerce became involved when they realized that the town, with its name, had a unique opportunity to share some love and friendship with people across America on Valentine's Day. Guy Lombardo was named honorary mayor of Loveland on February 14, 1950, giving this program nationwide exposure. Each year the Loveland Chamber of Commerce invites locals to submit designs and verses to be stamped on the Valentine envelopes. More than 200,000 cards are remailed each year. People from all 50 states and over 110 countries send their pre-addressed, stamped Valentine's cards in a separate mailer to the Loveland Post Office. Volunteers gently hand-stamp the design and four-line verse over the stamp and then remail the cards to their intended recipients.

D. R. Trail to Mahoney Park

Bobcat Ridge Natural Area opened to the public in 2006, with new trails added in 2007. Starting in prairie between a hogback and Green Ridge (the beginning of the foothills), the hike follows the Valley Loop Trail to a spur trail leading to an old cabin built in the early 1900s. Then it follows the D. R. Trail, which climbs through a ponderosa pine forest to Mahoney Park, a beautiful meadow ringed with hills and granitic rock formations. You'll hike through the scars of the 2000 Bobcat Gulch Fire, an area that is recovering with new trees and colorful wildflowers.

Start: Bobcat Ridge Natural Area trailhead kiosk
Distance: 8.4-mile lollipop
Hiking time: 3.25 to 5 hours
Difficulty: Difficult due to distance
Elevation gain: 1,260 feet
Trail surface: Accessible-grade (crusher fine and concrete) and natural surface trail
Seasons: Year-round
Other trail users: Mountain bikers on some sections; D. R. Trail open to hikers and equestrians only
Canine compatibility: Dogs not allowed at Bobcat Ridge Natural Area
Land status: City of Fort Collins Natural Areas Program
Fees and permits: None required
Schedule: Sunrise to sunset
Maps: USGS Masonville and Drake

Trail contact: City of Fort Collins Natural Areas Program, 1745 Hoffman Mill Road, Fort Collins; 970-416-2815; Bobcat Ridge Ranger Office 970-461-2700; fcgov.com/naturalareas
Other: Trails may be closed if they become very muddy during late winter/early spring due to snowmelt or after heavy summer rains. The cabin area may be closed for raptor nesting on nearby cliffs. Any trail or site closings will be posted at fcgov.com/naturalareas/status.php

Special considerations: Beware of rattlesnakes. Bring water, as none is available along the trail. Mountain lions, bears, and, of course, bobcats live in this area. Hunters use the national forest lands through which the D. R. Trail passes.

Finding the trailhead: From I-25 exit 257-B, Loveland/US 34 West, drive west on US 34 (also known as Eisenhower Avenue) for 10.6 miles through town to Larimer County Road 27 (LCR 27), which is right before the Big Thompson Elementary School. Turn right onto LCR 27 and drive north for 4.6 miles to the BOBCAT RIDGE NEXT LEFT sign. Turn far left onto LCR 32C, not into the private drive. The road turns to dirt as it crosses through the hogback (Buffum Canyon). Avoid this road if there is any chance of flash flood. The parking lot is 0.5 mile west. Vault toilets are available at the trailhead. Loveland can also be reached via US 287.

THE HIKE

The City of Fort Collins named Bobcat Ridge Natural Area after the Bobcat Gulch Fire of 2000 and for the small, wild feline that lives in foothills, mesas, and canyons, wherever bushes and woods provide shelter and food. The bobcats' favorite food is cottontail rabbit, but they eat other small animals like mice, voles, ground squirrels, amphibians, and birds. Measuring about 3 feet long, they are about twice the size of a house cat and have a short, 6-inch tail that gives them their name. Shy and secretive, they're seldom seen and avoid open areas and thick woods. While you may not see one on your visit to Bobcat Ridge, they do live here. Bobcats carved in sandstone greet you at the trailhead kiosk, the work of artist Robert Tully.

Heading north on the Valley Loop Trail.

Native Americans occasionally stayed in the valley between the hogback and Green Ridge. You'll pass a stone circle and interpretive sign along this hike. The stones may have held down the edges of a tipi or possibly been used for ceremonial or spiritual uses. The Arapaho lived along the foothills and plains in tipis made of bison skins, and depended upon the bison for food and materials.

Back in the 1870s, George Buffum settled along Buckhorn Creek, including the canyon that now bears his name, and raised sheep. Around the turn of the twentieth century, the Smith brothers owned land to the northwest of Buffum Canyon, where they operated a successful cattle ranch. In 1917, Ed Kitchen, with the help of the Smith brothers, built the log cabin you'll visit on this hike. Kitchen sharecropped the Smiths' land, as did several other families who lived in the cabin over the years. The cabin has been structurally stabilized and is now used for educational programs. Picnic tables and a water pump (not for drinking) have been installed nearby.

George Cline homesteaded Mahoney Park and land to the south in 1904. The name "Mahoney" remains a mystery. The Cline cabin burned in the 2000 Bobcat Gulch Fire.

In 1961, David Rice (D. R.) Pulliam purchased the property where Bobcat Ridge is today. D. R. was a successful businessman in Loveland and was involved in many community organizations. Although he and his wife, Ginny, did not live on their U Lazy U Ranch, he leased his land to caretakers who irrigated the fields, raised hay, and managed the Limousin cattle.

View of Milner Mountain above the trailhead parking lot.

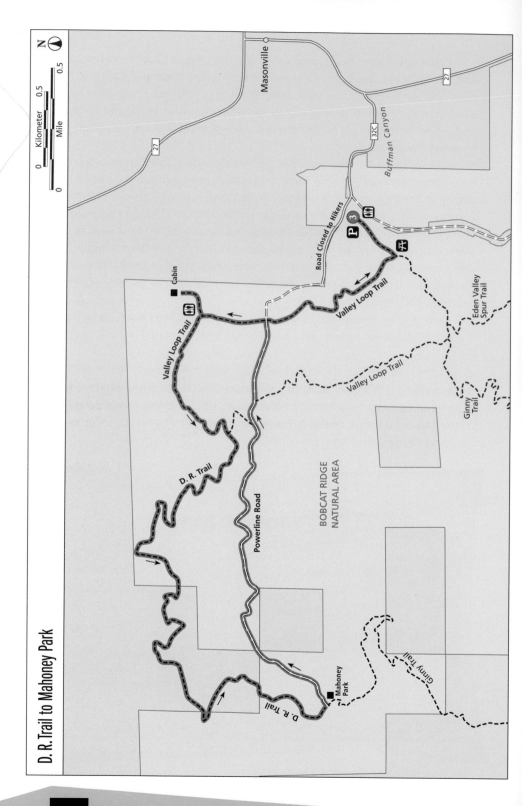

D. R. died in 1990 at the age of eighty-nine. The City of Fort Collins purchased the land in five phases starting in 2003. Valley Loop Trail opened in 2006, followed by the D. R. and Ginny Trails in 2007.

Hiking up the D. R. Trail, you'll come across ponderosa pines whose lower trunks were scorched in the Bobcat Gulch Fire in 2000. The bark of a mature ponderosa is fairly thick and fire-resistant. However, if the fire reaches the tree crown, the tree will burn, leaving skeleton-like remains. You can see these ghost trees to the south of D. R. Trail and in Mahoney Park. At least two other forest fires have occurred in the natural area in the last 200 years.

Pinkish humps of ancient igneous rocks, ponderosa pines, green grasses, and colorful wildflowers create the beauty of Mahoney Park. It's easy to understand why this gentle land surrounded by ridges became one of D. R.'s and Ginny's favorite spots.

The City of Fort Collins' Natural Areas Program offers many different programs and activities at Bobcat Ridge. Take advantage of these programs to learn more about the natural history and historical aspects of this beautiful area.

MILES AND DIRECTIONS

0.0 Start from the Bobcat Ridge Natural Area kiosk with interpretive signs about 0.1 mile from the vault toilet at the parking lot. This part of the trail is wheelchair-accessible pink concrete. Elevation: 5,440 feet. GPS: N40 28.76' / W105 13.59'.

0.1 Junction with Valley Loop Trail. Turn right (northwest) onto Valley Loop Trail. This part of the trail is wheelchair-accessible-grade gravel all the way to the cabin.

0.6 Several interpretive signs explain wetland and riparian habitat as the trail crosses a little drainage. The horse trail crisscrosses the hiking trail here.

0.9 Junction with Powerline Road. Continue straight ahead on Valley Loop Trail. At the next trail junction, continue straight ahead to see the cabin or turn left to continue on the Valley Loop.

1.2 Junction with spur trail to the cabin. Turn right here to see the old house and interpretive signs about the hogback and its residents, 0.3 mile out and back. Or, turn left to find a vault toilet. Picnic tables and a water pump (not for drinking) are available near the cabin. GPS: N40 29.46' / W105 13.85'. Return the way you came.

1.5 Arrive back at Valley Loop Trail and turn right to continue the hike. Please stay on the trail. You'll soon pass another spur trail on the right marked "Cabin." Stay to the left.

2.3 Junction with D. R. Trail. Turn right onto D. R. Trail, which will take you to Mahoney Park. This trail is open to hikers and equestrians only.

4.0 The trail weaves in and out of Roosevelt National Forest for the next mile. You'll start seeing evidence of the Bobcat Gulch Fire. Look at the bases of the ponderosa pines for bark blackened by fire. To the south, across the gulch, many trees died. GPS: N40 29.46′ / W105 15.37′.

5.0 Around a curve, a view of pretty Mahoney Park opens up. Come to an interpretive sign about the fire.

5.3 Interpretive sign about Mahoney Park.

5.5 Three-way junction in Mahoney Park where D. R. Trail, Ginny Trail, and Powerline Road converge. Elevation: 6,620 feet. GPS: N40 28.93′ / W105 15.77′. This area is great for a picnic, with big rocks to sit on. Turn left onto Powerline Road to return to the trailhead. Powerline Road is multiuse, but mountain bikers must ride uphill only. The road is fairly steep with some slippery sections (loose little rocks), especially when very dry. The trail goes in and out of national forest for the next 0.7 mile. There are nice views to the east along most of this trail.

6.1 The road reaches a Y. Single-track goes right and road continues straight ahead. Turn right onto the single-track trail (you could also hike down the road).

6.2 The road and trail merge back onto the road.

7.1 Junction with the west side of Valley Loop Trail. Continue straight ahead on Powerline Road.

7.2 A spur trail from Valley Loop Trail just about merges with Powerline Road. Continue straight ahead and downhill on Powerline. Just beyond is an interpretive sign about stone circles and the Native Americans who lived in this area. GPS: N40 29.20′ / W105 14.28′.

7.5 Junction with the east side of Valley Loop Trail. Turn right and return the way you came to reach the trailhead. (**Option:** Take a few moments to walk over to The Shelter and read the interpretive signs by the picnic tables; one describes the 2000 Bobcat Gulch Fire. Look through the binoculars to see close-up views of the area.)

8.4 Arrive back at the trailhead kiosk.

Option

For an easy 2.7-mile hike, follow the directions to the old cabin and return the way you came.

HIKE INFORMATION

Local Information: Fort Collins Convention and Visitors Bureau; 800-274-3678, 970-232-3840; visitftcollins.com

Visit Loveland; 970-667-3882, 800-258-1278; visitlovelandco.org

Local Events/Attractions: Anheuser-Busch Brewery Tours, Fort Collins; 970-490-4691; budweisertours.com

New Belgium Brewing, Fort Collins; 888-622-4044, 970-221-0524; newbelgium.com

Rocky Mountain Raptor Program, Fort Collins; 970-484-7756; rmrp.org

Loveland Stone Age Fair, Loveland Archaeological Society; 970-667-6311; stoneagefair.com

Hike Tours: City of Fort Collins Natural Areas Program; 970-416-2815; fcgov.com/naturalareas; register for activities at naturetracker.fcgov.com

Organizations: Volunteers for City of Fort Collins Natural Areas Program; 970-416-2480; fcgov.com/naturalareas/volunteers.php

The mission of Fort Collins' Natural Areas Program is "to conserve and enhance lands with existing or potential natural area values, lands that serve as community separators, agricultural lands, and lands with scenic values. Conservation of natural habitats and features is the highest priority while providing education and recreation for the Fort Collins community."

Eagle Wind Trail—Rabbit Mountain

With a little luck, you might see a golden eagle soaring above Rabbit Mountain, look-ing for a tasty lunch. The cliffs of Rabbit Mountain are one of the few places in Boul-der County where the magnificent birds still build their nests. The trail climbs through a variety of shrubs, grasses, and patches of ponderosa pine where Native Americans once lived and hunted. Views extend to Longs Peak and Mount Meeker, the Indian Peaks, Boulder's foothills, and down along the southern Front Range. They include a panoramic view of the plains to the north, east, and south. Spring brings colorful wildflowers to this peaceful island in the sky.

Start: Trailhead bulletin board
Distance: 4.0-mile lollipop
Hiking time: 1.5 to 2.5 hours
Difficulty: Easy
Elevation gain: 340 feet
Trail surface: Natural surface trail and old roads (closed to the motorized public)
Seasons: Best Apr through Nov. Avoid hot summer days—visit in the evening or early morning.
Other trail users: Equestrians and mountain bikers
Canine compatibility: Dogs must be on leash
Land status: Boulder County Parks and Open Space
Fees and permits: None required
Schedule: Open year-round from sunrise to sunset
Maps: USGS Hygiene, Carter Lake Reservoir; National Geographic Trails Illustrated 100 Boulder/ Golden; Latitude 40°: Boulder County Trails
Trail contact: Boulder County Parks and Open Space, 5201 Saint Vrain Road, Boulder; 303-678-6200; bouldercountyopenspace.org
Other: Camping and ground fires prohibited. Several parts of Rabbit Mountain Open Space are conser-vation easements and are closed to the public. The southeast part of Rabbit Mountain has a seasonal closure from Dec 15 through July 15 to protect nesting golden eagles. This hike does not go through the seasonal closure area. Please respect these closures.
Special considerations: Beware of rattlesnakes. Bring water with you because none is available along the trail.

Finding the trailhead: In Boulder, from 28th Street (US 36) and Canyon Boulevard (SH 119), head north on US 36 to its junction with SH 66, east of Lyons. Turn right (east) onto SH 66 and drive 0.9 mile to North 53rd Street. Turn left onto North 53rd Street and drive north 2.9 miles to Rabbit Mountain Open Space. (*Note:* North 53rd Street curves right onto Vestal Road, which curves left onto North 55th Street before reaching Rabbit Mountain Open Space.) Turn right into the parking lot. A vault toilet, group shelter, and picnic tables are available at the trailhead, but water is not.

THE HIKE

Rabbit Mountain rises out of the plains, but it's a little different from the other hogbacks along the foothills to the south. Rabbit is steeper on its east side, while the others rise slowly from the east to a steep drop-off on the west. The Fountain Formation, from which the Boulder Flatirons eroded, is still buried under Dakota sandstone, the Morrison Formation, and the Lykins Formation. Many moons from now some part of Rabbit Mountain may wear down into a Devil's Backbone formation or a flatiron.

The hogback is a mosaic of grasslands, shrubs, and patches of ponderosa pine. Prickly pear cactus and yucca, with its long bayonet leaves, also grow here, where plains and mountains intersect. A variety of wildlife lives here, from little mice, rabbits, and prairie dogs to prowling coyotes, foxes, and bobcats. Deer find shelter and elk visit. In the fall, listen for the high, eerie bugles of bull elk.

In order to determine how many of which type of carnivores live on Rabbit Mountain, Boulder County performed a two-year scent station survey. Four different habitat types were chosen and within each, nine stations were set up roughly 1,000 feet apart. Plots about 11 feet square were cleared of vegetation and rocks, and

A nice place to rest and take in the views of the Continental Divide.

then came the fun part: carrying fifty-pound bags of sand across uneven terrain, not to mention coming upon rattlesnakes. The sand was poured in the cleared area and smoothed so any critter traversing it would leave paw prints, and a pellet whose smell mimics animal urine was placed in the center. Each plot was checked the next day to see what inquisitive animals had walked across. The study ran monthly from June to October, and each month the plot was smoothed before placing another pellet.

Foxes and coyotes had visited most frequently, but bears, bobcats, and mountain lions had also wandered through. More elk tracks were seen than expected, so perhaps elk live at Rabbit Mountain year-round rather than only in winter. Researchers discovered that rabbits enjoyed dust baths in the sand.

The hike starts past a prairie dog village and climbs to a saddle through a land of mixed rocks, bushes, cactus, and flowers. In the saddle, the route crosses a dirt road (closed to the motorized public) and joins the Eagle Wind Trail. The Saint Vrain Supply Canal runs under the mountain, and an interpretive sign explaining the canal project sits along the trail, near where the tunnel carries the water underground.

The loop on Rabbit Mountain continues to bring interesting views at every twist and turn. Longs Peak and Mount Meeker poke their summits over intervening ridges. Farther along the trail, look back—you can see why French trappers called the two peaks *Les Deux Oreilles*, "the two ears." The Arapaho Indians called them *Nesótaieux*, "two guides." To the right are two lower, mostly forested peaks that appear symmetrical: Twin Sisters in Rocky Mountain National Park.

Many bushes line the trail. Mountain mahoganies' yellowish flowers produce a small fruit with a long, skinny plum. Skunkbush (a type of sumac) berries were used to make pemmican, a mixture of dried and pounded meat, melted fat, and fruits or berries pressed into small cakes or loaves; Indian women often wove the shrub's stems into baskets. Bitterbrush, sometimes called "deer ice cream"

Equestrians enjoying the Indian Mesa Trail near the Eagle Wind Trail.

because deer love to eat it, has leaves that look like a three-toed track. These three shrubs provide both food and cover for smaller animals, like rabbits.

Spring and fall are the best times to enjoy Rabbit Mountain. Summer days can be very hot. An excellent brochure about the history, geology, plants, and wildlife, along with a trail map, is available at the trailhead.

MILES AND DIRECTIONS

0.0 Start from the Rabbit Mountain Trailhead bulletin board. Elevation: 5,510 feet. GPS: N40 14.80' / W105 13.42'. To the right of the bulletin board, head up the trail that winds past the picnic shelter.

0.5 Junction of Little Thompson Overlook Trail and Indian Mesa Trail/Eagle Wind Trail. Turn right onto Indian Mesa/Eagle Wind.

0.6 Junction of Indian Mesa Trail (road) and Eagle Wind Trail. GPS: N40 14.97' / W105 13.03'. Cross the road to continue on Eagle Wind Trail.

0.8 Interpretive sign about the Saint Vrain Supply Canal. Soon after it, come to a bench on the left. The trail heads uphill and curves to the left. On the right is a spur trail to an overlook.

1.0 Start/end of Eagle Wind Loop. GPS: N40 14.69' / W105 12.79'. Turn right.

2.1 About the high point of the hike. Elevation: 5,850 feet. GPS: N40 14.28' / W105 12.17'. Seasonal closure sign for critical wildlife habitat to the east.

2.4 An old road comes in from the left and merges with the trail.

2.6 Old road goes to the left. Go right on Eagle Wind Trail.

2.9 Old road crosses the trail. Go straight ahead on Eagle Wind Trail.

3.0 Start/end of Eagle Wind Loop. Turn right to head back to the parking lot, cross the Indian Mesa Trail (road) and return the way you came.

3.5 At the junction of Little Thompson Overlook Trail and Indian Mesa Trail/ Eagle Wind Trail, turn left.

4.0 Arrive back at the trailhead.

Option

For a longer, moderate 5.9-mile hike, when you arrive back at the junction with Little Thompson Overlook Trail, 0.5 mile from the trailhead, turn right and follow this trail 1.0 mile to a bench and overlook. Return the way you came.

HIKE INFORMATION

Local Information: Lyons Area Chamber of Commerce; 303-823-6622 ext. 2; lyons-colorado.com

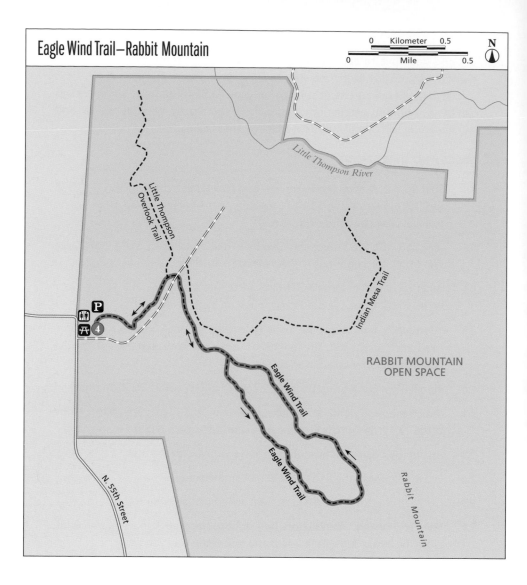

Local Events/Attractions: Oskar Blues Grill & Brew—Live Music, Lyons; 303-823-6685; oskarbluesfooderies.com/grill-and-brew

Rocky Mountain Folks Festival, Lyons; 303-823-0848, 800-624-2422; bluegrass.com/folks

RockyGrass Bluegrass Festival, Lyons; 303-823-0848, 800-624-2422; bluegrass.com/rockygrass

Hike Tours: Boulder County Parks and Open Space Hikes and Events; 303-678-6214; bouldercounty.org/os/events

Organizations: Boulder County Parks and Open Space Volunteer Program; 303-678-6216; bouldercountyopenspace.org/volunteer

Ponderosa pines have 4- to 7-inch-long needles that come in packets of two or three. These trees can grow 150 feet tall and live 300 to 500 years. Look for the dark gray Abert's squirrel, with its tufted ears. This little mammal lives exclusively in ponderosa pine forests.

The Colorado–Big Thompson Project

The Colorado–Big Thompson Project diverts 213,000 acre-feet of water from the west slope to northeastern Colorado to be used for agriculture, municipal water supplies, and industry. Water stored in Willow Creek Reservoir and from the Windy Gap Project is pumped uphill to Lake Granby (which is actually a reservoir). The Farr Pumping Station moves water from Lake Granby to Shadow Mountain Reservoir. Water then flows into Grand Lake, the largest natural lake in Colorado. From here the precious liquid is conveyed through the West Portal of the Adams Tunnel under the Continental Divide to Mary's Lake near Estes Park. A diagram on the interpretive sign along Eagle Wind Trail describes the distribution system on the eastern plains.

Although water is diverted from the Colorado River Basin, downstream users with water rights are still entitled to their share. When water is being diverted from the west slope reservoirs, Green Mountain Reservoir on the Blue River near Kremmling provides replacement water for those users. The Blue River flows into the Colorado River just downstream of Green Mountain Reservoir. The power plant below the dam has the capacity to generate 25.8 megawatts of electricity.

Big Bluestem Loop

Wander through tallgrass and mixed-grass prairie where cattle still graze, then hike up into the foothills thick with vegetation, in view of spectacular rock formations. In spring, the wildflowers and flowering bushes send sweet-scented fragrances wafting across the air. Fall brings colorful leaves and berries, which bears eagerly eat to fatten up before winter arrives. Devil's Thumb and The Maiden rock formations poke their heads into the sky as the land rises abruptly from the Mesa Trail. Sample the various ecosystems of Boulder's Open Space & Mountain Parks while hiking this scenic, moderate loop.

Start: South Boulder Creek West Trailhead

Distance: 6.8-mile loop

Hiking time: 2.7 to 3.5 hours

Difficulty: Moderate due to distance

Elevation gain: 940 feet

Trail surface: Natural surface trail and old road (closed to the motorized public), with some rocky sections

Seasons: Best Apr through Nov. Avoid hot summer days—hike in the evening or early morning.

Other trail users: Equestrians

Canine compatibility: Dogs must be leashed before exiting a vehicle at and around trailheads. Dog regulations vary from trail to trail and even seasonally; check osmp. org for dog regulations or call 303-441-3440. For example, all dogs must stay on a hand-held leash and remain on the trail on the Lower Big Bluestem Trail. Seasonal or daily (weekend) leash requirements may also exist on different sections of this loop to protect nesting birds and black bears. Observe all signage.

Land status: City of Boulder Open Space & Mountain Parks

Fees and permits: Daily or annual parking permit required if your vehicle is not registered in Boulder County. See fee station at trailhead.

Schedule: Open year-round

Maps: USGS Eldorado Springs and Louisville; National Geographic Trails Illustrated 100 Boulder/ Golden; Latitude 40°: Boulder County Trails

Trail contact: City of Boulder Open Space & Mountain Parks, PO Box 791, Boulder, CO 80306; 303-441-3440; osmp.org

Special considerations: Bring water with you, as it is often scarce along this loop and requires filtering. Cattle graze at the beginning and end of this hike. Keep your distance and do not harass them or allow your dog to harass them. Please close all gates behind you.

Finding the trailhead: In Boulder, from the intersection of Table Mesa Drive and Broadway (SH 93), drive south on SH 93 for 2.0 miles to South Boulder Creek West Trailhead. Make a right turn, then a quick left turn into the trailhead parking lot. Vault toilets and picnic tables are available, but no water.

THE HIKE

Big bluestem grass, also known as turkeyfoot for its trident-shaped seed head, is native to the tallgrass prairie. Its bluish leaves, which turn red-purple with age, give the grass its name. Although most of eastern Colorado consisted of dry shortgrass prairie before settlers arrived, this ecosystem—where the plains meet the mountains—contains enough moisture for big bluestem to grow between 3 and 8 feet tall. Accompanying big bluestem are little bluestem and blue grama grasses. They start their growth in spring, then bloom later in summer. Little bluestem can reach a height of 3 feet. Both big and little bluestem provide shelter for small animals and birds. Blue grama, the Colorado state grass, is easy to recognize because of its sickle-shape seed head. It's more typical of shortgrass prairie, but often mixes with little bluestem near the foothills. Birds such as the grasshopper sparrow and spotted towhee build their nests in these grasses.

A rare flower, the Ute ladies' tresses orchid, is found in only a few places in the West, including the wet meadows in Boulder's Open Space & Mountain Parks (OSMP). Cattle grazing and prescribed burns actually help the orchid's habitat. As you hike on the Big Bluestem and South Boulder Creek West Trails, you may

View of the Flatirons from the South Boulder Creek West Trailhead.

Big Bluestem Loop

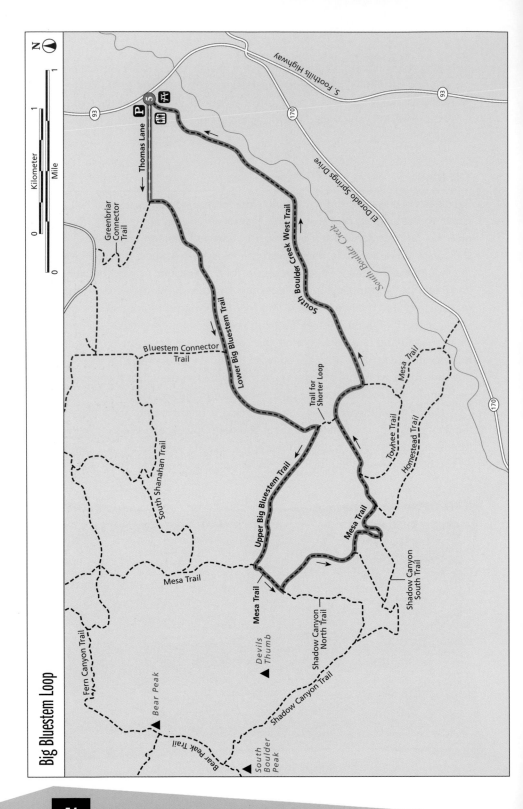

encounter grazing cattle. As explained in interpretive signs, livestock grazing is part of the management plan for the plains portion of OSMP.

Yucca, a member of the lily family, and prickly pear cactus, with its bright yellow flowers, grow among spring wildflowers such as blue to purple penstemon, pink geranium, yellow cinquefoil, and white chickweed. Where the earth retains more moisture, ponderosa pine, skunkbush, and Rocky Mountain juniper grow. Bushes flourish in drainages and gullies: chokecherry, wild plum, hawthorn, and many berry bushes—a gourmet restaurant for bears in the fall. Birds also love bushy places, and their songs produce a beautiful concert for your hike. Watch out for poison ivy in moister areas. Ferns flourish in wet shady spots.. This hike is great for watching how small changes in the lay of the land and a tad more moisture create different plant habitats.

Hiking across the open prairie affords great views of the flatiron-type rock formations and outcroppings such as Devil's Thumb and The Maiden, a skinnier version of another formation called The Matron. Boulder is famous for the tilted red rocks that jut from the east side of Green Mountain, like irons sitting on their sides. The slanted rocks near Bear Peak and South Boulder Peak have the same geologic history. About 300 million years ago, when Colorado straddled the equator, the Ancestral Rockies rose a little farther west of the current Front Range. Over time, erosion leveled the mountains, washing the red sand and gravel into alluvial fans. Buried later under the Cretaceous Interior Seaway, the eroded material was compressed into sandstone, now called the Fountain Formation. About 65 million years ago, the present Rocky Mountains started to rise and pushed the Fountain Formation up at an angle. As erosion wore down the overlying softer rock strata, the harder sandstone remained, creating interesting tilted formations.

As the trail becomes a single-track and heads up a drainage, you'll understand why Boulder is so named. The trail definitely becomes rockier. Water-bar steps help prevent erosion and make for a good leg workout. You can hike this loop year-round, though you may find some snowy and even icy spots depending on recent weather.

MILES AND DIRECTIONS

0.0 Start from the west end of the parking lot at the South Boulder Creek West Trailhead. Elevation: 5,460 feet. GPS: N39 57.61' / W105 14.21'. Turn right at the trail sign and walk to the dirt road, Thomas Lane. Turn left and walk west on Thomas Lane.

0.3 Arrive at a gate, which is the start of Lower Big Bluestem Trail, a double-track here. *Note:* Boulder OSMP personnel use this road for motor vehicle access.

Autumn colors painting the landscape.

0.5 Arrive at a gate. The double-track Lower Big Bluestem Trail curves to the left (south). Pass the junction with the Greenbriar Connector Trail on the right. (No dogs allowed on this connector).

0.9 Arrive at a gate, where a corral used to stand.

1.5 A trail comes in from the right, the Bluestem Connector to the South Shanahan Trail. Continue straight ahead on the Lower Big Bluestem Trail.

2.2 Come to the junction with the Upper Big Bluestem Trail. To the left, it connects with the Mesa Trail. Continue to the right (northwest) and ascend a gentle slope. GPS: N39 57.00′ / W105 16.02′. Pass through another gate, closing it behind you.

3.0 T-intersection with the Mesa Trail. Turn left (southwest) onto the Mesa Trail. Elevation: 6,330 feet. GPS: N39 57.21′ / W105 16.79′.

3.2 Junction with the Shadow Canyon North Trail. Continue to the left (southeast) on the Mesa Trail.

3.5 High point. Elevation: 6,400 feet.

3.7 Junction with another Shadow Canyon Trail. Continue to the left (southeast) on the Mesa Trail. GPS: N39 56.80′ / W105 16.79′.

3.9 Junction with the Shadow Canyon South Trail. Head to the left (north) on the Mesa Trail, which is now as wide as a road. GPS: N39 56.67′ / W105 16.60′.

4.1 Junction with the Homestead Trail on the right. Continue straight ahead (northeast) on the Mesa Trail.

4.3 Junction with the Towhee Trail on the right. (No dogs allowed on the Towhee Trail). Continue straight ahead (east) on the Mesa Trail. GPS: N39 56.74′ / W105 16.27′.

4.6 Junction with the Upper Big Bluestem Trail on the left. Continue to the right (southeast) on the Mesa Trail.

4.8 Junction with the South Boulder Creek West Trail. Turn left (northeast) onto this single-track. GPS: N39 56.72′ / W105 15.80′.

5.0 Arrive at a gate. Continue straight ahead on the South Boulder Creek West Trail.

5.5 Arrive at a gate. Continue straight ahead on the South Boulder Creek West Trail.

6.1 Arrive at a gate. Continue straight ahead on the South Boulder Creek West Trail.

6.5 Arrive at a gate. Continue straight ahead (north) on the South Boulder Creek West Trail.

6.6 Arrive at the last gate. Continue straight ahead (northeast) on the South Boulder Creek West Trail.

6.7 The trail joins another double-track. Turn left at the trail sign and continue to the trailhead.

6.8 Arrive back at the trailhead.

Option

For a shorter, easy 4.3-mile loop, start as above but make a left turn at mile 2.2, onto the Upper Big Bluestem Trail, and hike 0.1 mile to the Mesa Trail. Turn left onto the Mesa Trail and continue following the directions above from mile 4.6.

HIKE INFORMATION

Local Information: Boulder Convention and Visitors Bureau; 303-442-2911; bouldercoloradousa.com
Boulder Chamber of Commerce; 303-442-1044; boulderchamber.com
Local Events/Attractions: Colorado Shakespeare Festival, University of Colorado, Boulder; 303-492-8008; coloradoshakes.org

Colorado Music Festival, Chautauqua Auditorium, Boulder; 303-665-0599; comusic.org

Hike Tours: City of Boulder Open Space & Mountain Parks Nature Hikes & Programs; 303-441-3440; bouldercolorado.gov/osmp/nature-hikes

Organizations: City of Boulder Open Space & Mountain Parks Volunteer Program; 303-441-3440; bouldercolorado.gov/osmp/volunteer-program

Colorado Mountain Club, Boulder Group; 303-554-7688; cmcboulder.org

Frontcountry and Open Space Leave No Trace

Boulder and the Leave No Trace Center for Outdoor Ethics teamed up to create Leave No Trace on Open Space guidelines. Pick up a brochure at a trailhead.

1. Manage your dog

Wildlife, especially porcupines, can harm your pet. If your dog chases or harasses wildlife, the wild ones may get injured and definitely expend more energy than necessary, which can cause long-term health problems. Carry and use a leash as required.

2. Pick up poop

Dog poop is a health hazard and increases nitrogen in the soil, giving an edge to noxious weeds, which crowd out native plants. Please use a pick-up bag to pick up poop and deposit it in a trash can.

3. Trash your trash

Please remove all trash, including banana and orange peels, apple cores, and other food scraps. Scavengers attracted to trash can harm other wildlife.

4. Leave it as you find it

Please leave rocks, flowers, and arrowheads so others may enjoy them. Picking fruits and seeds deprives wildlife of a food source and seeds for new plants the next year.

5. Stick to the trail

Shortcutting trails causes erosion and can affect wildlife. When trail users walk around mud puddles, vegetation gets trampled, the trail and mud spot widen, and noxious weeds may take root, replacing native plants.

6. Share our trails

Please be courteous to other trail users.

Trails for Dinosaur Lovers

Dinosaur Ridge Trail, a National Natural Landmark, and the short Triceratops Trail are a must for dinosaur and ancient-life lovers of all ages. Dinosaur Ridge Trail is along West Alameda Parkway (closed to unauthorized vehicles), where the fossil remains of plants, footprints, and bones are impressive. Interpretive signs explain the journey through time presented by the various rocks and remains on the hogback. Triceratops Trail takes you to preserved remains of times long gone near Fossil Trace Golf Course. Both areas are outdoor natural history museums that provide a fun and educational journey close to home.

Dinosaur Ridge

Start: Dinosaur Ridge Visitor Center

Distance: 2.4 miles out and back

Hiking time: 1.5 to 2 hours

Difficulty: Easy due to distance and small elevation gain

Elevation gain: 170-foot gain and 40-foot loss

Trail surface: Dirt road shoulder, concrete sidewalk, and asphalt road

Seasons: Walkable all year when there's no snow on the ground

Other trail users: Tour buses and bicycles

Canine compatibility: Dogs must be on leash

Land status: Jefferson County Open Space

Trail contacts: Friends of Dinosaur Ridge, 16831 West Alameda Parkway, Morrison; 303-697-3466; dinoridge.org; Jefferson County Open Space, 700 Jefferson County Parkway, Golden; 303-271-5925; jeffco.us/open-space

Triceratops Trail

Start: Triceratops Trail parking lot

Distance: 0.85 mile out and back with short spur

Hiking time: 45 minutes

Difficulty: Easy due to length and minimal elevation gain

Elevation gain: 40 feet starting at trail's end

Trail surface: Concrete and gravel trail, with wooden stairs

Seasons: Walkable all year when there's no snow on the ground

Other trail users: Bikers on the recreation path

Canine compatibility: Dogs should be leashed (for safety) and kept off the golf course

Land status: City of Golden

Trail contact: Friends of Dinosaur Ridge, 16831 West Alameda Parkway, Morrison; 303-697-3466; dinoridge.org

For both

Fees and permits: None required

Schedule: Open year-round

Maps: USGS Morrison; National Geographic Trails Illustrated 100 Boulder/Golden

Other: You can purchase guidebooks for both trails at the Dinosaur Ridge Visitor Center.

For Dinosaur Ridge Trail, shuttle bus (Vanosaurus) transportation, which makes a loop about every 30 minutes, is available for a fee. Dinosaur Discovery Days are held the first or second Sat of each month May through Oct from 10 a.m. to 2:30 p.m.

Special considerations: Beware of rattlesnakes on both trails and falling rocks on Dinosaur Ridge Trail. No water is available on either trail. Please stay on Triceratops Trail and off the golf course and golf cart paths.

Finding the trailheads:

Dinosaur Ridge Visitor Center: From I-70 exit 260, C470/Colorado Springs, head south on C470 East for about 2.0 miles to the West Alameda Parkway exit. Turn right (west) onto West Alameda Parkway and drive 0.1 mile to the Dinosaur Ridge Visitor Center on the right. Turn into the Visitor Center parking lot. Vault toilets are available, but bring your own drinking water. The Stegosaurus Snack Shack is open seasonally. Before you start your hike, visit the Trek Through Time exhibit (small fee) to orient yourself to the age of the dinosaurs.

Triceratops Trail: From Dinosaur Ridge Visitor Center, drive 0.2 mile east on West Alameda Parkway and turn left to head north on C470 West. Stay to the left when C470 ends and take the two exits to West US 6 (6th Avenue). Drive to 19th Street in Golden, about 5.0 miles from the Dinosaur Ridge Visitor Center. Turn right onto 19th Street and drive 0.1 mile to Jones Road. Turn right onto Jones Road, then right into a Colorado School of Mines parking lot. Parking is free on weekends but not during the week. Walk west to the bike path, turn left and follow the path to the Triceratops Trail on the left. No facilities are available at the trailhead or along the trail.

Fossil exhibit at Fossil Trace Golf Club Clubhouse: From the Triceratops Trail parking lot, retrace your route to US 6. Turn left onto US 6 and drive 1.3 miles east to the first traffic light with Jefferson CO Parkway (West 10th Avenue) on the left; Heritage Drive will be to the right. Turn left, then take the first left onto Illinois Street. Go halfway around the traffic circle and turn right. You can see the entrance to Fossil Trace Golf Club—turn right into the parking lot. The exhibit is in the clubhouse.

THE HIKE

For anyone who wonders about dinosaurs or ancient life, a walk along Dinosaur Ridge and Triceratops Trail will surely provide some enlightenment. As you follow the green dinosaur tracks from the Dinosaur Ridge Visitor Center, you first walk along the Walk Through Time, a series of interpretive signs describing life during the last 300 million years. The rocks of Dinosaur Ridge showcase dinosaur tracks and bones, ripple marks, burrows, and trails preserved between 100 and 150 million years ago. The east side contains the younger fossils.

A most fascinating stop along the trail is the dinosaur tracksite. Similar dinosaur "roadways" have been found in the Dakota Formation from Boulder to the Oklahoma/New Mexico border. This phenomenon has been dubbed the "Dinosaur Freeway." The concept of "freeway" came about in the 1980s when paleontologists began to realize how many footprints exist along Dinosaur Ridge. The imprints were first exposed in 1937 during the construction of Alameda Avenue. The Spanish word *alameda* translates to "treelined avenue" or "promenade." In the 1980s, C470 was being built nearby, and many cars, analogous to the traveling dinosaurs, would soon drive along the new freeway. The combination of "alameda" and the new freeway gave paleontologists the idea to call the tracksite "dinosaur freeway."

An inland sea covered part of Colorado a hundred million years ago, and dinosaurs may have migrated along miles of broad coastline. Rivers crossed the wide, lush coast that also contained swamps, lakes, and mudflats, and the dinosaurs left footprints in the mud. Layers of rock reveal tracksites created over many years.

Fossilized dinosaur bone on Dinosaur Ridge.

Tracks left by individual dinosaurs help paleontologists study dinosaur behavior. Traits such as animal size, whether it walked on two feet or four feet, and how many toes it had can be revealed by analyzing tracks. Groups of tracks suggest that a family or several families may have walked together. Many dinosaurs were probably social, perhaps like elephants today.

When you cross the hogback (ridge) and head down the west side, you'll see rocks and fossils that are 150 million years old. The bones from a plant-eating dinosaur that grew up to 66 feet long and weighed up to twenty tons are visible in the cutaway rock at the last stop.

Walking on the Triceratops Trail fast-forwards you 32 million years from Dinosaur Ridge. Trace fossils—impressions, casts, and footprints—are found in the Laramie Formation (sandstone) along the trail. The hadrosaur and theropod tracks at the second stop are reverse tracks or bulges—they may take you a minute to find. One print may have been made by a Tyrannosaurus rex! The rocks here are tilted vertically, instead of slanted like at Dinosaur Ridge. Softer layers of clay eroded away or were removed by mining. Instead of foot indents like those at the tracksite at Dinosaur Ridge, these tracks are seen as if you were under the foot. Other unusual fossils include raindrop impressions or gas bubbles and beetle tracks. The first ever champsosaur track, made by a crocodile-like reptile, was discovered in the Fossil Trace area. The first triceratops was unearthed in 1887 in Denver, near today's Federal Boulevard, and the horned dinosaur left tracks along the trail named for it near Golden. The trail ends at a display of palm frond impressions, which take you to a tropical climate 68 million years ago.

Looking south along the hogback from the Dakota Ridge Trail, above the interpretive displays.

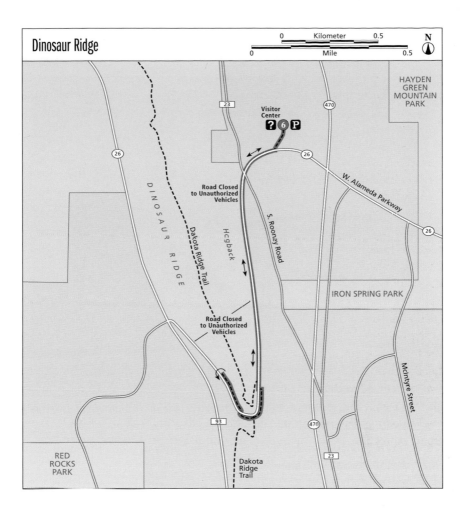

Dinosaur Ridge

Be sure to visit Trek Through Time at the Dinosaur Ridge Exhibit Hall. The exhibit explains what you see along Dinosaur Ridge and the Triceratops Trail, and the hands-on displays are fun for kids of all ages.

MILES AND DIRECTIONS

Dinosaur Ridge

0.0 Start from the bulletin board in front of the Visitor Center. Elevation: 6,030 feet. GPS: N39 41.33' / W105 11.43'. Walk south to West Alameda Parkway and turn right. The first part of the hike is a Walk Through Time, presented with a series of interpretive signs, beginning 300 million years ago.

0.2 Start of Dinosaur Ridge Trail. GPS: N39 41.18' / W105 11.55'. The trail starts on the right side of the road. Eighteen interpretive signs explain points of interest along the route.

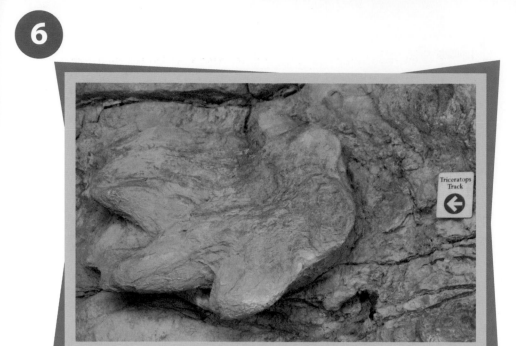

A reverse track (seen as if you were under the foot) of a Triceratops footprint on the Triceratops Trail.

0.9 Junction with Dakota Ridge Trail. Cross the road in the provided crosswalk to more interpretive signs and an overlook with a shelter.

1.0 Another junction with Dakota Ridge Trail. Continue along the roadway to the Cretaceous Time interpretive sign.

1.15 Cross the road on the provided crosswalk.

1.2 End of the trail at the fossilized bones. Elevation: 6,160 feet. GPS: N39 40.70′ / W105 11.70′. Return the way you came.

2.4 Arrive back at the Visitor Center.

Triceratops Trail

0.0 Start from the Triceratops Trailhead parking lot at Parfet Prehistoric Preserve. Elevation: 5,880 feet. GPS: N39 44.69′ / W105 13.32′. Walk onto the paved recreation path along West 6th Avenue and turn left (southeast).

0.15 Turn left at the trailhead signs onto Triceratops Trail, a dirt path. Follow the signs and ignore any side roads.

0.25 Duckbills, Carnivores, Beetles, and Raindrops site. Turn right and walk down the stairs to the sheltered exhibits. Return back to the trail after reading the interpretive signs and checking out the tracks and raindrop impressions. At the top of the stairs, turn right to continue on Triceratops Trail. Stop at three different interpretive signs.

0.45 End of the trail at the Prehistoric Plants impressions and interpretive signs. Elevation: 5,840 feet. GPS: N39 44.61′ / W105 13.15′. Return the way you came.

0.85 Arrive back at the parking lot.

HIKE INFORMATION

Local Information: Town of Morrison; 303-697-8749; town.morrison.co.us
Greater Golden Chamber of Commerce; 303-279-3113; goldencochamber.org
Local Events/Attractions: Paleontological Exhibit, Fossil Trace Golf Club, Golden; 303-277-8750; fossiltrace.com/the-experience
Morrison Natural History Museum; 303-697-1873; mnhm.org
Red Rocks Park and Amphitheater, Morrison; 303 697-4939; redrocksonline.com. Tours available May through Oct or by appointment, 303-697-6910.
Hike Tours: Friends of Dinosaur Ridge, Morrison; 303-697-3466; dinoridge.org/fieldtrips.html
Organizations: Friends of Dinosaur Ridge, Morrison; 303-697-3466; dinoridge .org/membership.html

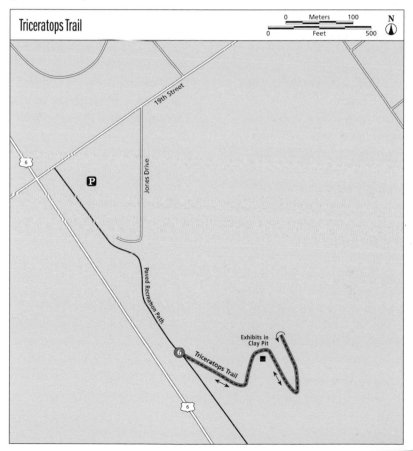

Triceratops Trail

South Valley Park Loop

This short and easy loop takes you past towering rock formations created by erosion of the Ancestral Rocky Mountains. Early Native Americans created shelters under overhanging rocks. While hiking along, use your imagination to find various shapes in the red towers. Golden eagles and cliff swallows find nesting sites on rock ledges, where white droppings betray their homes. Interpretive signs explain the park's natural features and geologic history. For people in the south Denver metro area, this park provides a convenient place for a quick workout or just to enjoy a beautiful piece of hogback valley.

Start: Trailhead in South Valley Park (north end)

Distance: 2.5-mile loop with spur

Hiking time: 1 to 1.5 hours

Difficulty: Easy due to length and terrain

Elevation gain: 100-foot loss and 160-foot gain

Trail surface: Gravel and natural surface trail

Seasons: Best Mar through Nov. Avoid hot summer days—visit in the evening or early morning.

Other trail users: Hikers only on Swallow Trail; equestrians and mountain bikers on other trails

Canine compatibility: Dogs must be on leash

Land status: Jefferson County Open Space

Fees and permits: None required, though large groups and unique activities require special permits. Check jeffco.us/open-space or call 303-271-5925.

Schedule: Open year-round, 1 hour before sunrise to 1 hour after sunset

Maps: USGS Indian Hills; National Geographic Trails Illustrated 100 Boulder/Golden

Trail contact: Jefferson County Open Space, 700 Jefferson County Parkway, Golden; 303-271-5925; jeffco.us/open-space

Other: Climbing on the rocks is prohibited. Please stay on designated trails to avoid damage to fragile geological features and wildlife habitat. Charcoal fires are allowed in provided grills only.

Special considerations: No water is available along the trail. Come prepared for an outdoor experience. Leave valuables at home.

Finding the trailhead: From C470, exit at Ken Caryl Avenue and head west. In 0.3 mile the road comes to a Y. Turn left onto South Valley Road. In 1.0 mile, turn left into South Valley Park. Restrooms, picnic tables, and water are available at the trailhead, along with a doggie water fountain.

THE HIKE

When the present Rocky Mountains rose about 70 million years ago, layers of sedimentary rock lying on top were thrust into an arch shape. Softer dirt and rock eroded away over the following years, while harder rock in the Fountain Formation and Lyons Formation remained as sky-reaching flatirons. The Dakota sandstone became a tilted ridge called a "hogback," which runs intermittently along the Front Range from Douglas County to the Wyoming border. The valley that formed between the hogback and the higher foothills is called the "Hogback Valley," and herein lies South Valley Park.

Hunter-gatherers probably wintered in South Valley and similar areas in the Hogback Valley as long as 12,000 years ago. They built shelters against the south- or southwest-facing red rocks, which absorbed afternoon heat that kept them warm at night. Mammoth remains have been found, along with those of smaller animals, in this area. By 7,000 years ago, the mammoth and giant bison had disappeared. The Archaic Indians used spears, atlatls, or traps to kill bison, deer, antelopes, rabbits, mice, and birds for food. Berries and roots supplemented their diet. They cooked food in hide bags, animal stomachs, or tightly woven water-proofed baskets by dropping heated rocks inside to boil water.

By about AD 100, Native Americans learned to make pottery. This period is known as the Woodland Culture. People made pots by pressing thin slabs of clay together, using a flat stone on the inside while paddling the outside with a piece

Dakota sandstone formations along the Coyote Song Trail.

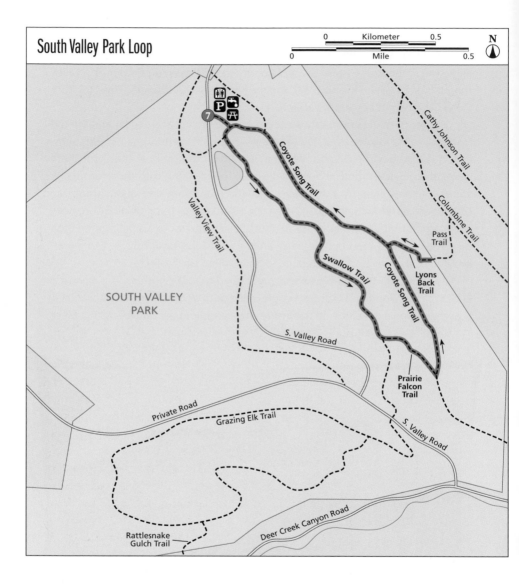

South Valley Park Loop

0 Kilometer 0.5

0 Mile 0.5

N

Cathy Johnson Trail

Coyote Song Trail

Columbine Trail

Pass Trail

Lyons Back Trail

Valley View Trail

Swallow Trail

Coyote Song Trail

SOUTH VALLEY PARK

S. Valley Road

Prairie Falcon Trail

Private Road

Grazing Elk Trail

S. Valley Road

Rattlesnake Gulch Trail

Deer Creek Canyon Road

Approaching the intersection with the Lyons Back Trail.

of wood. Plant fiber was braided into a cord, which was pressed into the soft clay slabs before firing. Clay deposits were found east of the hogback.

Bows and arrows replaced the atlatl, and chert for arrows and spearheads was found nearby. When snow melted in the high country, people left the Hogback Valley, crossed the Front Range into the high plains of North Park, and then headed south to Middle Park. They hunted game and gathered grains and roots along the way. By late August, they crossed the Continental Divide, hunting summer-fattened elk and bighorn sheep. Archaeologists have found sandstone grinding slabs from the hogback region at timberline, evidently left behind by the hunters hauling hides and meat back to their low-elevation homes before the snows fell.

In the early 1900s, white-faced English cattle roamed the large Ken-Caryl Ranch. In 1971, part of the ranch was sold to the Johns-Manville Corporation, which built its corporate headquarters just west of South Valley Park. The building now belongs to Lockheed-Martin. The Ken-Caryl Ranch subdivision was developed in the 1980s. Jefferson County purchased the property for South Valley Park in 1997.

While you hike around the tilted red rocks, imagine life here thousands of years ago and the contrasts with life today in the Hogback Valley. The rocks take on various shapes from different aspects. One looks like an angel, another, a goose. Gambel oaks (oakbrush) grow large here. Their acorns are very nutritious and help bears fatten up before their winter sleep. Deer enjoy browsing on the leaves. Native Americans ground the acorns into meal to make mush and bread. Rocky Mountain junipers grow among the oakbrush, especially as you head up the Lyons Back Trail. Birds and small animals eat the little berries, which Native Americans also enjoyed.

Although the loop hike is fairly short, South Valley Park is long on history. Watch for eagles circling above or swallows swooping after insects while you enjoy this special place.

MILES AND DIRECTIONS

0.0 Start from the trailhead bulletin board. Elevation: 5,980 feet. GPS: N39 33.97′ / W105 09.17′.

185 feet T-intersection. Turn right onto Swallow Trail (hikers only), a wide gravel path. Interpretive signs along the trail explain wildlife habitats in the rocks and Native history.

0.8 Junction with connecting trails. The right branch heads to Grazing Elk Trail (seasonal closure may apply). Turn left onto Prairie Falcon, a multiuse connector trail.

1.1 Junction with Coyote Song Trail. Turn left onto Coyote Song (multiuse), a natural surface trail.

1.5 Junction with Lyons Back Trail. Turn right and hike up to the ridge for views to the west and south.

1.7 South Valley Park boundary. Elevation: 6,040 feet. GPS: N39 33.63′ / W105 08.53′. Turn around here and enjoy the view on the way down.

1.9 Arrive back at Coyote Song Trail. Turn right.

2.4 Trail reaches a Y and Coyote Song Trail continues north. Turn left to head past the picnic tables.

2.5 Turn right, walk a few feet, and arrive back at the trailhead bulletin boards.

HIKE INFORMATION

Local Information: South Metro Denver Chamber of Commerce, Centennial; 303-795-0142; bestchamber.com
Local Events/Attractions: Chatfield State Park, Littleton; 303-791-7275; cpw.state.co.us/placestogo/parks/chatfield
Organizations: Jefferson County Open Space Volunteers, Golden; 303-271-5922; jeffco.us/open-space/volunteer

Roxborough State Park Loops

Roxborough State Park is a land of red rock slabs sticking up like upside-down spear points. The Fountain Valley Trail provides a close-up view of the rocks and the historic Persse Place. The South Rim Trail circles Roxborough's south end, winding through oakbrush past some of the huge rocks. Crossing over grasslands and past ponderosa pines, it ascends a ridge for an almost aerial view of the interesting rock formations. The geology is easy to see and examine from the rim. Skyscrapers to the north form a contrasting backdrop to the natural "buildings" of the tilted rocks.

Start: WILLOW CREEK and FOUNTAIN VALLEY trailhead interpretive signs just southwest of the Roxborough State Park Visitor Center

Distance: 5.5-mile figure-8 loop with one spur

Hiking time: 2.25 to 3 hours

Difficulty: Moderate due to length; easy if loops are done separately

Elevation gain: 440 feet

Trail surface: Natural surface trail and dirt road (closed to the motorized public)

Seasons: Best Apr through Nov

Other trail users: Hikers only

Canine compatibility: Dogs not permitted in Roxborough State Park

Land status: Colorado state park, Colorado natural area

Fees and permits: Daily entrance fee or annual pass required

Schedule: Open year-round, day use only. Park hours change with the seasons. Check the website or call.

Maps: USGS Kassler; National Geographic Trails Illustrated 135, Deckers/Rampart Range

Trail contact: Roxborough State Park, 4751 East Roxborough Drive, Littleton; 303-973-3959; cpw .state.co.us/placestogo/parks/ roxborough

Other: You can cross-country ski or snowshoe on designated trails when there is enough snow.

Special considerations: Bring water with you, as no potable water is available on the trails. No pets (dogs included) are allowed in Roxborough State Park. Beware of rattlesnakes and poison ivy.

Finding the trailhead: From C470 and Wadsworth Boulevard (SH 121), drive south on Wadsworth 4.5 miles to Waterton Road (Douglas County Road 217 [DCR 217]). Turn left onto Waterton Road, drive 1.7 miles to North Rampart Range Road, and turn right. Drive another 2.1 miles on North Rampart Range Road, then turn left onto Roxborough Park Road. Turn right immediately after the fire station and follow the road into the Park. Stop at the entrance station to pay the fee, or if it is unattended, stop at the self-serve station. The Visitor Center parking lot is 2.2 miles from the fire station. Water and restrooms are available at the Visitor Center, a 0.1-mile walk from the main parking lot.

THE HIKE

Roxborough State Park has received several designations over and above state park: Colorado Natural Area, National Natural Landmark, and National Archaeological District. Once you arrive, you'll understand why so many "labels" have been bestowed upon the area. The tilted red slabs of sandstone immediately catch your eye, but look around this small area and you'll discover other geologic formations that developed over 500 million years. The area also exemplifies the transition zone between prairie and mountains. Around and between the towering rocks, many natural microcosms provide a home for very diverse vegetation like yucca and Gambel oak (oakbrush), stately ponderosa pine, aspen and wild rose, and marshes. With a variety of food available, mule deer, foxes, rock squirrels, coyotes, and black bears populate the area, with an occasional visit from a mountain lion. Raptors love the ridges. Opportunities to learn about geology, natural history, prehistoric peoples, and early Colorado history give you an excuse to return time and again.

Rock formations near the trailhead in autumn, an especially nice time of year to visit Roxborough.

To truly experience this unique area, visit Roxborough at various times of the year. Towering rocks, wet from melting snow, contrast sharply against a brilliant blue Colorado sky and snow-draped hills and trees. Spring brings fragrant blossoms and colorful flowers, with changing variety throughout summer. Oakbrush turns reddish brown in fall, while aspens don regal gold. Although you may not always see wildlife when you visit, you might catch a glimpse of a new fawn or fledgling (young bird) spreading its wings. No matter the season, something is always new for the observant hiker!

Start your hike on the easy Fountain Valley Trail that wanders among the tilted rocks. A borrowed trail guide from the Visitor Center will give you additional insight into the various numbered posts. Take a few minutes to hike up to Lyons Overlook, which provides almost a bird's-eye view of the rock formations. The Persse Place is about halfway around the loop. Henry Persse, owner of much of the land that is now the park, suggested renaming the area Roxborough, after his family's estate in Ireland. Originally called Washington Park (see if you can find the rock that looks like George Washington), confusion with Denver's Washington Park necessitated the name change. Denver's elite enjoyed the Persse Resort in the early 1900s.

Back at the trailhead, head south on Willow Creek Trail—a separate trail guide is available. While walking you can learn about geology and the plants and animals that live in the grasslands and oakbrush along the trail. You pass a couple of large Fountain Formation rock slabs that create the "feel small" perception.

A chicken house and tool shed built on Henry Persse's homestead in the early 1900s, on the Fountain Valley Trail.

Poison ivy and rattlesnakes live here, so be careful not to tangle with either. Watch for deer along the way.

At the junction, head south on South Rim Trail. It gently climbs past ponderosa pines, eventually gaining a ridge (rim) that gives you a unique perspective of the park's standing rock formations. On a clear day you can see tall buildings in the south metro area and out onto the plains. Dropping down from the ridge, switchback to a junction with the Willow Creek Trail and stay to the right. The trail crosses a bridge over Willow Creek. Return to the Visitor Center via a trail north of the entrance road.

Enjoy the special features of Roxborough State Park and return often to watch the seasons change!

MILES AND DIRECTIONS

0.0   Start from the WILLOW CREEK and FOUNTAIN VALLEY trailhead interpretive signs just southwest of the Roxborough State Park Visitor Center. Start to the right down the old dirt road, which is the Fountain Valley Trail. Elevation: 6,200 feet. GPS: N39 25.77' / W105 04.17'.

0.1   Junction with Fountain Valley Overlook Trail on the left. (**Option:** A less than 0.1 mile out-and-back spur to an overlook.) Continue straight ahead on Fountain Valley Trail.

0.2   Start/end of Fountain Valley Loop. Hike to the right first. GPS: N39 25.94' / W105 04.21'.

0.6   South end of Lyons Overlook spur trail. Turn left onto the spur. In about 200 feet, turn left and continue uphill to the overlook. Go left at a bench and in 0.2 mile arrive at an observation deck with nice views of the tilted rocks, ridges, and trail. Elevation: 6,240 feet. GPS: N39 26.13' / W105 04.29'. Return to the last turn at the bench and go right; then turn left and walk downhill 0.2 mile to Fountain Valley Trail via the north leg of the Lyons Overlook Trail.

1.0   Turn left onto Fountain Valley Trail.

1.4   Persse Place to the right. Elevation: 6,040 feet. GPS: N39 26.60' / W105 04.37'.

2.4   Back at the start/end of Fountain Valley Loop. Turn right to return to the trailhead.

2.6   Arrive back at the trailhead. For South Rim Trail, hike down Willow Creek Trail to the left of the large trail sign.

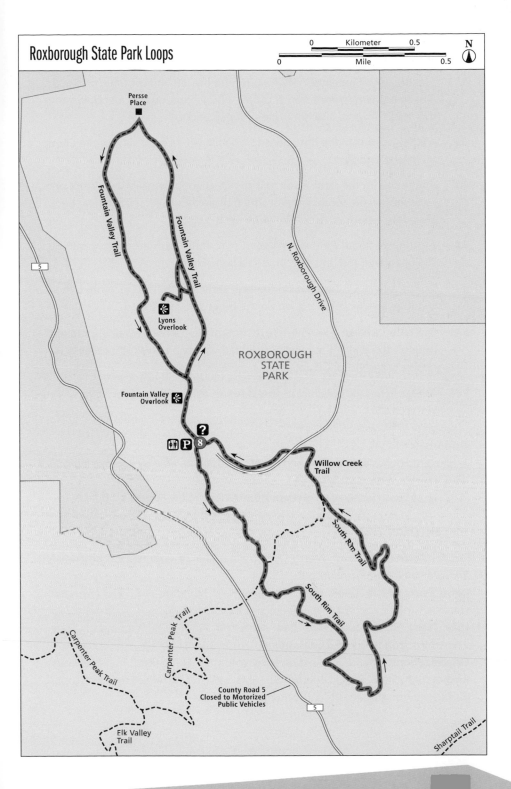

Roxborough State Park Loops

Persse
Place

Fountain Valley Trail

Fountain Valley Trail

Lyons
Overlook

Fountain Valley
Overlook

N. Roxborough Drive

ROXBOROUGH
STATE
PARK

5

8

Willow Creek
Trail

South Rim Trail

South Rim Trail

Carpenter Peak Trail

Carpenter Peak Trail

County Road 5
Closed to Motorized
Public Vehicles

5

Elk Valley
Trail

Sharptail Trail

0   Kilometer   0.5

0   Mile   0.5

N

3.05 Junction with Willow Creek Trail. Turn right on South Rim Trail/Carpenter Peak Trail.

3.1 Junction with Carpenter Peak Trail. Turn to the left and continue on South Rim Trail. There's a nice bench under a huge cottonwood just down the trail. Head down to a seasonal creek with a bridge.

3.6 A little spur trail to the right goes to a bench with a great view of the tilted rocks to the north.

4.1 A little trail to the right leads to a bench shaded by oakbrush. There are nice views to the south and east. The trail reaches its high point near here. Elevation: 6,480 feet. GPS: N39 25.24' / W105 03.57'.

5.0 Junction of South Rim and Willow Creek Trails, with a bench. Continue straight ahead and downhill. There's a bench here.

5.2 Trail arrives at a Y. Turn left on the trail and cross the entrance road, then continue on the trail to the left on the other side of the road.

5.4 Trail enters a parking lot. There's a restroom here. Continue walking straight through the parking lot, which will lead you to a trail to the parking lot closest to the Visitor Center.

5.5 Arrive back at the parking lot closest to the Visitor Center. GPS: N39 25.74' / W105 04.08'.

Options

1. Hike just Fountain Valley Trail and Lyons Overlook for an easy 2.6-mile lollipop with spur. Elevation gain: 200 feet.
2. Hike just South Rim Trail for an easy 2.9-mile loop. Elevation gain: 280 feet.

HIKE INFORMATION

Local Information: South Metro Denver Chamber of Commerce, Centennial; 303-795-0142; bestchamber.com

Local Events/Attractions: Chatfield State Park, Littleton; 303-791-7275; cpw.state.co.us/placestogo/parks/chatfield. Has a campground.

Hike Tours: Roxborough State Park, Littleton; 303-973-3959; cpw.parks.state.co.us/placestogo/parks/roxborough

Organizations: Friends of Roxborough, Volunteer Naturalists, Trail Stewards, Roxborough State Park, Littleton; 303-973-3959; cpw.state.co.us/placestogo/parks/roxborough/pages/friendsofroxborough.aspx

Colorado natural areas preserve special sites that meet at least one of four criteria of statewide significance: native plant communities, geologic formations or processes, paleontological localities, and habitat for rare plants or animals.

Protecting Roxborough State Park

Because Roxborough Park is so special, its different designations require conservation for present and future generations. Emphasis is placed on protecting the total park resource. For example, assuring grasses grow undisturbed by humans means the local mice and other little critters have enough to eat. These small mammals are an important food source for the many raptors in the area, including golden eagles. Therefore, restrictions and regulations, such as day use only, have been instituted.

Everyone can help preserve the uniqueness of Roxborough by staying on the trails, not feeding or disturbing wildlife, and leaving what you find. With so many visitors, hiking off-trail can lead to vegetation damage and destruction. Collecting samples of vegetation and rocks only robs others of the chance to see nature at its best, and picking flowers or fruits deprives wildlife of needed nutrients. One autumn day, a woman visiting the park loudly challenged the various rules. People later observed her leaving with some bright red branches, presumably for home decoration. Imagine her surprise when she discovered she had an armful of poison ivy!

Swallowtail Trail

Starting in Roxborough State Park, this hike takes you southeast past the old Sundance Ranch. Nelson Ranch Open Space, situated between the hogback and the foothills, provides habitat protection for foxes, elk, bears, coyotes, spotted towhees, migratory birds, and, of course, swallowtail butterflies. The butterfly shape of the Swallowtail Trail winds around a towering red rock of the Fountain Formation, up and over rimrock, passing by ponderosa pine, Douglas fir, oakbrush, smooth sumac, hawthorn, chokecherry, and wild plum, with a touch of prairie full of rabbitbrush for good measure. What shapes do you see while hiking around the red rock?

Start: WILLOW CREEK and FOUNTAIN VALLEY trailhead interpretive signs just southwest of the Roxborough State Park Visitor Center
Distance: 6.7-mile figure-8 lollipop
Hiking time: 2.75 to 3.5 hours
Difficulty: Moderate due to length
Elevation gain: 520 feet
Trail surface: Natural surface and rocky trail, and dirt road (closed to the motorized public)
Seasons: Best Apr through Nov. Avoid hot summer days—visit in the evening or early morning.
Other trail users: Access through Roxborough State Park is hiker-only. Swallowtail Trail allows hikers, equestrians, and mountain bikers.
Canine compatibility: Dogs not allowed in Roxborough State Park, where this hike starts
Land status: Douglas County Open Space, Colorado state park
Fees and permits: Daily entrance fee or annual pass required for Roxborough State Park
Schedule: Open year-round. Roxborough State Park is day-use only. Park hours change with the seasons; check the website or call. Douglas County Open Space is open 1 hour before sunrise to 1 hour after sunset. You can cross-country ski or snowshoe Swallowtail Trail in winter if there is enough snow, but the trail is neither marked nor maintained for winter use. Call the Roxborough State Park Visitor Center for snow conditions.
Maps: USGS Kassler; National Geographic Trails Illustrated 135, Deckers/Rampart Range
Trail contacts: Douglas County Open Space, 100 Third Street, Castle Rock; 303-660-7495; douglas.co.us/openspace. Roxborough State Park, 4751 East Roxborough Drive, Littleton; 303-973-3959; cpw.state.co.us/placestogo/parks/roxborough
Special considerations: Bring water with you, as no potable water is available on the trails. No pets (including dogs) are allowed in Roxborough State Park or on Sharptail Trail. Beware of rattlesnakes and poison ivy.

Finding the trailhead: From C470 and Wadsworth Boulevard (SH 121), drive south on Wadsworth 4.5 miles to Waterton Road (DCR 217). Turn left onto Waterton Road, drive 1.7 miles to North Rampart Range Road, and turn right. Drive another 2.1 miles on North Rampart Range Road, then turn left onto Roxborough Park Road. Turn right immediately after the fire station and follow the road into the Park. Stop at the entrance station to pay the fee or, if it is unattended, stop at the self-serve station. The Visitor Center parking lot is 2.2 miles from the fire station. Water and restrooms are available at the Visitor Center, a 0.1-mile walk from the parking lot.

THE HIKE

Douglas County, with help from Friends of Roxborough and Great Outdoors Colorado, purchased the Nelson Ranch in 2001, creating 695 acres of Open Space. This undulating valley behind a low, tilted ridge (hogback) is anchored by a prominent red rock, a remnant of the Fountain Formation, like the uplifted red rock towers in nearby Roxborough State Park. The Nelson family called it Bottle Rock. This property provides a buffer for Roxborough State Park and protects wildlife habitat. Red foxes, mule deer, rock squirrels, and coyotes live here, while elk pass through. Bears enjoy the plentiful berries and acorns before turning in for their winter deep sleep. In spring and summer, spotted towhees feed under the many different bushes lining the valley.

View of Red Rock, also known as Bottle Rock, from the Sharptail Trail. It stands at a height of 6,500 feet.

The autumn colors of the foliage complement the rock colors on a ridge along the Swallowtail Trail.

Fly back in time 300 million years when the land we call Colorado straddled the equator. The Ancestral Rockies were eroding, leaving reddish sediment along their east and west flanks. Shallow seas bordered the shrinking range. As sea level dropped, the land dried out and sand dunes developed. Millions of years later, shallow seas would ebb and flow across a flat "Colorado." Over time the reddish coarse-grained sediment hardened into the Fountain Formation. The buff- to salmon-colored sand dunes became the Lyons Formation. Shales and sandstones from the shallow sea were compressed into the Lykins Formation. These formations are visible across Nelson Ranch in the towering red rock and in the rocky ledges.

Swallowtail Trail loops like a gentle roller coaster around the remote hogback valley—"remote" because access to the area is long, 4.0 miles from Sharptail Trailhead and 7.9 miles from Indian Creek Trailhead in the Pike National Forest. Entrance through Roxborough State Park is about 2.0 miles one-way, but the hike through this picturesque area is worth the effort. The trail winds in and out of Gambel oak (oakbrush) thickets, with mountain mahogany and berry bushes in the mix. An occasional ponderosa pine or Rocky Mountain juniper rises above the smaller shrubs.

After crossing a grassy area full of wildflowers, the trail climbs a ledge of red and buff sandstones with a good view of the valley and Red Rock. A ponderosa pine grows against the rocks. As the trail drops off the ledge, trees shelter a picnic table. You will traverse another section of rocky trail, walking over sandy spots that eroded from the sandstone.

After crossing Rainbow Creek, which is often dry, you'll arrive at the junction with the lower (southern) loop. The first section is open grassland, full of yellow-flowered rabbitbrush, which rabbits eat and use for shelter. You'll cross another set of sandstone ledges as the trail heads back north. Hawks and prairie falcons soar overhead in the blue Colorado sky, looking for lunch.

As you start back on the upper loop, you'll reach the junction with Ringtail Trail, where the smooth sumacs turn bright red in fall—a beautiful time to hike. The trail changes to pink feldspar and shiny mica for a short distance. Look for the western tiger swallowtail butterfly. This large yellow-and-black butterfly with blue and red spots near its tail lays its eggs in the chokecherry bushes.

After you leave Nelson Ranch, look to the left for a rock wall with a window. It is near the southeastern end of Sharptail Trail and is all that remains of an old homestead, slowly being covered with bushes and branches.

Swallowtail Trail provides a quiet and peaceful escape from the hustle and bustle of the nearby Denver metro area.

MILES AND DIRECTIONS

0.0 Start from the WILLOW CREEK and FOUNTAIN VALLEY trailhead interpretive signs just southwest of the Roxborough State Park Visitor Center. Start to the left of the trail sign on Willow Creek Trail. Elevation: 6,200 feet. GPS: N39 25.77' / W105 04.17'.

0.45 Junction with the lower loop of Willow Creek Trail on the left. Head straight onto South Rim Trail/Carpenter Peak Trail.

0.5 Junction with South Rim Trail. Head right onto Carpenter Peak Trail/Colorado Trail.

0.6 T-intersection with Douglas County Road 5. GPS: N39 25.38' / W105 04.02'. Turn left (southeast) and walk on DCR 5. This road is closed to the motorized public, except private inholders and Roxborough State Park personnel.

0.7 The old Sundance Ranch houses.

1.0 Although the sign says NO TRESPASSING, DCR 5 is public right-of-way. Please stay on the road.

1.2 Exit private property.

1.5 Junction with Sharptail Trail, which comes in from the left. Continue hiking to the right on the southernmost leg of Sharptail Trail, which merges with DCR 5.

1.6 Turn left (south) on the single-track Sharptail Trail, which is closed to mountain bikers, dogs, and motorized equipment. Pass through a fence. GPS: N39 24.70' / W105 03.46'.

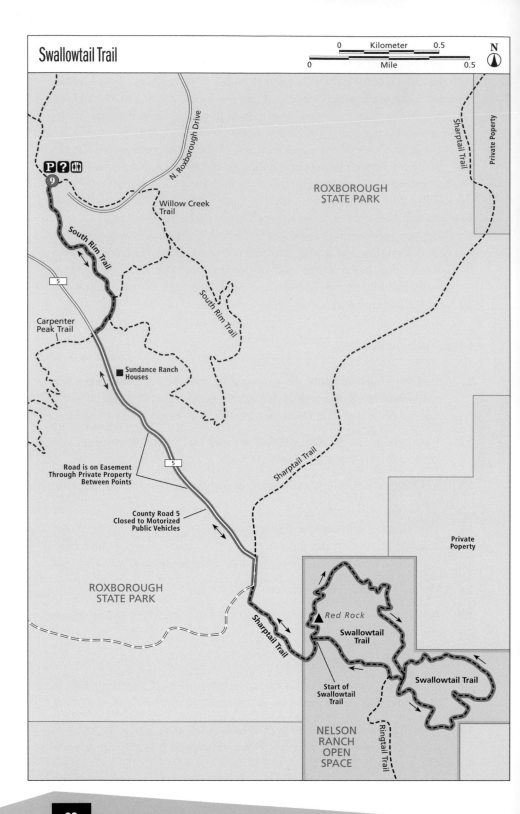

Swallowtail Trail

0 Kilometer 0.5

0 Mile 0.5

N

ROXBOROUGH
STATE PARK

Private Property

Sharptail Trail

N. Roxborough Drive

P **?** 🚻
9

Willow Creek
Trail

South Rim Trail

5

South Rim Trail

Carpenter
Peak Trail

■ Sundance Ranch
Houses

Road is on Easement
Through Private Property
Between Points

5

County Road 5
Closed to Motorized
Public Vehicles

Sharptail Trail

Private
Poperty

ROXBOROUGH
STATE PARK

Sharptail Trail

▲ Red Rock

**Swallowtail
Trail**

Swallowtail Trail

Start of
Swallowtail
Trail

Ringtail Trail

NELSON
RANCH
OPEN
SPACE

1.9 Trail enters Nelson Ranch Open Space and becomes Swallowtail Trail. This trail is open to hikers, horses, mountain bikers, and pets on leash. There's a picnic table down a little trail to the right.

2.0 Start/end of Swallowtail Trail loops. Turn left here to hike around the Red Rock.

2.1 Trail splits. You can go either direction around the Red Rock.

2.2 Trail splits again. Turn left if you went left around the Red Rock; turn right if you went right around the Red Rock. Head north on Swallowtail Trail.

2.5 The trail takes you up on a sandstone ledge (rimrock).

3.1 Arrive at the middle of the figure-8 and trail signs. Follow the "Loop Connection." GPS: N39 24.45' / W105 02.94'. Go straight ahead about 100 feet to the next junction, after a hitch rail and bench, then turn left onto the lower loop, heading south.

3.7 The trail climbs up along sandstone ledges in switchbacks. At one place you might think the trail goes straight ahead, but it switchbacks to the right.

4.3 Arrive back at the middle of the figure-8. Go left about 100 feet to the next junction, then turn right onto the upper loop, heading west.

4.4 T-intersection with Ringtail Trail. Turn right (northwest) and continue on the upper loop of Swallowtail Trail.

4.7 Arrive back at the start/end of Swallowtail Trail loops. Turn left and return the way you came to the Roxborough State Park trailhead near the Visitor Center.

6.7 Arrive back at the trailhead.

Option

For a shorter, 5.5-mile hike, just hike the upper loop of Swallowtail Trail. At the 3.1-mile direction above, skip to mile 4.3 and follow the directions from there.

HIKE INFORMATION

Local Information: South Metro Denver Chamber of Commerce, Centennial; 303-795-0142; bestchamber.com

Local Events/Attractions: Chatfield State Park, Littleton; 303-791-7275; cpw. state.co.us/placestogo/parks/chatfield. Has a campground.

Hike Tours: Douglas County Open Space, Castle Rock; 303-660-7495; douglas. co.us/openspace

Organizations: Volunteer Program, Douglas County Open Space, Castle Rock; 303-660-7495; douglas.co.us/openspace

Great Outdoors Colorado (GOCO)

The Great Outdoors Colorado Trust Fund was created in 1992 when the citizens of Colorado voted to dedicate a portion of the state's lottery proceeds to preserve, protect, and enhance Colorado's wildlife habitats, parks, rivers, trails, and open space heritage. The rest of the proceeds go to the Conservation Trust Fund and Colorado State Parks. GOCO disburses funds to local governments, nonprofit conservation groups, the Colorado Division of Wildlife, and Colorado State Parks through various grant opportunities.

Since its inception, GOCO has helped protect over 1 million acres of land, helped finance projects in over 1,000 community parks and outdoor recreation areas, and helped build and maintain over 900 miles of trails. GOCO funds have added over 47 acres to the State Parks system and protected over 750 miles of rivers. GOCO has funded over 4,500 projects throughout the state, in both rural and urban areas, and in all 64 counties. Visit goco.org to learn more.

Prickly pear cactus.

Starting at an old homestead, this trail takes you over Cherry Creek and then through a great example of shortgrass prairie before heading up the mesa. You wander through a juniper ecosystem with some ponderosa pine and prickly pear cactus on this mesa rimmed by Castle Rock Conglomerate, with its cemented cobbles. Views from the top start at Pikes Peak to the south and follow the Front Range to Longs Peak in the north. The Black Forest around Franktown pleases the eye to the east. This 1,224-acre open space buffer between Castle Rock and Franktown protects prairie dogs, pronghorns, mule deer, elk, and many raptors.

Start: Hidden Mesa Trailhead

Distance: 6.9-mile lollipop

Hiking time: 2.75 to 3.5 hours

Difficulty: Moderate due to length

Elevation gain: 470 feet

Trail surface: Natural surface trail and paved recreation path

Seasons: Best Apr through Nov. Avoid high-wind and hot summer days--visit in the evening or early morning.

Other trail users: Equestrians and mountain bikers

Canine compatibility: Dogs must be on leash

Land status: Douglas County Open Space

Fees and permits: None required

Schedule: Open year-round from 1 hour before sunrise to 1 hour after sunset

Maps: USGS Castle Rock North

Trail contact: Douglas County Open Space, 100 Third Street, Castle Rock; 303-660-7495; douglas.co.us/openspace

Other: A picnic shelter is available at the trailhead.

Special considerations: There is no water along the trail except for Cherry Creek (not potable) near the trailhead. Beware of rattlesnakes-- stay on existing trails.

Finding the trailhead: From I-25, take exit 193, Lincoln Avenue, to SH 83/South Parker Road. Turn right (south) and follow SH 83 almost to Franktown. After mile marker 51 (1.3 miles north of the junction of SH 86 and SH 83), turn right (west) onto the Hidden Mesa Open Space access road leading into the parking lot. A portable toilet is available. Bring your own water.

THE HIKE

As more people find Colorado attractive and the Denver metro area a good place to live and work, open lands, farms, and ranches are quickly disappearing. People once predicted that homes and towns would sprawl continuously from Fort Collins to Colorado Springs, forming a huge megalopolis. However, Front Range counties, municipalities, and the State of Colorado, in conjunction with private groups, have continuously worked to preserve lands as buffers between communities and as wildlife habitats. Hidden Mesa is one such preserve, a joint effort between Douglas County and the Town of Castle Rock.

The old barn and the log part of the house at the trailhead were built in 1872 by William Brian. This Irishman and his family cultivated about 20 acres of their 160-acre homestead and raised stock on the rest. Their land included the low area and land just west of Cherry Creek.

After much revegetation, the riparian area along Cherry Creek is recovering from over a century's worth of cattle munching on the bushes. The willows had disappeared, but now native chokecherries, wild plums, and willows thrive again, providing nesting and hiding places and "restaurants" for birds and small animals. Hidden Mesa sustains habitat for prairie dogs, pronghorns, elk, coyotes, mule deer, and a variety of raptors. A few burrowing owls make their homes in abandoned prairie dog tunnels. In addition, Douglas County has built natural surface trails for hikers, equestrians, and mountain bikers. This land purchase also provided public land for a missing link in the 40-mile-long Cherry Creek Regional

Impressive view of Pikes Peak from the Mesa Rim Loop on Hidden Mesa.

The Mesa Rim Loop trail on Hidden Mesa.

Trail that connects Castlewood Canyon State Park to the south and downtown Denver to the north.

While you're hiking across the grassland and along the mesa top, try to imagine over a thousand homes here. Instead you can enjoy a remnant of prairie and mesa, with its marvelous views of the Front Range Mountains.

Eagle Scouts have been active at Hidden Mesa. One built the bluebird houses you see along the trail; volunteers from the Audubon Society maintain them. Other Eagle Scouts provided the directional signs and benches at strategic locations.

The rock that rims the mesa and has prevented its erosion to the level of Cherry Creek's floodplain is Castle Rock Conglomerate, the same rock you can see at the top of Castle Rock itself and in Castlewood Canyon. Small rocks eroded from this formation are strewn along some parts of the trail, especially close to the rim. The deep red stones contain iron oxide. Roundish rocks once rolled around in a streambed, possibly the ancestor of the South Platte River.

You'll find some interesting features during your hike. A small pond full of cattails seems out of place in the seemingly dry grassland punctuated with yucca and prickly pear cactus. A table formation of rocks creates a great frame for a photo of Pikes Peak. Hidden Mesa is a great place to daydream while hiking. Rounded rocks become dinosaur gizzard stones, and the breeze evokes visions of prairie schooners sailing across miles of open plains. At the base of the mesa is a grove of large Gambel oaks (oakbrush) that are taller than a typical bush. In the cool shade under their branches sit a picnic table, two benches, and a horse hitch rail. What a great place to have a bite to eat and enjoy the breeze before heading back to the mechanized world!

MILES AND DIRECTIONS

0.0 Start from the Hidden Mesa Trailhead on the west side of the picnic table shelter. Elevation: 6,040 feet. GPS: N39 24.55' / W104 45.76'.

0.5 Cross Cherry Creek on a nice bridge before reaching a T-intersection with the concrete Cherry Creek Trail. GPS: N39 24.51' / W104 46.26'. Turn right (north) and head up the Cherry Creek Trail. A natural surface single-track runs along the right of the concrete trail.

0.9 Junction with the Hidden Mesa Trail. GPS: N39 24.79' / W104 46.52'. Turn left (west) onto the natural surface double-track trail.

1.4 Pass through a gate.

1.7 In a grove of oakbrush are a picnic table, two benches, and hitching post. The trail starts climbing more.

1.8 Junction with the Pleasant Pass Trail to the right. Go left to continue on the Hidden Mesa Trail up to Rocky Pass.

2.3 Start of Mesa Rim Loop. GPS: N39 24.34' / W104 47.54'. There's a bench here. Turn right and head uphill toward the Pleasant View Entrance.

2.7 Junction of Mesa Rim Loop and the Pleasant View Entrance trail. There's a bench here. Turn left to continue on Mesa Rim Loop. When the trail crosses the rimrock, keep an eye out for cairns (little rock piles) and trail markers that show the way.

3.0 Nice view of Pikes Peak to the south.

4.6 Arrive back at the start of Mesa Rim Loop. Turn right and head downhill. Return the way you came.

6.9 Arrive back at the trailhead.

Option

For a shorter, easy 3.4-mile out-and-back route, hike only to the picnic table and return the way you came.

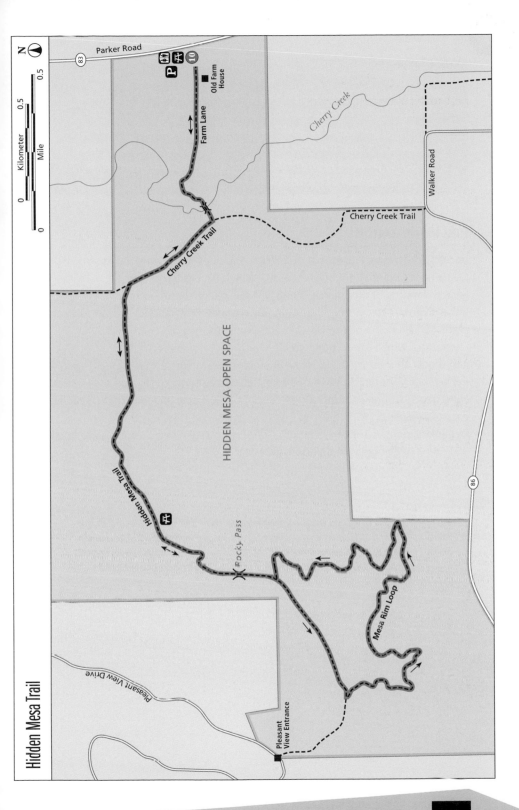

Hidden Mesa Trail

> 🌿 **Green Tip:**
> *When you just have to go, dig a hole 6-8 inches deep and at least 200 feet from water, camps, and trails. Carry a zip-lock bag with you to pack out toilet paper (and feminine products), or use a natural substitute such as leaves instead (but not poison ivy!!!). Fill in the hole with soil and other natural materials when you're done.*

HIKE INFORMATION

Local Information: Franktown; colorado.com/cities-and-towns/franktown.
Castle Rock Chamber of Commerce; 303-688-4597; castlerock.org
Parker Chamber of Commerce; 303-841-4268; parkerchamber.com
Local Events/Attractions: Colorado Renaissance Festival and Artisan Market-place, Larkspur; 303-688-6010; coloradorenaissance.com
Castle Rock Wine Fest; 303-688-4597;
castlerockculture.com/castle-rock-winefest
Castle Rock Museum; 303-814-3164; castlerockmuseum.org
Hike Tours: Douglas County Open Space, Castle Rock; 303-660-7495; douglas.co.us/openspace
Organizations: Volunteer Program, Douglas County Open Space, Castle Rock; 303-660-7495; douglas.co.us/openspace

Burrowing owls received their name because they live underground in bur-rows, usually adopting a tunnel abandoned by ground squirrels or prairie dogs. They weigh less than 6 ounces. Active day and night, burrowing owls enjoy eating tiny animals like mice and insects, especially beetles and grasshoppers.

10

Douglas County Open Space

The Douglas County Open Space program is a relative newcomer to the impressive collection of Denver metro area Open Space programs. In 1994, voters approved a 0.6 percent sales and use tax, the proceeds of which would be used to acquire land. In addition to preserving wildlife habitat and creating buffers between communities, DCOS also conserves the rural landscape, historic properties, archaeological sites, and the agricultural heritage of the county.

Since approval of the tax, 48,741 acres have been obtained for open space preservation. Land management includes treating noxious weeds and restoring native vegetation. An important aspect of the program is education through interpretive programs and guided hikes to develop a sense of ownership and stewardship of the lands. Trails enable the public to enjoy most of the open-space properties for passive or nonmotorized recreation. Some properties are open only during special programs or by prearrangement, such as Prairie Canyon Ranch, which is managed as a working cattle ranch. Other parcels are conservation easements on private properties that are not open to the public.

Keep an eye on the website douglas.co.us/openspace for information about new trails and properties opening to the public, or call 303-660-7495 for further information.

A lizard basking in the warm sunshine on Hidden Mesa.

Hidden Mesa Trail

Castlewood Canyon State Park Loops

This beautiful figure-8 hike drops down to Cherry Creek and the remains of the Castlewood Dam, which provided water for irrigation and recreation for over forty years. The dam broke in 1933, leaving tattered remains and scars in the canyon downstream. You'll walk past big hunks of Castle Rock Conglomerate, full of imbedded rocks and pebbles. Watch for birds of prey like turkey vultures and various hawks while you amble through four ecosystems in this canyon on the plains. The Visitor Center offers two excellent movies to help you appreciate this amazing state park.

Start: Lake Gulch Trailhead
Distance: 6.2-mile figure-8
Hiking time: 3 to 4 hours
Difficulty: Moderate due to distance and some steep sections
Elevation gain: 680 feet, including two gains
Trail surface: Natural surface and rocky trails, with some wooden stairs
Seasons: Best Apr through Nov. Avoid hot summer days—visit in the evening or early morning.
Other trail users: Hikers only
Canine compatibility: Dogs must be on leashes no longer than 6 feet
Land status: Colorado state park, Colorado natural area
Fees and permits: Daily fee or annual pass required

Schedule: Open 8 a.m. to 9 p.m. in summer; changes seasonally. Check the website or call for current hours.
Maps: USGS Castle Rock South, Russellville Gulch
Trail contact: Castlewood Canyon State Park, 2989 South Highway 83, Franktown; 303-688-5242; cpw.state.co.us/placestogo/parks/castlewoodcanyon
Special considerations: Beware of rattlesnakes. Bring water because some parts of the trail have none—treat any water you take from Cherry Creek. When hiking the Inner Canyon Trail and the Creek Bottom Trail, beware of poison ivy. Also be aware that flash floods can occur on Cherry Creek.

Finding the trailhead: From I-25, take exit 193, Lincoln Avenue, to SH 83/South Parker Road. Turn right (south) and follow SH 83 to its junction with SH 86 at Franktown. At the junction of SH 86 and SH 83, continue straight (south) on SH 83 and drive 5.0 miles to the entrance of Castlewood Canyon State Park. Turn right onto the park road and drive 0.5 mile to the Entrance Station/Visitor Center. After paying the fee, drive straight ahead past the next intersection (or turn left to stop at the Visitor Center) and head for Canyon Point. The parking lot is 0.2 mile from the Visitor Center. Restrooms and water are available at the trailhead.

THE HIKE

Driving south from Franktown to Castlewood Canyon, a gash appears in the landscape. Around 34 million years ago, an ancient river, perhaps a young South Platte River, deposited sand and gravel in an alluvial fan–type formation around today's Castle Rock. The sand, gravel, and cobbles cemented together to become the Castle Rock Conglomerate, very obvious along the Creek Bottom and Inner Canyon Trails. In the same time frame, the Thirty-Nine Mile Volcanic Field near Salida erupted, sending volcanic ash over the alluvial fan. Cherry Creek, which begins near the town of Black Forest to the south, eroded its way through softer layers of rock created by the volcanic ash. The harder Castle Rock Conglomerate became a rimrock cliff above the creek.

In the late 1800s truck farms, orchards, and potato fields north of Franktown helped provide food to the growing city of Denver. However, precipitation averages only about 17 inches per year here, so in 1890 the Denver Water Storage Company built a dam at a narrow point in Castlewood Canyon, below the confluence of Lake Gulch and Cherry Creek, to provide irrigation water. Denver residents loved to visit the reservoir. They camped along its shores, canoed on its waters, hiked in the canyon below the dam, fished, and hunted waterfowl. People interviewed after the dam broke in 1933 shared fond remembrances of days spent at the lake and in the canyon. One person remembered eagles flying overhead, their nest in the top of a huge pine that had been struck by lightning. Hundreds of rattlesnakes reportedly enjoyed sunning themselves on the eastside rocks. People remembered a beautiful canyon with colorful cliffs.

Pikes Peak (14,110') towers over Castlewood Canyon State Park.

The canyon is still beautiful, the eastern cliffs hanging over its depths. Rattlesnakes remain, but apparently in lesser numbers. Golden eagles still fly overhead looking for prey, along with several species of hawks and prairie falcons. Turkey vultures soar on morning updrafts.

The Lake Gulch Trail travels along a high divide between Lake Gulch and Cherry Creek. On clear days, there's a nice view of Pikes Peak and Devil's Head. The trail winds down slabs of conglomerate, past some interesting rock formations. The old reservoir once covered the green fields below. The hike proceeds to Rimrock Trail and passes the smidgeon of the dam that remains on the east side. Vegetation is sparse up here, with intermittent patches of ponderosa pine, Rocky Mountain juniper, mountain mahogany, prickly pear, yucca, and Gambel oak (oakbrush). When the trail drops down the caprock, it passes fallen hunks of rock, through what seems like a verdant rock garden.

Partway up the Creek Bottom Trail, there is a picnic table at an overlook of a waterfall. Upstream from here you'll pass boulders of Castle Rock Conglomerate, full of imbedded rocks, some larger than fist-size. Cottonwoods thrive along Cherry Creek, which along with oakbrush, make this loop a colorful fall hike. You'll pass below the bottom of the dam's larger remains. After the junction with the Lake Gulch Trail, the Inner Canyon Trail climbs slowly along Cherry Creek, filled with huge boulders. You'll scramble over some rocky areas as you hike through pleasant forest. The hike climbs out of the canyon via a staircase.

Enjoy your journey through the various facets of this beautiful canyon!

Remains of the Castlewood Dam can be seen from the Rimrock Trail.

0.0 At the west end of the parking lot, start out northwesterly from the Lake Gulch Trailhead at Canyon Point. Elevation: 6,600 feet. GPS: N39 20.00' / W104 44.69'. The first 100 feet or so is a concrete path.

0.4 Trail appears to Y across a rocky area. The left trail goes to a little overlook. Continue to the right on the Lake Gulch Trail.

0.8 Lake Gulch Trail goes to the left to cross Cherry Creek on some big sandstone boulders. On the other side, turn right to reach the trail junction at mile 0.9 below.

0.9 Junction of Lake Gulch Trail and Inner Canyon Trail. GPS: N39 20.39' / W104 45.15'. Turn left (west) onto the Inner Canyon Trail and ascend some wooden steps.

1.1 Junction of Inner Canyon Trail, Creek Bottom Trail, and Rimrock Trail. Head to the right (northeast) on the Rimrock Trail. You'll find good views of the Castlewood Dam ruins.

1.3 As you climb out of the canyon, the trail makes a right switchback. If you miss this switchback, you'll be ducking under the branches of a big ponderosa pine. Back up and turn right. When you reach the rim of the canyon, turn left. The trail is dirt, sand, or slabs of the rimrock. Cairns (small rock piles) mark the way.

1.7 There's a great view of the dam ruins from the edge of the canyon rim, a little to the left of the trail. GPS: N39 20.70' / W104 45.35'.

2.6 The trail comes to a Y. Continue slightly to the right. The trail soon starts stair-stepping down into a ponderosa pine and oak woodland.

3.2 Cross Cherry Creek on a nice bridge. This is the low point of the hike. Elevation: 6,100 feet.

3.3 Three-way junction of Rimrock Trail, Homestead Trail, and Creek Bottom Trail. Turn left (south) onto the Creek Bottom Trail.

3.9 Junction with the trail to the Westside Trailhead. GPS: N39 21.07' / W104 45.80'. Turn left and walk down steps of wooden water bars to continue on the Creek Bottom Trail.

4.1 The Falls Spur Trail comes in from the right. Continue straight ahead on the Creek Bottom Trail. In a few feet, the trail passes very close to South Castlewood Canyon Road. As the trail curves to the left, a picnic table is to the right. GPS: N39 20.87' / W104 45.74'. You can see the falls from this viewpoint.

4.8   Junction with the Dam Historic Trail and a good view of the north side of the dam ruins. Continue straight ahead on the Creek Bottom Trail, which takes you past the broken edge of the dam. You'll soon pass another access trail coming down from Dam Historic Trail.

4.9   Junction with the other end of the Dam Historic Trail. Continue to the left on the Creek Bottom Trail. The trail crosses Cherry Creek and climbs up wooden stairs.

5.1   Arrive back at the junction of Inner Canyon Trail, Creek Bottom Trail, and Rimrock Trail. Turn right onto the Inner Canyon Trail.

5.3   Arrive back at the junction of Inner Canyon Trail and Lake Gulch Trail. Continue straight ahead on the Inner Canyon Trail.

5.5   The trail climbs up some wooden stairs. There are several side trails to the right that go down to Cherry Creek. Ignore these and continue on the Inner Canyon Trail.

5.8   The trail goes under an overhanging rock and then up some rocks.

6.0   The trail curves to the right and crosses Cherry Creek. The trail soon climbs a set of stairs, complete with handrails, to the canyon rim.

6.1   Top of stairs and the Inner Canyon Trailhead. The trail splits. Take the right branch to return to the parking lot.

6.2   Arrive at the parking lot. GPS: N39 20.02′ / W104 44.65′.

Options

1. For an easy 1.8-mile loop with a 200-foot gain, hike Lake Gulch Trail to Inner Canyon Trail, then turn right and return to the parking lot via the Inner Canyon Trail.

2. Add a spur to the Castlewood Dam ruins to Option 1 for a 2.7-mile lollipop hike. Hike Lake Gulch Trail to Inner Canyon Trail and turn left. At the junction with Creek Bottom Trail, Rimrock Trail, and Inner Canyon Trail, turn left and follow the Creek Bottom Trail to the second (northernmost) junction with the Dam Historic Trail to get a bottoms up view of the ruins. Return the way you came to the junction of Lake Gulch Trail and Inner Canyon Trail, but continue straight ahead on Inner Canyon Trail back to the parking lot.

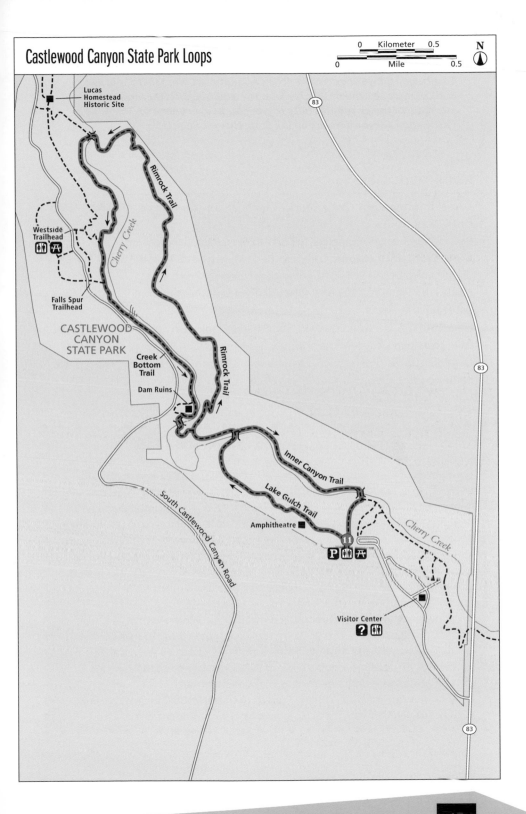

Castlewood Canyon State Park Loops

0   Kilometer   0.5

0   Mile   0.5

N

83

Lucas
Homestead
Historic Site

Rimrock Trail

Cherry Creek

Westside
Trailhead

Falls Spur
Trailhead

CASTLEWOOD
CANYON
STATE PARK

Creek
Bottom
Trail

Rimrock Trail

Dam Ruins

83

Inner Canyon Trail

Lake Gulch Trail

South Castlewood Canyon Road

Amphitheatre

11

P

Cherry Creek

Visitor Center

?

83

Castlewood Canyon has received the designations Colorado Natural Area and Colorado Watchable Wildlife Site. The park supports the largest summer roost of turkey vultures (fifty to one hundred) in Colorado. The ruins of Castlewood Canyon dam are on the State Historic Register.

HIKE INFORMATION

Local Information: Castle Rock Chamber of Commerce; 303-688-4597; castlerock.org

Parker Chamber of Commerce; 303-841-4268; parkerchamber.com

Local Events/Attractions: Colorado Renaissance Festival and Artisan Marketplace, Larkspur; 303-688-6010; coloradorenaissance.com

Castle Rock Wine Fest; 303-688-4597; castlerockculture.com/castle-rock-winefest

Castle Rock Museum, Castle Rock; 303-814-3164

Hike Tours: Castlewood Canyon State Park, Franktown; 303-688-5242; parks. state.co.us/parks/castlewoodcanyon

Organizations: Friends of Castlewood Canyon State Park, Franktown; castlewoodfriends.org

Friends of Castlewood Canyon State Park

The Friends of Castlewood Canyon State Park is an independent, nonprofit, 501(c)(3) organization whose mission is "to support and promote Castlewood Canyon by raising funds to preserve and enhance the park's natural and recreational resources, protect its boundaries, increase public awareness, and to enhance educational and interpretive activities which increase understanding and public appreciation of the park." The group has a cooperative agreement with Castlewood Canyon State Park. They raise funds for various park projects and help enhance educational activities and displays for the public. These funds supplement state appropriations.

One recent project was completed through a coalition with other public and private partners. The Friends raised $100,000 and worked with Great Outdoors Colorado and the Colorado Division of Parks to obtain another $1.35 million to procure a buffer zone of 397 acres to protect the canyon's pristine ecosystems from potential nearby developments.

For more information, contact Friends of Castlewood Canyon State Park, PO Box 403, Franktown, CO 80116, or visit castlewoodfriends.org.

Blackmer Loop—Cheyenne Mountain State Park

Twist and turn up and down along the pleasant Blackmer Loop on the toe of Cheyenne Mountain. After passing a group of car-size boulders, you'll come upon one with a ponderosa pine growing out of it. The trail generally travels in ponderosa pine and Douglas fir forest, but occasional openings present expansive views of Fort Carson and the eastern plains and of rugged Cheyenne Mountain to the west. Rustic remnants of ranching lie unused in fields along the north section of trail. Interpretive signs along Blackmer Loop and Zook Loop explain different park features.

Start: Day Use Trailhead

Distance: 4.7-mile lollipop

Hiking time: 2 to 2.5 hours

Difficulty: Moderate due to distance and elevation gain

Elevation gain: 525 feet

Trail surface: Natural surface and rocky trail

Seasons: Best Apr through Nov

Other trail users: Mountain bikers

Canine compatibility: Dogs not allowed

Land status: Colorado state park

Fees and permits: Daily fee or annual pass required

Schedule: Open year-round. Check website or call for current conditions.

Maps: USGS Cheyenne Mountain

Trail contact: Cheyenne Mountain State Park, 410 JL Ranch Heights Road, Colorado Springs; 719-576-2016; cpw.state.co.us/placestogo/parks/cheyennemountain

Other: Visitor Center hours are 9 a.m. to 5 p.m. daily. Fort Carson Army Base is east of Cheyenne Mountain State Park (CMSP). If severe weather is in the area, you may hear a siren that alerts soldiers in the field. At noon, reveille (a bugle call), resounds across the park.

Special considerations: Bring water because none is available on this hike. Beware of rattlesnakes. Smoking is not allowed on the trails or in the backcountry.

Finding the trailhead: From I-25 exit 140, head southbound on SH 115 (Nevada Avenue). In 5.5 miles, just past mile marker 42, turn right at the traffic light onto JL Ranch Heights Road. At the roundabout, drive halfway around so you continue heading west. The Visitor Center is 0.7 mile and the Entry Station is 0.8 mile from SH 115. After paying the fee, drive 0.1 mile and turn left into the Day Use Trailhead parking lot (A new sign says LIMEKILN GROVE TRAILHEAD.). There are restrooms and water at both the Visitor Center and the trailhead. There are also picnic tables and a small playground for kids at the trailhead.

THE HIKE

To access the Blackmer Loop, hike on the Zook Loop from the Day Use Trail-head along the Limekiln Valley. Gambel oaks (scrub oaks) grow tall here, more like trees than their usual bush form. A few ponderosa pines and Rocky Mountain junipers grow between the scrub oaks. Interpretive signs tell about the mountain lions and black bears that live in Cheyenne Mountain State Park (CMSP). A short trail climbs a little drainage connecting Zook Loop with Blackmer Loop. Along the loop, you can occasionally see 9,565-foot Cheyenne Mountain and some interesting rock formations. See if you can find a camel shape in one of them.

Within Cheyenne Mountain lies a fortified command center of the North American Air Defense Command (NORAD). Excavation through solid granite to build the underground post started in 1961 and took three years to complete. The operations center began its mission in 1966. It originally provided command and control for potential incoming Soviet bombers, which later changed to incoming nuclear warheads on intercontinental ballistic missiles (ICBMs). Various American and Canadian military agencies used the facility. When the Cold War ended, NORAD started tracking all aircraft, especially those without flight plans, including drug-smuggling planes. They also monitored over 8,200 objects orbiting the earth, alerting various world militaries if one entered the atmosphere, in order to avoid misunderstandings or panic.

Cheyenne Mountain from the Blackmer Loop trail.

12

Passing the trail to the campground and heading back down the Blackmer Loop trail.

In 2006, most operations were moved to nearby Peterson Air Force Base. The command center remains on "warm" standby, watching once again for missiles. NORAD may be best known for tracking Santa's flight on Christmas Eve. The northern section of Blackmer Loop is only about 0.15 mile from the NORAD access road.

One showpiece of this hike is the ponderosa pine growing out of a large granitic boulder. An interpretive sign describes ponderosa pines, Abert's squirrels, and porcupines. Farther along, the trail crosses green fields of tall grass growing around an old ranch fence and a huge tire with a pipe sticking out of it. The ranchers used the tire to try to catch water for their cattle.

Lloyd and Dorothy Jones once owned 1,500 acres here and operated a cattle ranch called the JL Ranch, until the mid-1900s. They lived in a house near the present-day entrance to NORAD. The Broadmoor Hotel took guests on trail rides through the area during part of that time. Since the 1950s, the area has been closed to the public, with little ranching activity.

In 1997, Colorado Springs voters approved a 0.1 percent increase in sales tax to fund open space. When 2,500 home sites were planned on the JL Ranch, the City of Colorado Springs' Trails and Open Space Commission (TOPS) campaigned to purchase the land. Collected sales tax funds helped the City of Colorado Springs partner with Colorado Parks and Wildlife, Great Outdoors Colorado (GOCO), and other private organizations to purchase the JL Ranch in June 2000. Now called Cheyenne Mountain State Park, it is the first state park in El Paso County. The

Blackmer Loop—Cheyenne Mountain State Park

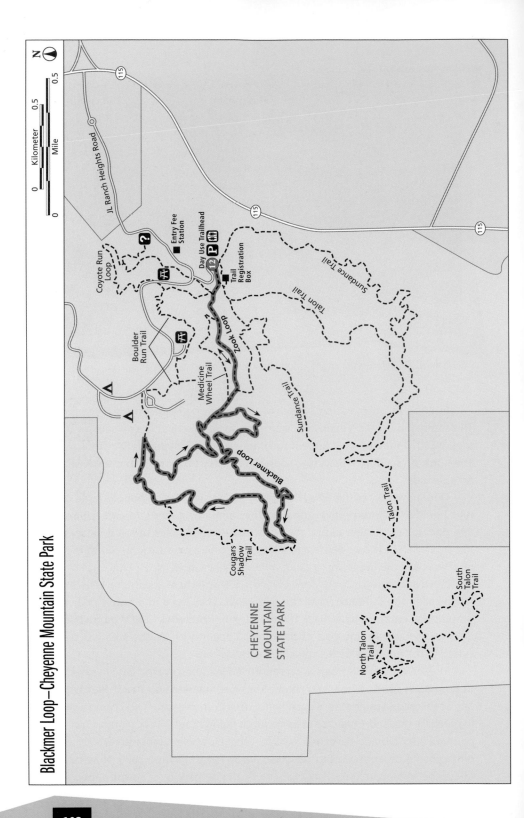

1,680-acre park opened to the public in 2006 with 20 miles of trails that were designed to protect wildlife and rare species. Only 80 acres contain development such as the Visitor Center, an outdoor amphitheater, campground, picnic grounds, and an archery range. GOCO has invested close to $24 million in the park.

Between 2007 and 2009, about 1,000 acres along the east side and top of Cheyenne Mountain were purchased by the City of Colorado Springs and Colorado Parks and Wildlife as additions to CMSP. This unique park is now considered one of the "crown jewels" of Colorado's State Park system. If you'd like to camp here, plan ahead and reserve your campsite as soon as possible!

MILES AND DIRECTIONS

0.0 Start from the Day Use Trailhead to the right (west) of the restrooms at the edge of the pavement. Elevation: 6,055 feet. GPS: N38 43.88' / W104 49.28'. Walk about 200 feet to the trail registration box and sign in. Turn right here onto the Zook Loop (blue).

0.1 Junction with Coyote Run. Head left to continue on Zook Loop.

0.2 Junction with Medicine Wheel. Continue straight ahead on Zook Loop.

0.5 Junction with Blackmer Loop (dark purple). GPS: N38 43.81' / W104 49.78'. There's a bench here and an interpretive sign about black bears. Turn right onto Blackmer. You can see the round trail marker above some small boulders.

0.6 Junction with Medicine Wheel. Continue straight ahead on Blackmer Loop.

0.7 Start/end of Blackmer Loop. Turn left.

1.3 Viewpoint to the east with a metal bench, and as you curve right, there is a good view of Cheyenne Mountain and some interesting rock formations. GPS: N38 43.84' / W104 50.02'. The trail twists and turns while climbing.

2.1 Junction with Cougar's Shadow Trail. Turn right to continue on Blackmer Loop. The trail winds past some huge boulders.

2.4 Ponderosa pine growing out of a huge boulder. There's a bench and nice rest spot. GPS: N38 43.74' / W104 50.20'.

2.9 Junction with Cougar's Shadow Trail. Continue straight ahead here.

3.3 Junction with Boulder Run Trail, which goes to the campground. Turn right and head downhill to finish the Blackmer Loop.

4.0 Start/end of Blackmer Loop. Turn left and return the way you came.

4.7 Arrive back at the trailhead.

Options

1. If you are staying at the campground, a combination of Boulder Run Trail and Blackmer forms a 3.7-mile lollipop. From the campground, hike down the road to the Boulder Run crosswalk. Turn right onto Boulder Run (gold). GPS: N38 44.11′ / W104 49.77′. Hike 0.2 mile to the junction with Blackmer Loop (dark purple). Turn left and hike down Blackmer 0.7 mile to the junction with the Blackmer spur to Zook Loop. Walk straight ahead to continue on Blackmer back to Boulder Run. Follow the directions above, starting at mile 0.7.

2. The many trails in CMSP offer a variety of hiking options.

> 🌿 **Green Tip:**
> *Pack out what you pack in, even food scraps because they can attract wild animals. Orange peels and other food items do not readily decompose in Colorado's high and dry climate.*

HIKE INFORMATION

Local Information: Colorado Springs Convention and Visitors Bureau; 800-888-4748, 719-635-7506; visitcos.com

Local Events/Attractions: Cheyenne Mountain Zoo, Colorado Springs; 719-633-9925; cmzoo.org

Florissant Fossil Beds National Monument; 719-748-3253; nps.gov/flfo

Garden of the Gods Visitor & Nature Center, Colorado Springs; 719-634-6666; gardenofgods.com

United States Air Force Academy, Visitor Center; 719-333-2025; usafa.af.mil

Hike Tours: Cheyenne Mountain State Park, Colorado Springs; 719-576-2016; cpw.parks.state.co.us/placestogo/parks/cheyennemountain

Organizations: Friends of Cheyenne Mountain State Park, Colorado Springs; friendsofcmsp.org

When Cheyenne Mountain State Park was established in 2000, the property's shape looked like a bear with one paw and nose pointing east, an ear to the north, the other paws to the south, and tail to the west.

Talon Loops—Cheyenne Mountain State Park

From prairie grasslands through oak shrublands to montane forests, a loop on the Talon, North Talon, and South Talon trails provides a sampling of Cheyenne Mountain State Park's variety. At 9,565 feet, Cheyenne Mountain towers above you to the west. Various raptors, including peregrine falcons, prairie falcons, and golden eagles, soar overhead. Interpretive signs along the way explain the park's many features. One overlook with a bench is a great place for lunch as you enjoy an outcrop of pink Pikes Peak granite. The hike crosses an interesting rock fin on North Talon before looping through thick forest on South Talon and returning back to Talon.

Start: Day Use Trailhead
Distance: 7.9-mile multiple loops
Hiking time: 3.25 to 4.5 hours
Difficulty: Moderate due to distance
Elevation gain: 820 feet, plus a lot of undulations
Trail surface: Natural surface and rocky trail
Seasons: Best Apr through Nov
Other trail users: Mountain bikers
Canine compatibility: Dogs not allowed
Land status: Colorado state park
Fees and permits: Daily fee or annual pass required
Schedule: Open year-round. Check website or call for current conditions.
Maps: USGS Cheyenne Mountain

Trail contact: Cheyenne Mountain State Park, 410 JL Ranch Heights Road, Colorado Springs; 719-576-2016; cpw.parks. state.co.us/placestogo/parks/ cheyennemountain
Other: Visitor Center hours are 9 a.m. to 5 p.m. daily. Fort Carson Army Base is east of Cheyenne Mountain State Park. If severe weather is in the area, you may hear a siren that alerts soldiers in the field. At noon, reveille (a bugle call) resounds across the park.
Special considerations: Bring water because none is available on this hike. Beware of rattlesnakes. Smoking is not allowed on the trails or in the backcountry.

Finding the trailhead: From I-25 exit 140, head southbound on SH 115 (Nevada Avenue). In 5.5 miles, just past mile marker 42, turn right at the traffic light onto JL Ranch Heights Road. At the roundabout, drive halfway around so you continue heading west. The Visitor Center is 0.7 mile and the Entry Station is 0.8 mile from SH 115. After paying the fee, drive 0.1 mile and turn left into the Day Use Trailhead (LIMEKILN GROVE TRAILHEAD) parking lot. There are restrooms and water at both the Visitor Center and the trailhead. Picnic tables and a small playground for kids are also at the trailhead.

13

THE HIKE

With a little imagination, the outline of the Talon Trail, with its north and south loops, resembles a raptor's foot—the back talon and three front ones. This is perhaps appropriate, because the nearby Air Force Academy's mascot is a falcon.

This loop provides a sample of the different ecosystems in Cheyenne Mountain State Park (CMSP). The first part of the trail crosses grasslands punctuated with Gambel oak (scrub oak) and Rocky Mountain juniper. Hungry raptors can choose dinner from the black-tailed prairie dog colony along the trail. Currant bushes, skunkbush (a type of sumac), and mountain mahogany, with its curly-tailed fruits, grow along the trail as it slowly gains elevation. Boulder raspberry (thimbleberry), with its big white rose-like flowers, and wild roses bloom in spring. Wild turkeys live and breed in the park, where they eat acorns, nuts, seeds, fruits, and insects.

After the trail passes the westernmost Sundance Trail junction, it undulates past scrub oak, ponderosa pine, common juniper, prickly pear cactus, yucca, and a variety of bushes. Douglas firs grow along the north-facing part of North Talon. The climbing trail twists and turns, becoming rockier. White firs also grow along here. This is a true fir, with cones that stick up, and has longer needles than the Douglas fir, whose cones hang down, meaning it is not a true fir. White fir cones have smooth scales, unlike the "mouse tail and feet" bracts of the Douglas fir cone.

The overlook at 3.2 miles makes a great lunch stop. An interpretive sign explains Pikes Peak granite, with some good examples across the drainage. Just

Heading to the Zoop Loop trail.

past the high point of this hike is an interesting rock fin of sandstone. The South Talon Trail travels like a roller coaster through a thick fir forest in shadier areas, and scrub oaks and ponderosa pines on sunnier exposures. It's a great place to observe the response of vegetation to different slope aspects.

On the way down Talon, take a few minutes to walk to the interpretive sign about raptors. Birders have spotted prairie falcons, peregrine falcons, red-tailed hawks, golden eagles, American kestrels, and sharp-shinned hawks in CMSP. The sign provides fascinating facts about falcons.

Red-tailed hawks range over most of North America. About 19 inches long, they have upper tails that are red with brown-gray banding on the lower edge. While hunting they hover and glide, looking for a tasty morsel of a small mammal, bird, or reptile.

American kestrels are small falcons about 9 inches long with blue-gray wings. They eat small prey like mice, voles, little birds, and insects. They live in woodpecker holes and natural cavities in cliffs.

Sharp-shinned hawks are slightly larger than kestrels and have short, rounded wings. Their breasts look like a brownish-red and white checkerboard. They catch small birds in midair and take them home for dinner.

Golden eagles, at 30 inches long, are impressive birds. They are dark-colored, easy to distinguish from bald eagles with their white heads and white tails. Rabbits and rodents such as prairie dogs are snatched by diving eagles. The raptors build large platform nests on cliff ledges, on the ground, or in trees.

The Sundance Trail on the lower loop.

Talon Loops–Cheyenne Mountain State Park

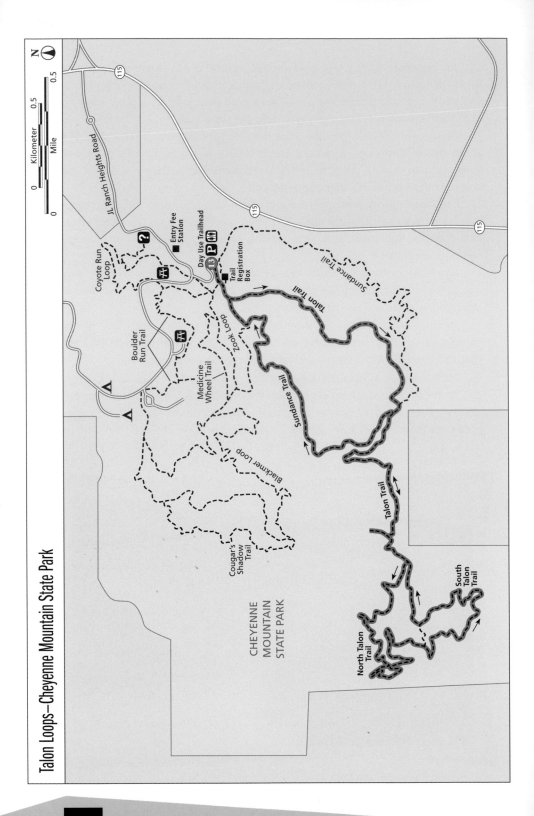

This loop hike ends by returning on the north side of the Sundance Trail; you'll see different landscape as the trail weaves between two small hills and down a ridge.

Geocache sites (see geocaching.com) are located in CMSP. You can rent GPS units at the Visitor Center and go on a treasure hunt.

MILES AND DIRECTIONS

0.0 Start from the Day Use Trailhead to the right (west) of the restrooms at the edge of the pavement. Elevation: 6,055 feet. GPS: N38 43.88' / W104 49.28'. Walk about 200 feet to the trail registration box and sign in. Turn left here onto the Zook Loop (blue).

0.1 Junction with Talon (yellow). Turn left onto the Talon Trail.

0.3 Junction with Little Bear. Head left to continue on Talon.

0.5 Interpretive sign about Pikes Peak. A few feet farther is the junction with Turkey Trot. Head left to continue on Talon.

1.25 Junction with the southern section of Sundance Trail. Turn right and head uphill.

1.3 Junction with the northern section of Sundance. Keep left on Talon.

1.6 A metal bench with a nice view of the lower part of the park.

2.1 A spur trail goes to the right to an interpretive sign about raptors. About 275 feet out and back.

2.3 Junction with North Talon (green). Turn right.

3.2 Spur trail heads right to a lunch spot and view of the rocky cliffs of Cheyenne Mountain. GPS: N38 43.39' / W104 50.94'. Return to North Talon at 3.3 miles.

3.4 A flat area that's the high point of the hike. Elevation: 6,860 feet. GPS: N38 43.33' / W104 50.95'. In a few hundred feet, you'll cross an interesting rock fin.

4.0 Three-way junction of Talon, North Talon, and South Talon. Turn right onto South Talon (reddish brown).

5.0 Junction of South Talon and Talon. Turn right and head down Talon.

5.3 Junction of Talon and North Talon. Continue straight downhill on Talon.

6.4 Junction with Sundance. Turn left on Sundance (red).

6.75 Spur trail to the right. Stay to the left on Sundance.

7.4 In about 200 feet is the junction with Turkey Trot. Turn left and head downhill on Sundance. In another 150 feet is a spur trail to the right. Stay left.

7.6 Junction with Little Bear. Continue left on Sundance.

7.7 Junction with the Zook Loop. Turn right onto Zook.

7.8 Four-way junction with Talon, Zook Loop, and Sundance. Go straight ahead on the Zook Loop to the parking lot.

7.9 Arrive back at the trailhead.

Options

1. For a 7.2-mile lollipop, hike Talon and North Talon, turning left on Talon at mile 4.0 above.

2. For a 6.6-mile lollipop, hike Talon and South Talon heading straight ahead at mile 2.3 above, then turning right at mile 4.0 to head downhill on Talon.

3. For a shorter, easy 2.8-mile loop, hike Talon to Sundance north (mile 1.3 above), turn right, and follow the directions starting at mile 6.4.

> 🌿 **Green Tip:**
> *Don't take "souvenirs" home with you. This means natural materials such as plants, rocks, shells, and driftwood as well as historic artifacts such as fossils and arrowheads.*

HIKE INFORMATION

Local Information: Colorado Springs Convention and Visitors Bureaus; 800-888-4748, 719-635-7506; visitcos.com

Local Events/Attractions: Cheyenne Mountain Zoo, Colorado Springs; 719-633-9925; cmzoo.org

Florissant Fossil Beds National Monument; 719-748-3253; nps.gov/flfo

Garden of the Gods Visitor & Nature Center, Colorado Springs; 719-634-6666; gardenofgods.com

United States Air Force Academy, Visitor Center; 719-333-2025; usafa.af.mil

Hike Tours: Cheyenne Mountain State Park, Colorado Springs; 719-576-2016; cpw.parks.state.co.us/placestogo/parks/cheyennemountain

Organizations: Friends of Cheyenne Mountain State Park, Colorado Springs; friendsofcmsp.org

The Friends of Cheyenne Mountain State Park is a nonprofit, 501(c)(3) organization that serves "to protect, enhance, and preserve for all time the natural state and spectacular beauty of the park. We are also dedicated to working in partnership with the park staff to promote recreational and educational activities as well as advocating for important park issues."

Honorable Mentions

A. Valley Loop at Bobcat Ridge Natural Area

Valley Loop explores the grasslands section of the Bobcat Ridge Natural Area, with a taste of ponderosa pine and Douglas fir forest included for good measure. You'll also pass through the lower edge of the 2000 Bobcat Gulch Fire and can take side trips to a stone circle and the Kitchen cabin built in 1917. The cabin has been stabilized for use in educational programs.

The trail starts at the Bobcat Ridge Natural Area kiosk about 0.1 mile from the vault toilet at the parking lot. Elevation: 5,440 feet. GPS: N40 28.76' / W105 13.59'. In 0.1 mile turn left onto the Valley Loop. Pass the junction of Eden Valley Spur at 0.6 mile and the junction with Ginny Trail at 0.7 mile. The trail undulates along the edge of the valley as it crosses little drainages. At 1.8 miles, the trail reaches a Y. Head right for an optional look at the stone circle and interpretive sign. Otherwise, head left to the junction with Powerline Road at 2.0 miles at about 5,720 feet. Continue north on the Valley Loop past the junction with D. R. Trail in another 0.2 mile. The trail heads downhill and into the grasslands. At 3.0 miles turn left on the trail to the Kitchen cabin, which is about 0.3 mile out and back. After returning from the cabin, head left on the Valley Loop and hike 1.2 miles back to the trailhead.

The total loop, including the cabin, is a moderate 4.4 miles due to distance. Elevation gain is about 280 feet, plus lots of little undulations. The trail is also used by equestrians and mountain bikers. Dogs are not allowed in Bobcat Ridge Natural Area.

Finding the trailhead: From I-25 exit 257-B, Loveland/US 34 West, drive west on US 34 for 10.6 miles through town to Larimer County Road 27, which is right before the Big Thompson Elementary School. Turn right onto LCR 27 and drive north for 4.6 miles to the BOBCAT RIDGE NEXT LEFT sign. Turn far left onto LCR 32C, not into the private drive. The road turns to dirt as it crosses through the hogback (Buffum Canyon). Avoid this road if there is any chance of flash flood. The parking lot is 0.5 mile west. Vault toilets are available at the trailhead.

B. Flatirons Vista Trails

With numerous trails on the Flatirons Plateau, Greenbelt Plateau, Doudy Draw, and the Community Ditch, you can create several loop hikes of different lengths from this trailhead to suit your mood. The Flatirons Vista South and North Trails make a 3.5-mile loop through grasslands and open stands of ponderosa pine. A longer 6.5-mile loop includes Flatirons Vista North, Doudy Draw, Community Ditch, and Greenbelt Plateau Trails. You'll cross SH 93 twice on this loop—once while going through the new underpass on the Community Ditch Trail and the other in a traditional crosswalk at the intersection of SH 93 and SH 128. This loop is often dry when other area trails are still muddy or snowy. Views of the Flatirons and the eastern plains are excellent, and you may meet some grazing cattle along the way. Mountain bikers and equestrians also use these trails. Dog regulations vary with season and trail, so check them out at osmp.org or call 303-441-3440.

Finding the trailhead: In Boulder, from the intersection of Table Mesa Drive and Broadway (SH 93), drive south on SH 93 for 4.6 miles. Soon past the intersection with SH 128, turn right into the trailhead parking area. GPS: N39 55.45' / W105 14.13'. Vault toilets are available. Bring water, as none is available along the trail. This is a parking permit fee area; see the self-serve fee station near the toilets. If your vehicle is not registered in Boulder County, you have to pay for a daily or annual permit and display it on your windshield. For more info: osmp.org or 303-441-3440.

Flatirons Vista Pond.

The Foothills

The Rawhide Trail in White Ranch Park northwest of Golden.

These fifteen hikes explore the foothills, where many a dream was born and then died, but a few came true. Several trails climb to summits or high points, a great workout rewarded by wonderful views. Other hikes take you on historical tours to burned mansions, old mines, and remains of old ranches. One hike follows a former railroad route. Native Americans passed through the foothills valleys, camping for a while and performing their ritual ceremonies. Some hikes take you past interesting geological features.

The foothills are the lower mountains and hills that rise abruptly from the plains. Roughly speaking, the northern foothills "strip" is east of the north/south line drawn by Colorado SH 119, SH 72, and SH 7, and west of the "flat" plains. It ranges from Larkspur in the south to Estes Park in the north. These hikes start as low as 5,500 feet and rise to 8,720 feet. Trails vary in length from 2.8 to 10.2 miles. When the plains begin to heat up but snowdrifts still linger in the mountains, the foothills trails provide a great escape. Lower trails might be hikable year-round, except after a big snowstorm. If there's enough snow, higher trails provide opportunities for snowshoeing and cross-country skiing.

The foothills are typically covered in ponderosa pine and Douglas fir, with a wide variety of bushes, depending on the lay of the land and water availability. Rocky Mountain juniper, common juniper, Gambel oak (oakbrush), and mountain mahogany grow on lower, warmer slopes. Aspens start appearing at about 5,600 feet in moist areas, becoming more common above 8,000 feet.

Rocky, lumpy ridges form part of the area's geology. Magma gathered under an ancient Colorado about 1.4 billion years ago and cooled before ever reaching the surface. Over the years—as the land rose, was buried in sediment, and rose again numerous times—the hardened rock (various types of granite) emerged and eroded again. When erosion uncovers granite, the rock expands, and joints or fractures form along large exposed surfaces. Freeze-thaw cycles take over, causing joints to expand, and eventually rock surfaces break off, much like layers being peeled off an onion. The granite erodes into interesting shapes.

During the Laramide mountain-building episode starting about 70 million years ago, mineral-rich solutions heated by magma moved into the cracks formed by the uplift. As these solutions cooled, gold, silver, lead, and zinc ores formed. These ores are mostly found in a 60-mile-wide zone called the Colorado Mineral Belt that starts at Telluride in southwestern Colorado; moves through Aspen, Leadville, Fairplay, Breckenridge, Georgetown, and Central City; and ends north of Boulder.

While Native Americans mostly passed through the foothills, miners flocked to the Colorado Mineral Belt in search of their fortunes. Others decided mining wasn't for them and started ranches and farms to raise food to sell to the miners. Several of these foothills ranches were sold to county open space programs or to the Colorado state park system, as the owners wished to preserve their land "as it was." How fortunate for us twenty-first century hikers!

Homestead Meadows

Several hiking options allow you to explore the peaceful and quiet remains of different farms and ranches in Homestead Meadows National Historic District (including one with a sunken bathtub!). Old relics like stoves and cars lie abandoned in the flower-filled meadows. Cattle ranching, farming, and logging provided income to the families who settled here. A newer and easier access to this outdoor history museum is through Hermit Park Open Space, opened in 2008 by Larimer County. The USDA Forest Service manages Homestead Meadows, a unique property that provides an insight into the past as well as critical winter habitat for elk.

Start: Homestead Meadows Connector Trailhead

Distance: 7.9 miles out and back with loops and spurs

Hiking time: 3 to 4.5 hours

Difficulty: Moderate due to length

Elevation gain: 720 feet, including various ups and downs

Trail surface: Natural surface trail and nonmotorized dirt roads (closed to the motorized public)

Seasons: Best mid-May through Oct

Other trail users: Mountain bikers and equestrians

Canine compatibility: Dogs must be on leash in Hermit Park Open Space and under voice control on national forest lands

Land status: Larimer County Parks and Open Space, national forest

Fees and permits: Day use fee or annual pass required for Hermit Park Open Space

Schedule: Open year-round

Maps: USGS Panorama Peak; National Geographic Trails Illustrated 101 Cache La Poudre/Big Thompson; Latitude 40°: Colorado Front Range

Trail contacts: Roosevelt National Forest, Canyon Lakes Ranger District, 2150 Centre Avenue, Building E, Fort Collins; 970-295-6700; www.fs.usda.gov/arp. Hermit Park Open Space, Larimer County Department of Natural Resources, 1800 South County Road 31, Loveland; 970-619-4570; larimer.org/naturalresources

Other: Advise staff at Hermit Park Open Space if you plan to leave a vehicle overnight at the trailhead (otherwise they call Search and Rescue). Leave all artifacts that you find so others may enjoy them.

Special considerations: Bring water with you because none is available along the trails. People cross-country ski in Homestead Meadows; however, the trail is neither marked nor maintained for winter use. Winter access to the trailhead in Hermit Park will be "as conditions allow." The winter closure gate is near the group-use area, 0.7 mile from this trailhead.

THE HIKE

Homestead Meadows today is quiet and full of flowers and wildlife. Trying to visualize life as a farmer or rancher here in the early 1900s without electricity, plumbing, high-speed cars on good roads, cell phones, and computers challenges the imagination.

Hermit Park Open Space (OS) had been privately owned and protected for many years. A trail from Hermit Park OS to Grizzly Gulch was constructed to access Homestead Meadows in Roosevelt National Forest. In 2008, Larimer County built a new trailhead in Hermit Park OS and improved the trail, which provides easier and shorter access than Lion Gulch Trail 949, which was heavily damaged in the 2013 flood and is now closed. Once in Homestead Meadows, numerous interpretive signs, installed by the Forest Service, inform hikers about each homestead and its various owners.

The route follows a dirt road, then becomes a single-track as it crosses a grassy area. It slowly climbs through ponderosa pine, Douglas fir, and aspen forest before dropping down to a dirt road (closed to the motorized public) in Grizzly Gulch, Homestead Meadow Trail 971. The road climbs steadily to Homestead Meadows.

The first homestead, which sits at the bottom of a nice meadow, belonged to the Irvins. It is the best preserved, with the most buildings. Frank Irvin earned his land in 1917 but died soon after. Another owner was R. J. Nettleton, who logged the area using a team of hefty black Percheron horses to drag huge timbers to the sawmill. The remains of the old sawmill lie along a spur trail near the Irvin house. Take some time to explore the old buildings and poke your head in the old barn. The house still sports some green roofing as well as nice flooring. The most fascinating building is the old bathhouse with a sunken bathtub. The trail to this interesting relic starts on the right side of the house as you face it.

After exploring the Irvin Homestead, hike down to the Griffith Homestead. The remains of the cabin lie snuggled among ponderosa pines at a meadow's

The remains of a barn at the Irvin Homestead.

edge. The trail descends through seemingly terraced meadows. Keep an eye out to the left for an old rusted stove amid the wildflowers. In another 0.1 mile, down on the right is the interpretive sign about Sarah Walker's homestead, of which very little remains. Imagine Sarah, a widow who outlived both of her children, walking down the Lion Gulch Trail to SH 36, hitching a ride into Lyons to sell her eggs and cream, and then buying supplies before reversing her morning adventure.

Below the Walker Homestead, the trail intersects Lyons Park Trail 949-1, which heads right (south) to the Engert, Laycook, Hill, and Boren home-steads. Unfortunately, the Engert house burned in the Big Elk Fire in 2002. If you look to the southeast, you can see several burned patches. Travel a little farther down Lion Gulch to the interpretive sign about the Homestead Act of 1862, the incentive that brought settlers to this area, then return to the Griffith cabin.

Beyond the Griffith cabin you'll return to Homestead Meadow Trail 971. Head left (west) at the junction, which winds through forest and across a lush, grassy meadow on the way to the remains of the Brown Homestead. Harry Brown raised registered Hereford cattle here. During the Depression, cattle prices dropped by about 90 percent, forcing Harry to sell the herd.

You can camp in Homestead Meadows, away from the buildings, to have more time to explore all the homesteads and feel the spirit of this long-ago lively place.

MILES AND DIRECTIONS

0.0 Start from the Homestead Meadows Connector Trailhead. Elevation: 8,380 feet. GPS: N40 20.12' / W105 28.31'. Go around the metal gate and continue straight on the road when it intersects the access roads to two cabins.

0.4 The road splits. The right branch is blocked off; continue on the left branch. Hike down to where the single-track trail starts. Elevation: 8,280 feet (low point). GPS: N40 20.11' / W105 27.83'. Turn right onto the single-track trail and hike across a grassy meadow.

0.7 A HOMESTEAD MEADOWS sign points to the right to keep you on the trail.

0.9 The trail intersects a dirt road in Grizzly Gulch, which is Homestead Meadow Trail 971. Elevation: 8,320 feet. GPS: N40 19.88' / W105 27.48'. Turn right and hike uphill on the road.

1.75 This becomes Forest Road 120. GPS: N40 19.38' / W105 27.43'. Continue straight ahead on FR 120.

2.6 Junction of FR 120 and Irvin Homestead Trail 971.1. GPS: N40 18.94' / W105 26.88'. Turn left onto the Irvin Homestead Trail.

3.0 Junction of the trail to the old sawmill and the trail to the Irvin Homestead. In about 50 feet is the interpretive sign; the house itself is less than 0.1

The Homestead Meadow Trail, on the way to the Brown Homestead.

mile from the sign. The Forest Service requests that you not enter the old buildings. Take some time to wander around this old homestead, the best preserved of the four along this hike.

Option: You can make a 0.6-mile loop and side trip to the sawmill remains. Start at the interpretive sign and walk toward the house, but first check out the barn on your right. Continue to what looks like the chicken house on the right, then return to the house. Walk to the right around the house, past what probably was a root cellar. Follow the stone path to the right, down past the spring to the bathhouse with the sunken bathtub. Head north across the meadow to the two cabins. From the west cabin, take the trail to the southwest, which returns to the interpretive sign. Then head back toward Meadow Loop Trail, but take the right trail to check out the strange remains of the sawmill.) Return to Irvin Homestead Trail 971.1 and turn right to return the way you came from FR 120.

3.4 Junction of FR 120 and Irvin Homestead Trail 971.1. Continue left.

3.8 Junction of Irvin Homestead Trail and Homestead Meadow Trail. GPS: N40 18.83' / W105 27.20'. Turn left (south) onto the Homestead Meadow Trail.

4.0 Junction of Homestead Meadow Trail and the single-track Griffith Homestead Trail 949.2. GPS: N40 18.69' / W105 27.08'. Turn left onto single-track and head downhill.

4.2 Arrive at the Griffith Homestead. Take a few minutes to read the interpretive sign on the right along Lion Gulch Trail 949. Turn around to the east and head downhill on Lion Gulch Trail 949.

4.4 The WALKER HOMESTEAD interpretive sign is down on the right; the Walker Homestead ruins are to the left. Here, you can see how the trail was slightly re-aligned due to flood damage. Continue downhill to the interpretive signs about the Big Elk Fire and the Homestead Act of 1862.

4.5 Junction of Lion Gulch Trail 949 and Lion's Paw Trail 949.1. Elevation: about 8,400 feet. GPS: N40 18.47' / W105 26.73'. Continue left downhill on the trail, straight ahead to the HOMESTEAD ACT OF 1862 interpretive sign.

4.6 Stop and read the interpretive sign about the Homestead Act of 1862 for background on why these people worked hard to tame these meadows. GPS: N40 18.44' / W105 26.63'. Turn around and retrace your steps northeast toward the Irwin Trail.

5.4 Junction of Homestead Meadow Trail and Irvin Homestead Trail 971.1. Turn left to finish the Homestead Meadow Trail and explore the Brown Homestead. The high point of the trail (8,720 feet) is along this stretch.

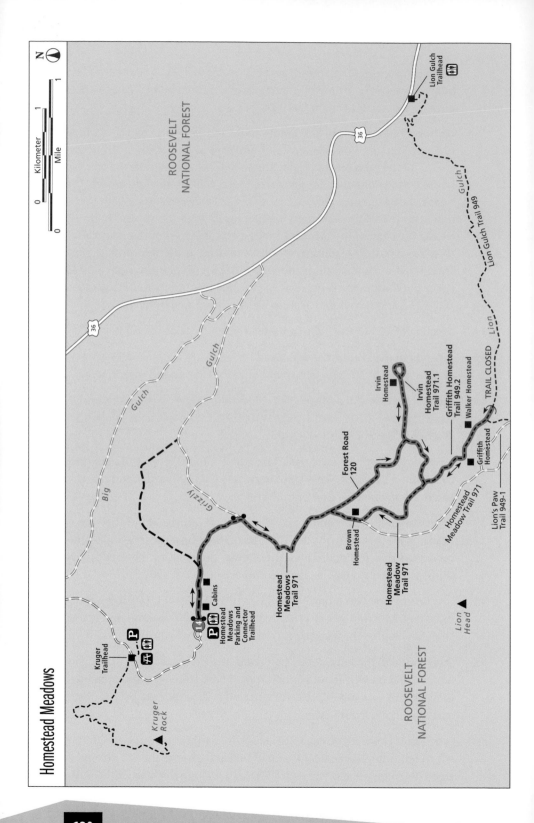

Homestead Meadows

N

Kilometer

Mile

ROOSEVELT
NATIONAL FOREST

Lion Gulch
Trailhead

36

Gulch

Lion Gulch Trail 949

Lion

Big

Gulch

Grizzly

Gulch

TRAIL CLOSED

Irvin
Homestead

Irvin
Homestead
Trail 971.1

Griffith Homestead
Trail 949.2

Walker Homestead

Griffith
Homestead

Forest Road
120

Homestead
Meadow Trail 971

Lion's Paw
Trail 949-1

Brown
Homestead

Homestead
Meadow Trail 971

Homestead
Meadows
Trail 971

Cabins

Kruger Trailhead

P

14

P

Homestead
Meadows Parking and
Connector Trailhead

Lion
Head

ROOSEVELT
NATIONAL FOREST

Kruger
Rock

5.6   The trail crosses a meadow with very tall grass. Follow the little posts across this meadow to reach the forest.

5.8   Arrive at a T-intersection with an old road, which merges here with the Homestead Meadow Trail. Turn right (north) onto the Homestead Meadow Trail.

5.9   Arrive at the Brown Homestead.

6.1   Arrive back at the junction of FR 120 and the Homestead Meadow Trail. Turn left onto FR 120 (the road down Grizzly Gulch) and return the way you came.

7.9   Arrive back at the trailhead.

Options

1. For a shorter, 3.9-mile out-and-back hike, follow the instructions to mile 1.75 above. Then turn right and hike 0.2 mile to the Brown Homestead. Return the way you came.

2. To visit only the Irvin Homestead is a 6.0-mile lollipop hike. Follow the directions to mile 3.4 above, then turn right and return the way you came to the trailhead in Hermit Park OS.

3. To see two homesteads, this option is 6.8 miles with a loop and spur to the Irvin Homestead and the Brown Homestead. Follow the directions to mile 3.4 above. Turn right and head back the way you came 0.9 mile to the junction of FR 120 and Homestead Meadow Trail. Turn left and hike 0.2 mile to the Brown Homestead. Return the 0.2 mile to the junction of FR 120. Turn left onto Homestead Meadow Trail, the road down Grizzly Gulch, and return to Hermit Park OS the way you came.

HIKE INFORMATION

Local Information: Estes Park Visitor Center; 800-443-7837, 970-577-9900; visitestespark.com

Local Events/Attractions: MacGregor Ranch, Estes Park; 970-586-3749; macgregorranch.org

Longs Peak Scottish-Irish Highland Festival, Estes Park; 800-903-7837, 970-586-6308; scotfest.com

Elk Fest, Estes Park; 800-443-7837, 970-577-9900; visitestespark.com/events-calendar/special events/elk-fest

Organizations: Friends of Larimer County Parks and Open Lands, Loveland; 970-493-4791; larimer.org naturalresources/friends

Larimer County Natural Resources Volunteer Program, Loveland; 970-619-4552; larimer.org/naturalresources/volunteer

The Hewlett-Packard Corporation, and then Agilent Technologies, owned Hermit Park for about forty years. The land was used for recreation, including campsites, cabins, picnic areas, and trails. Employees wanted to preserve the land for public use and approached Larimer County to purchase their special place.

The Homestead Act of 1862

In the mid-1800s Congress attempted several times to make homesteading laws for the western territories more fair and affordable. However, factory owners in the North were concerned that if homesteading was more appealing, their cheap factory labor would leave; Southern slave owners worried that new states created in the West by homesteaders would oppose slavery.

During the Civil War, Congress finally passed the Homestead Act, which President Abraham Lincoln signed into law on May 20, 1862. Settlers could lay claim to 160 acres of surveyed public land by filing an application. The applicant had to live on the land for the next five years, making improvements such as growing crops and building at least a 12-by-14-foot dwelling. After five years, the settler would file proof of residency and documentation that he or she had made the required improvements. If the claims proved valid, the homesteader received free and clear title to the land for a $15 filing fee. For people with more money, 160 acres could be purchased for $1.25 per acre after living on the land for six months and making minor improvements.

Nighthawk Trail—Hall Ranch

This long hike climbs to the old Nelson Ranch in Antelope Park, where Native Americans lived and hunted. The trail winds through beautiful valleys, grasslands, and forest. Rock ridges rise like ships' prows, one higher than the other. Peace and quiet take you away from the hustle and bustle of nearby cities. Most of the hike is open to hikers and equestrians only. As you enter Antelope Park, a stunning view of Longs Peak and Mount Meeker appears. Hall Ranch provides critical wildlife habitat, so keep your eyes and ears open for the wild residents.

Start: Trailhead bulletin board by the upper parking lot

Distance: 10.2 miles out and back

Hiking time: 4.5 to 6.5 hours

Difficulty: Difficult due to distance and elevation gain

Elevation gain: 1,410-foot gain and 320-foot loss to the Nelson Ranch house

Trail surface: Natural surface trail and old roads (closed to the motorized public)

Seasons: Best May through Oct

Other trail users: Equestrians on all sections; mountain bikers on Nelson Loop Trail only.

Canine compatibility: Dogs not permitted in Hall Ranch

Land status: Boulder County Parks and Open Space

Fees and permits: None required

Schedule: Open year-round from sunrise to sunset

Maps: USGS Lyons; National Geographic Trails Illustrated 100 Boulder/Golden; Latitude 40°: Boulder County Trails

Trail contact: Boulder County Parks and Open Space, 5201 Saint Vrain Road, Boulder; 303-678-6200; bouldercountyopenspace.org

Other: Collecting plant materials, even for personal use, is prohibited at Hall Ranch Open Space. Camping, ground fires, and smoking are prohibited. Several parts of Hall Ranch Open Space are critical wildlife habitats and are closed to the public. Please respect these closures.

Special considerations: Beware of rattlesnakes. Bring water with you—very little to none is available along the trail.

Finding the trailhead: In Boulder, from 28th Street (US 36) and Canyon Boulevard (SH 119), head north on US 36 to its junction with SH 66. Turn left on SH 66 and drive through Lyons to the stop sign at the T-intersection (US 36 and SH 7). Turn left onto SH 7 and drive 1.5 miles to Hall Ranch North Foothills Open Space, just past mile marker 32. Turn right onto the Hall Ranch access road and drive to the upper trailhead. If no parking is available, drive back to the lower parking lot. The trail starts at the west end of the lot. Hike 0.15 mile to the upper trailhead. A vault toilet, group shelter, and picnic tables are located at the upper parking lot, but no water.

THE HIKE

Nighthawk Trail winds through different ecosystems with views back into geologic history. The lower part of Hall Ranch is populated by different grasses, such as little bluestem, big bluestem, and western wheatgrass. Prickly pear cactus thrives in the warm, dry southern exposure. In spring, big yellow waxy-looking flowers bloom on the cactus. By fall, red spiny fruits stick up in clusters from the green pads.

A few small Rocky Mountain juniper trees are slowly growing in open areas. The little grayish blue-green berries are used to flavor gin. Native Americans ground or cooked the berries into meal or mush for winter food or for flavoring meat dishes. Rabbitbrush, with its golden fall flowers, lines the trail. Chewing gum was prepared from the lower bark and roots of some rabbitbrush species. Tea was steeped from the leaves to treat fevers, coughs, and colds, while flowers created a yellow dye.

Where rocks protrude from the surrounding hills or the little canyon that the trail climbs, larger Rocky Mountain junipers and ponderosa pines punctuate the land. Early peoples stripped bark from ponderosas for the cambium, or inner bark, a sweet treat. Seeds from the cones were ground into a meal to make bread. Tea made from the needles provided vitamins A and C. Native Americans used the sap for torches, chewing gum, and waterproofing baskets.

Trees grow larger where rocks channel moisture to the roots. You can tell where water stays year-round, either under a dry creek bed or low depression, by the cottonwood trees growing in small clusters. The rounded and lumpy rocks are granite, once magma that slowly cooled beneath the earth's surface. These

Autumn view from the Nighthawk Trail.

ancient igneous rocks that formed 1.3 to 1.7 billion years ago were thrust up starting 70 million years ago to become the current Rocky Mountains.

The trail winds around a hump of land then drops into a drainage only to climb again, traversing little hills to a higher meadow. As the land undulates, ponderosa forest appears, interspersed with grassy areas. Old ranch roads, closed to the motorized public, provide emergency and park maintenance access to the area. The trail switchbacks up a ridge to a nice viewpoint to the east, then drops into a little drainage in a higher meadow lined by ponderosa pines. You'll pass an old stone wall, probably a remnant of early ranching days.

Lumpy rock humps dot the landscape along this hike. The high point of the trail is along a little bump of forested land. As the trail descends into Antelope Park, a spectacular view of Longs Peak and Mount Meeker suddenly appears. The high peaks of the Continental Divide that border the west side of Wild Basin in Rocky Mountain National Park seem like dwarfs compared to the two massive peaks on the right.

Antelope Park's grassy meadows have been home to deer, antelope, elk, and maybe even bison over the years. The Arapaho and Cheyenne lived here at least part of the year. The berries of the skunkbush, wild plum, chokecherry, and various currant bushes provided food for the long winter. The old Nelson Ranch house sits silently near the silo that still stands tall and proud, looking down on a trough that fills with water after rain. Red sandstone rocks to the southeast of the structure make a great lunch spot.

Hall Ranch is a beautiful place. Please remember that collecting plant materials, even for personal use, is prohibited here. About 4,465 acres provide not only recreation for people weary from hectic lifestyles, but also a haven for wildlife that has lost much habitat to agriculture and modern society.

View of Mount Meeker and Longs Peak from the Nelson Loop trail.

Nighthawk Trail–Hall Ranch

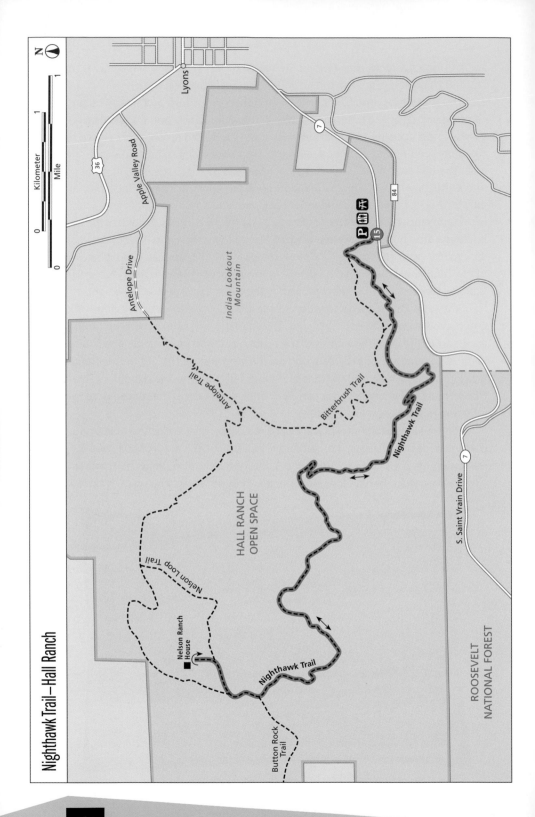

0.0   Start from the bulletin board at the upper parking lot. Elevation: 5,480 feet. GPS: N40 12.73' / W105 17.37'. The trail from the lower parking lot comes in from the left in about 60 feet.

375 feet   Junction of Nighthawk and Bitterbrush Trails. Turn left onto double-track Nighthawk Trail, which is open to hikers and equestrians (no mountain bikers).

0.35   Nighthawk Trail crosses a dirt road. Continue straight ahead across the road to continue on Nighthawk.

0.6   Junction with a trail that connects with Bitterbrush Trail. Go straight ahead on Nighthawk Trail.

1.1   The trail crosses a little creek fairly close to SH 7.

1.75   You'll notice remnants of an old road. For the next 2.0 miles, the trail goes on and off this wider track a few times. The trail is well signed.

3.6   A rocky viewpoint. Elevation: 6,520 feet. GPS: N40 12.95' / W105 19.50'. At the end of this rocky area, the trail curves to the left and a road goes to the right. Stay left.

4.2   The trail switchbacks around an old stone fence or wall.

4.6   Four-way intersection with the Button Rock Trail (left) and a dirt road (right). GPS: N40 13.15' / W105 19.97'. Continue across the road and a tad right to continue on the Nighthawk Trail.

4.7   T-intersection with Nelson Loop. Turn right onto Nelson Loop. There's a nice bench here to rest and take in the views.

5.0   Junction with the trail to the Nelson Ranch house remains. Turn left and head to the old ranch house.

5.1   Nelson Ranch house interpretive sign. Elevation: 6,570 feet. GPS: N40 13.42' / W105 19.76'. Take some time to explore the area. Behind the house is an old water trough and silo. To the right of the house are some nice rocks to sit on for lunch. Return the way you came.

10.2   Arrive back at the trailhead.

Option

For a shorter, moderate 7.2-mile out-and-back hike, hike to the viewpoint at 3.6 miles above and return the way you came.

HIKE INFORMATION

Local Information: Lyons Area Chamber of Commerce; 303-823-6622 ext. 26; lyons-colorado.com

Local Events/Attractions: Oskar Blues Grill & Brew—Live Music, Lyons; 303-823-6685; oskarbluesfooderies.com/grill-and-brew

Rocky Mountain Folks Festival, Lyons; 303-823-0848, 800-624-2422; bluegrass.com/folks

RockyGrass Bluegrass Festival, Lyons; 303-823-0848, 800-624-2422; bluegrass.com/rockygrass

Hike Tours: Boulder County Parks and Open Space; 303-678-6216; bouldercounty.org/os/events

Organizations: Boulder County Parks and Open Space Volunteer Program; 303-678-6216; bouldercountyopenspace.org/volunteer

Boulder County recruits volunteers to help with various projects on their Open Space properties. Some projects include native seed collection, forest restoration, and native plant revegetation. Trail projects are organized as necessary for maintenance or even to build new trail tread. Go to bouldercountyopenspace.org or call 303-678-6216 for information about future projects.

Boulder County Parks and Open Space

Boulder County Parks and Open Space's mission is "to conserve natural, cultural, and agricultural resources and provide public uses that reflect sound resource management and community values." Boulder County, the City of Boulder and other municipalities, the USDA Forest Service, the National Park Service, the Bureau of Land Management, and conservation easements protect about 67 percent of the county's land from development. Nineteen county parks, from foothills to plains, are on that list, including the County Fairgrounds.

Boulder County POS administers or manages over 103,000 acres, including more than 24,000 acres of land that are leased for agricultural uses. Since 1993, Boulder County voters have approved various sales and use taxes, earmarked recycling and composting taxes, and added an open space tax to fund open space purchases and maintenance costs. The County leverages these monies with funds from the Conservation Trust Fund and Great Outdoors Colorado (both funded by Colorado State Lottery proceeds) and property taxes. Occasional funding sources include grants from the Land and Water Conservation Fund and the Federal Farmland Protection Program.

Green Mountain West Ridge Trail

This short but steep trail is good training for those aspiring to climb higher mountains. For others, the view of Boulder and the eastern plains beyond is worth the effort. Plus there's a great view of the Indian Peaks and Rocky Mountain National Park peaks to the west and north. The rumble and whistles of trains traveling above Eldorado Canyon to the south waft through the air. The trail traverses through the Western Mountain Parks Habitat Conservation Area, which requires on-trail travel unless you obtain an off-trail permit. Staying on-trail helps protect and preserve sensitive or rare plants and animals.

Start: Green Mountain West Ridge Trailhead
Distance: 2.8 miles out and back
Hiking time: 1.25 to 2 hours
Difficulty: Most Difficult due to steepness in short distance
Elevation gain: 544 feet
Trail surface: Natural surface and rocky trail, with many water bars and steep steps
Seasons: Best Apr through Nov
Other trail users: Hikers only
Canine compatibility: Dogs must be leashed before exiting a vehicle at trailheads and in the area of the trailheads. Dogs must remain on leash and stay on the trail; check osmp.org or call 303-441-3440 for current dog regulations.
Land status: City of Boulder Open Space & Mountain Parks
Fees and permits: None required for groups of fewer than twenty-five people, unless you plan to travel off-trail. Free off-trail permits are available online.
Schedule: Open year-round; day use only
Maps: USGS Eldorado Springs; National Geographic Trails Illustrated 100 Boulder/Golden; Latitude 40°: Boulder County Trails
Trail contact: City of Boulder Open Space & Mountain Parks, PO Box 791, Boulder; 303-441-3440; osmp.org
Other: This trail travels through the Western Mountain Parks Habitat Conservation Area. Please hike only on designated trails. Off-trail travel requires a permit.
Special considerations: Bears and mountain lions are active in this area throughout the year. Bring your own water, as none is available along the trail. The trail may be icy in spots in winter.

Finding the trailhead: In Boulder, from Broadway and Baseline Road, travel west on Baseline Road (which becomes Flagstaff Road) for 6.0 miles, where you can park on either side of the road by the Green Mountain West Ridge Trailhead. Parking is limited; do **not** park on nearby private roads. This area is just beyond and out of the fee area for the Boulder Open Space and Mountain Parks. No facilities are available at the trailhead, but there is a bike rack.

THE HIKE

Green Mountain West Ridge is the fastest and shortest way to summit Green Mountain, and enjoy its views of Boulder, the eastern plains, and the rugged Continental Divide. The first part of the trail is like a roller coaster, undulating over and around little ridges and drainages.

The trail crosses through the Western Mountain Parks Habitat Conservation Area (HCA). This special area was created by Boulder Open Space & Mountain Parks (OSMP) to protect the habitat of some rare and threatened species of plants and animals. OSMP has designated nine HCAs. These special areas have few, if any, trails in them and few visitors. Each represents a large block of a naturally functioning ecosystem that has experienced only a small amount of human disturbance. Grasslands, tallgrass prairie, a marsh, wetlands, and foothills/mountain ecosystems are preserved. Some HCAs protect rare species found only on OSMP lands.

Looking west at the Indian Peaks from the Green Mountain West Ridge Trail.

View of Mount Toll, Paiute Peak, and Mount Audubon, with Sugarloaf Mountain in the foreground.

One species protected in this HCA is the white adder's-mouth orchid, Colorado's rarest orchid, growing only on Green Mountain. In 1895, Ernst Bessey first documented this orchid in Colorado in El Paso County, but it has not been found in that area since then. In 1970, three scientists spent a full day searching in the Boulder OSMP and found seven white adder's-mouth orchid plants, which grow only 3 to 4 inches high in certain wet areas.

Another protected species is the paper birch, a tree that typically flourishes in the northern states and in Canada and Alaska. In the OSMP, they are remnants of the last ice age that ended about 12,000 years ago, growing only in small pockets in the right cool environment. Their white bark peels off in horizontal strips like paper, giving them their name.

Back to your hike up Green Mountain. After you pass the junction with the Green Bear Trail first and then with the Ranger Trail, the Green Mountain West Ridge Trail starts its climb to the summit. Numerous log and stone steps, with some "flat" dirt trail in between, carry you upward. This trail could replace a StairMaster workout at the gym.

When you complete the last rock-step climb to the top, take time to explore the area around the summit boulder with its cairn. You might want to scramble up different boulders for better views. Please remember not to go off-trail from the summit or designated trails without an off-trail permit. The red-roofed buildings of the University of Colorado ("CU," as it's called) lie to the northeast. You can see Baseline Reservoir almost straight east. Below, to the right, lies the

National Center for Atmospheric Research (NCAR). Farther right is Fairview High, Southern Hills Middle School, and Viele Lake. You can gaze down on the tops of a Flatiron or two, and perhaps a glider will soar through the air either below or above you. A trail register tube is cemented into a big cairn on the summit boulder—the protective cap reads NOT TOO TIGHT! To the north of the summit there's a wonderful view of Longs Peak and the Indian Peaks.

The return trip continues to provide a workout for your downhill muscles, with views west through the trees.

MILES AND DIRECTIONS

0.0 Start from the Green Mountain West Ridge Trailhead. Elevation: 7,680 feet. GPS: N39 59.00' / W105 19.40'.

0.7 A faint double-track road comes in from the right. Walk to the left on Green Mountain West Ridge Trail.

0.9 Junction with the Green Bear Trail on the right.

1.2 Junction with the Ranger Trail on the left. Continue straight ahead and uphill. There's a good view of Longs Peak and Mount Meeker from near the RANGER TRAIL sign.

1.4 Top of Green Mountain. Elevation: 8,144 feet. GPS: N39 58.93' / W105 18.09'. On the summit, to both the right and left, are boulders on which to scramble for views of Boulder and out to the east. To the left is a big boulder with a cairn on top. On the north side of this big rock lump is a great view of Longs Peak, Twin Sisters, and south to Mount Audubon. The E. M. Greenman Trail heads downhill from this point. Return the way you came.

2.8 Arrive back at the trailhead.

Option

For a longer, 4.6-mile lollipop hike with a total of 1,624 feet gain, you can hike down E. M. Greenman Trail from the top of Green Mountain. At the junction with Saddle Rock Trail, go to the left and continue on E. M. Greenman Trail to Ranger Trail (elevation 6,960 feet). Turn left onto Ranger Trail and hike uphill until you arrive back at the junction at mile 1.2 above. Turn right and return to the trailhead the way you came.

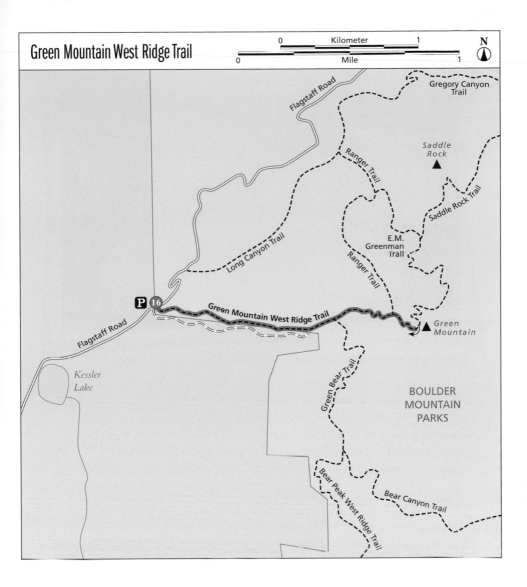

Green Mountain West Ridge Trail

HIKE INFORMATION

Local Information: Boulder Convention and Visitors Bureau; 303-442-2911; bouldercoloradousa.com

Boulder Chamber of Commerce; 303-442-1044; boulderchamber.com

Local Events/Attractions: Colorado Shakespeare Festival, University of Colorado, Boulder; 303-492-8008; coloradoshakes.org

Colorado Music Festival, Chautauqua Auditorium, Boulder; 303-665-0599; comusic.org

Plaque atop the summit cairn of Green Mountain, identifying several Front Range peaks.

Hike Tours: City of Boulder Open Space & Mountain Parks Nature Hikes & Programs; 303-441-3440; bouldercolorado.gov/osmp/nature-hikes
Organizations: City of Boulder Open Space & Mountain Parks Volunteer Program; 303-441-3440; bouldercolorado.gov/osmp/volunteer-program
Colorado Mountain Club Boulder Group, Boulder; 303-554-7688; cmcboulder.org

🍂 Green Tip:
Pack out your dog's waste or dispose of it in a trash can. DO NOT leave plastic bags along the trail or at trailheads. Besides being unsightly, there are many environmental/ health reasons for picking up dog waste and disposing of it properly. As many have noted, "There is no poop fairy!" It's up to YOU to do the right thing and take care of your doggy doo. Also, dog waste left on or buried in the snow reappears in the spring—it does not decompose in the snow.

Walker Ranch Loop

The Walker Ranch Loop trail is the longest trail in Boulder County's Walker Ranch Open Space, which has 3,616 acres of meadows, mountainous terrain, and riparian habitat, with South Boulder Creek flowing through its southern sections. It's a beautiful setting with excellent trails for hikers, anglers, and other recreationists. On hot days, you can dip your feet into the cool, sparkling waters of the creek, picnic along its rocky banks, or walk amongst wildflowers, taking in views of the Indian Peaks to the west and the Plains to the east. The Loop trail winds in and out of forest, along the creek, and up and down ridges to provide a hike that is full of variety and a nice level of physical challenge. You won't be bored!

Start: Trailhead bulletin board
Distance: 7.6-mile loop
Hiking time: 3.5 to 6 hours
Difficulty: Difficult due to steep sections
Elevation gain: 892 feet
Trail surface: Natural surface trail and old roads (closed to the motorized public)
Seasons: Best Apr through Nov.
Other trail users: Equestrians and mountain bikers
Canine compatibility: Dogs must be on leash and under control; this is strictly enforced. If you have forgotten your leash, Boulder County graciously provides "loaners" at the trailhead. Borrow one and return it when you've finished your hike.

Land status: Boulder County Parks and Open Space, and Eldorado Canyon State Park
Fees and permits: None required
Schedule: Open year-round from sunrise to sunset. When closed, unattended vehicles will be ticketed or towed.
Maps: USGS Eldorado Springs; National Geographic Trails Illustrated 100 Boulder/Golden; Latitude 40°: Boulder County Trails
Trail contact: Boulder County Parks and Open Space, 303-678-6200; bouldercountyopenspace.org
Other: Smoking is strictly prohibited. Consuming marijuana or any marijuana derivative within any County Open Space property is unlawful. Camping and wood fires are prohibited. Violations will result in fines.
Special considerations: Bring water with you; water from the creek must be filtered/treated.

Finding the trailhead: In Boulder, from the intersection of Broadway (US 93) and Baseline Road, head west on Baseline for 1.4 miles, where it curves sharply right and becomes Flagstaff Road. Continue up the steep and winding Flagstaff Road for another 7.4 miles. Follow the speed limit and watch for cyclists and pedestrians. This road is heavily traveled on weekends. Turn left into the Walker Ranch Loop Trailhead parking lot. A vault toilet and picnic tables are available at the trailhead, but no water.

THE HIKE

Walker Ranch Open Space lies southwest of Boulder, in the Lower Montane—Foothill ecological zone, adjoining Eldorado Canyon State Park to the south. Boulder County began acquiring this property in 1977 and continued adding to it until 2006. It's valued for its rich cultural history, biodiversity, and recreational opportunities. It has hosted almost a hundred species of birds, and several mammal species: mountain lion, black bear, elk, mule deer, coyote, bobcat, red fox, and others. Bullsnakes and garter snakes also live here. Plant life includes ponderosa pine, Douglas fir, aspen, Boulder raspberry, mountain mahogany, and a rainbow of colorful wildflowers.

James Walker came to Colorado from the Midwest and homesteaded 160 acres of this land in 1882. By the following year, he and his young family were living in their newly completed ranch house; the property also had a barn and blacksmith shop to care for livestock. The Walkers designed their homestead to support a self-sufficient lifestyle, and built a smokehouse, granary, root cellar, pig barn, turkey and chicken houses, springhouse, and other amenities. The Walker family acquired more land and expanded the ranch over time; it eventually became one of the largest cattle ranches in this area of the state. In 1959, when the ranch was finally sold by the Walker family, it had reached a size of more than 6,000 acres.

Walker Ranch is now listed on the National Register of Historic Places. The homestead is closed to the general public but group tours can be arranged by calling 303-776-8848. You can also attend the Walker Ranch Autumn Heritage Days to see costumed volunteers demonstrate the lifestyle of an 1880s working ranch and to cheer on the players in a vintage "base ball" game.

The Loop hike begins at the southern end of the Walker Ranch Loop Trailhead parking lot. Start down the right-hand leg on a very nice, level, dirt trail. You'll immediately notice evidence of the Walker Ranch/Eldorado Wildland Fire that occurred in September of 2000. It lasted for five days and covered 1,062 acres but, fortunately, no homes were lost. Very effective fire mitigation had been done before it started, and good fire-fighting techniques were used to control it. It's believed that this fire was started by a careless cigarette smoker. All Boulder County Parks are smoke-free and smoking is not allowed **anywhere** on these properties.

Heading out on the Walker Ranch Loop.

The trail continues down into the forest, and soon to the banks of South Boulder Creek, where there are picnic tables and a nice, shady spot to relax and escape the summer heat. After following the creek for a while, the trail then climbs up the hillside, with views of the Indian Peaks opening up to the west. At the top of this ascent, the trail reaches beautiful alpine meadows with wildflowers and views down to the eastern flatlands. You'll traverse the meadows, then descend back down into the forest, and down some steep steps to the rocky banks of the creek. Once again, you'll follow the creek for a while, then ascend back up through the forest, where you'll eventually climb the ridge and follow it back to the parking lot.

MILES AND DIRECTIONS

0.0   Start from the Walker Ranch Loop Trailhead bulletin board. Elevation: 7,230 feet. GPS: N39 57.09' / W105 20.24'. The trail goes to the left of the bulletin board and then forks. Take the right-hand fork.

0.1   Head downhill to a switchback to the left. Come to an interpretive sign about the rock dike above the trail.

0.5   Spur trail on the right goes to a rocky overlook. GPS: N39 56.86' / W105 20.31'. The loop continues straight ahead. Continue downhill and come to an interpretive sign about forest fire.

1.0 Spur trail to the left goes down to South Boulder Creek and a picnic area. GPS: N39 56.59' / W105 20.20'. The loop continues straight ahead, along the creek and crosses a bridge.

1.5 Come to a left switchback, passing a bench and another nice resting place along the creek on the right. GPS: N39 56.30' / W105 20.45'. Head uphill to the left.

1.7 Trail curves to the right. Pass a spur trail on your left and continue uphill to the right. GPS: N39 56.39' / W105 20.31'. The trail weaves around, gaining altitude, and eventually leaves Boulder County Open Space land and enters Eldorado Canyon State Park.

2.6 Junction with a trail heading right to the Crescent Meadows parking lot. Turn left, continuing on the Loop trail. You'll soon come to a spur trail on the left, after a Colorado State Parks interpretive sign; head right to continue on the Loop trail.

3.0 Cross an alpine meadow and come to a 3-mile post on the right. Begin descending back into the forest, crossing some drainages along the way. GPS: N39 55.68' / W105 19.93'. In about a mile, the trail leaves the State Park and reenters Boulder County Open Space.

4.4 A fork in the trail with a sign indicating that the "Less Technical Route" is on the left. Take the left fork.

South Boulder Creek along the Walker Ranch Loop trail.

Looking east down to the plains from the upper part of the Walker Ranch Loop trail.

4.6 Start descending steeply down to the creek. A sign cautions "Staircase Ahead." The steps down are nicely constructed with dirt, wood, and rock, but take your time and be careful. At the bottom of most of the stairs, the trail switchbacks to the left but there is a spur trail to the right. Stay left. Reach the creek, following along its south side, and cross a bridge.

4.9 Come to a green metal fence on the right. Turn left to continue on the Loop trail. GPS: N39 56.51' / W105 18.90'. Reach a junction with a trail to Eldorado Canyon State Park, on the right. Continue straight ahead.

5.2 Turn left at a sign post and continue on the Loop trail. This is a nice, new section of single-track, heading up through forest with occasional mountain views.

6.1 Junction with a trail on the right leading to the Ethel Harrold Trailhead. Turn left and continue on the Loop trail, ascending a ridge with several switchbacks. GPS: N39 57.17' / W105 19.38'.

6.7 Reach the top of the ridge and turn right, continuing on the Loop trail as it winds to the west. Pass the 7-mile post on your right. The trail curves to the right and heads northwest.

7.6 Arrive back at the trailhead.

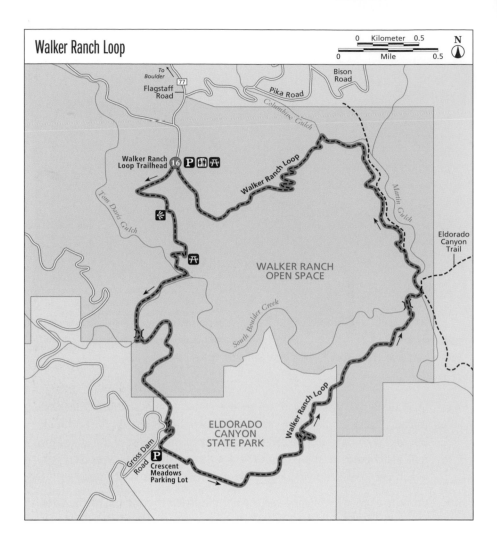

Walker Ranch Loop

HIKE INFORMATION

Local Information:
Boulder Chamber of Commerce; 303-442-1044; boulderchamber.com
Boulder Convention and Visitors Bureau; 303-442-2911; bouldercoloradousa.com

Local Events/Attractions:
Colorado Music Festival, Chautauqua Auditorium, Boulder; 303-665-0599; comusic.org
Colorado Shakespeare Festival, University of Colorado, Boulder; 303-492-8008; coloradoshakes.org

Walker Ranch Autumn Heritage Days, Boulder; 303-678-6200; bouldercounty.
org/os/parks/pages/walkerranch.aspx
Hike Tours:
Boulder County Parks and Open Space, Longmont; 303-678-6214;
bouldercountyopenspace.org
Organizations:
Colorado Mountain Club Boulder Group, Boulder; 303-554-7688; cmcboulder.org
Volunteer for Boulder County Parks and Open Space, Longmont; 303-678-6216;
bouldercountyopenspace.org

Blossom of a Boulder raspberry shrub.

Rattlesnake Gulch Trail—
Eldorado Canyon State Park

Follow old Crags Boulevard up Rattlesnake Gulch to the ghost of the Crags Hotel, a popular and luxurious resort in the early 1900s. Winding up the steep gulch, one wonders how early autos could make it! The trail provides wonderful views of the sheer walls of Eldorado Canyon, a world-renowned rock-climbing area. Golden eagles, bald eagles (winter), turkey vultures, red-tailed hawks, peregrine falcons, prairie falcons, and sharp-shinned hawks soar on thermals (upward currents of warm air) and swoop down on their prey. A higher loop takes you along the path that accessed the hotel from the railroad tracks.

Start: Fowler and Rattlesnake Gulch Trailhead

Distance: 3.8 miles out and back with spurs

Hiking time: 1.5 to 2.25 hours

Difficulty: Most Difficult due to elevation gain in short distance

Elevation gain: 1,000 feet

Trail surface: Natural surface and rocky trail

Seasons: Best Apr through Nov

Other trail users: Mountain bikers; wheelchairs to the junction of Fowler and Rattlesnake Gulch Trails

Canine compatibility: Dogs must be on leash

Land status: Colorado state park

Fees and permits: Daily fee or annual pass required

Schedule: Open year-round from sunrise to sunset

Maps: USGS Eldorado Springs; National Geographic Trails

Illustrated 100 Boulder/Golden; Latitude 40°: Boulder County Trails

Trail contact: Eldorado Canyon State Park, 9 Kneale Road, Eldorado Springs; 303-494-3943; cpw.state.co.us/placestogo/parks/eldoradocanyon

Other: If parking lots are full (typically summer weekends and holidays), you'll either have to wait until a space becomes available or return another day. Try to arrive before 10 a.m. or after 5 p.m. You can cross-country ski or snowshoe on the Rattlesnake Gulch Trail when there is enough snow. With a mostly northern aspect, the trail is cooler in summer and usually icy and snow-packed most of the winter.

Special considerations: Bring water with you, as none is available along the trail. Beware of rattlesnakes. Camping is not permitted.

Finding the trailhead: In Boulder, from the intersection of Table Mesa Drive and Broadway (SH 93), drive south on SH 93 for 2.5 miles to Eldorado Springs Drive (SH 170). Turn right onto SH 170 and drive 3.1 miles into the tiny town of Eldorado Springs, past the swimming pool on the right. Turn left into Eldorado Canyon State Park; pay the fee at the entrance station. A vault toilet is available at the parking lot. Drive another 0.5 mile on the narrow dirt road to the Fowler and Rattlesnake Gulch Trailhead, which is on the left. The road has pullouts so vehicles can pass—please park only in designated parking areas. There are no facilities at the trailhead. The Visitor Center is 0.3 mile west of the trailhead and has restrooms, water, and a picnic area.

THE HIKE

As you drive through the quiet little town of Eldorado Springs, it's hard to imagine a popular resort with dancing halls, a roller-skating rink, pool hall, and arcade. The resort opened on July 4, 1905. Visitors swam in outdoor pools fed by artesian wells with naturally warm water around 76°F. Rustic cabins were available for rent, as were big canvas tents with floors and frames. By 1908, the Grandview Rooming House and the forty-room New Eldorado Hotel offered lodging to visitors. Guests enjoyed a spectacular view of the canyon from the veranda. Special excursion trains brought as many as 2,000 people for a summer weekend of fun and relaxation.

A. D. Stencel purchased 40 acres on the south side of Eldorado Canyon, one of the few "flat" spots in the foothills near the new resort. Stencel platted lots and remodeled the Crags Hotel. People could take the train from Denver for $1.25 round-trip, disembark at a rail siding called Scenic, and descend by foot or horse-drawn buggy via a trail, which you can hike as part of the upper loop. Other people drove wagons or autos up Crags Boulevard (today's Rattlesnake Gulch Trail) from the bustling resort below. An incline railway provided the fastest route to the posh hotel. Guests would board the funicular at today's picnic area near the Visitor Center, and be whisked straight up the mountain. To the west, some people bought the lots and built private cabins.

The Crags Hotel rented rooms, furnished cabins, tents, and screened sleeping porches. Carpeted hotel rooms had brass beds, a dresser, and rocking chair; Coleman lanterns provided light at night. People enjoyed dining, dancing, and card games. But then, one night in November 1912, disaster struck. Guests at the resort noticed a big blaze up the hill—the hotel was on fire. Some suspect that it was torched for insurance money. The hotel had been closed for the season, so other reasons were hard to ascertain. As you'll see when you explore the site, a big stone fireplace, the courtyard fountain, and some rock walls remain.

Shirt Tail Peak and the Rattlesnake Gulch Trail.

In 1978, the State of Colorado purchased 272 acres from the Fowler family, who long owned and ran the resort. This acquisition became the Inner Canyon part of Eldorado Canyon State Park. Crescent Meadows, the western part of the park, was added in late 1979. You can access its rolling meadows via the Eldorado Canyon Trail through the City of Boulder Open Space and Mountain Parks land and the Walker Ranch Loop in Boulder County's Walker Ranch Open Space, or via the Gross Dam Road from SH 72 (Coal Creek Canyon).

The Rattlesnake Gulch Trail winds through a typical sunny foothills forest of ponderosa pine and Rocky Mountain juniper joined by mountain mahogany, skunkbush (a type of sumac), and currant bushes. Some nice views of the steep canyon cliffs occasionally appear between the trees. On the upper loop, the views are less obstructed and you can see east to Sawmill Ponds and Baseline Reservoir. Coal and passenger trains rumble by, going in and out of nearby tunnels. A few Douglas firs grow in shadier spots. At the Continental Divide Overlook, the view west is hampered by trees, but the views of the canyon cliffs are awesome. You can also see the flat area where the Crags Hotel once stood.

Eldorado Canyon State Park—with its historic sites, cliffs and rock climbers, bountiful wildlife, and a variety of plants—is a little gem. El Dorado means "the golden one" in Spanish. When the setting sun casts its last rays on the walls of the canyon, a golden glow reflects off the lichens and mosses. Eldorado Canyon State Park lives up to its name!

18

Redgarden Wall and The Bastille in Eldorado Canyon, from the Continental Divide Overlook.

MILES AND DIRECTIONS

0.0 Start from the Fowler and Rattlesnake Gulch Trailhead. Elevation: 6,040 feet. GPS: N39 55.77' / W105 17.41'. Head uphill and pass a unique interpretive display about rattlesnakes, treading lightly, butterflies, and other wildlife.

0.1 Junction of the Fowler and Rattlesnake Gulch Trails. Turn right (west) onto the Rattlesnake Gulch Trail.

0.4 Turn right onto a long bridge.

1.3 Intersection of the Rattlesnake Gulch Trail, the Rattlesnake Gulch Loop, and the Crags Hotel ruins. There's a bench and interpretive sign here. Elevation: 6,680 feet. GPS: N39 55.60' / W105 17.69'. Turn left onto the Rattlesnake Gulch Loop. (**Option:** You can explore the ruins and return the way you came for a 2.4-mile out-and-back trip.)

1.7 Switchback and trail junction. GPS: N39 55.31' / W105 17.66'. Continue right around the switchback. The trail straight ahead goes to the railroad tracks and was the old access trail for people riding the train to reach the Crags Hotel. Great views of Eldorado Canyon along this section, and the high point of the hike (7,040 feet).

2.1 Junction with a spur trail. Stay to the right.

Rattlesnake Gulch Trail—Eldorado Canyon State Park

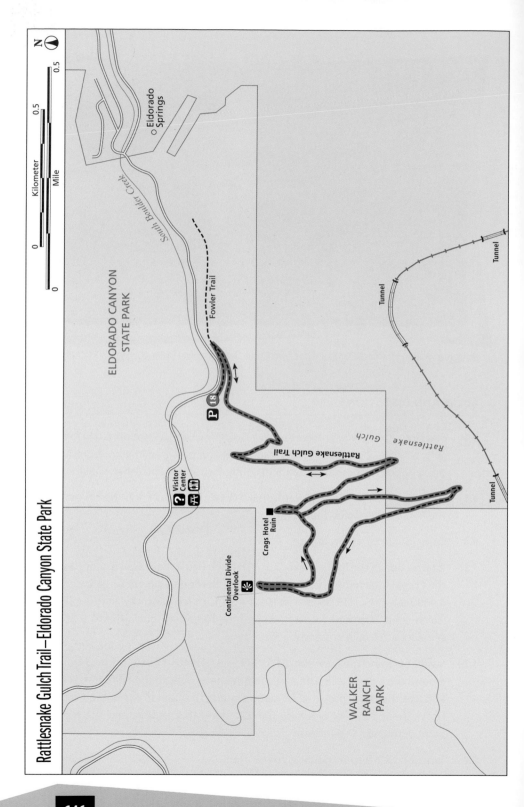

2.2 T-intersection at a switchback. Turn left for a 0.1-mile out-and-back walk to the Continental Divide Overlook and a great view of Eldorado Canyon State Park and the plains east of Boulder. GPS: N39 55.68' / W105 17.88'. Return to the Rattlesnake Gulch Loop, and continue straight ahead and downhill.

2.5 Arrive back at the Crags Hotel ruins intersection. Explore the ruins if you haven't already. Return the way you came from the trailhead.

3.8 Arrive back at the trailhead.

Options
1. Hike out and back to the Crags Hotel ruins for a shorter, 2.4-mile round-trip.
2. On the way back, turn right on Fowler Trail and hike 0.2-mile one-way to the interpretive displays about raptors and a telescope to watch both raptors and rock climbers. Easy trail; wheelchair accessible.

HIKE INFORMATION

Local Information: Boulder Convention and Visitors Bureau; 303-442-2911; bouldercoloradousa.com
Boulder Chamber of Commerce; 303-442-1044; boulderchamber.com
Local Events/Attractions
Colorado Shakespeare Festival, University of Colorado, Boulder; 303-492-0554; coloradoshakes.org
Colorado Music Festival, Chautauqua Auditorium, Boulder; 303-665-0599; comusic.org
Hike Tours: Guided hikes and programs are offered occasionally by park staff; inquire at the Visitor Center for information, 303-494-3943.
Organizations: Action Committee for Eldorado, Eldorado Springs; aceeldo.org
Colorado Mountain Club Boulder Group, Boulder; 303-554-7688, cmcboulder.org

Eldorado Canyon survived several threats that would have destroyed its scenic beauty. In the 1920s people planned to dam the canyon to provide water to Denver, and in the 1970s the canyon almost became a rock quarry. In 1978, citizens succeeded in their efforts to create a state park.

Ivy Baldwin and His Tightrope

In the early 1900s, Eldorado Springs had a reputation of being the "Coney Island of the West." One of the "acts" was Ivy Baldwin, a famous tightrope walker. In 1906, Frank Fowler, who owned the Eldorado Springs Resort, helped install a cable between Castle Rock (known today as the Bastille) and the Wind Tower, near the mouth of the canyon. Ivy walked the 635-foot-long, 7/8-inch cable, which hung 582 feet above the canyon floor, with no safety net below! Besides the significant height above South Boulder Creek, ferocious winds can come screaming down the canyon with little warning.

Ivy completed this feat eighty-one times during his life. He was small and wiry—5 feet, 3 inches tall and 112 pounds. An aerial performer with the Baldwin Brothers, his career of circus performer and tightrope artist, among other daring deeds, took him around the world. He even flew observation balloons during the Spanish-American War and was shot down by enemy fire. His last wire walk in Eldorado Canyon in 1948 was completed on a lower wire when he was eighty-two years old.

Mount Galbraith Park

Mount Galbraith is a close-to-town, hiker-only park with a pleasant trail through woods, shrubs, and open areas. You can see a long way from the southern flank of Mount Galbraith, which the trail encircles. With a lush riparian area, beautiful views in all directions, interesting rocky sections, forest, and green meadows, you get a lot of "bang" for your time. In the spring, colorful wildflowers and flowering bushes invite you to hike, while a large elk herd roams nearby. Bighorn sheep and numerous songbirds also visit the park. Come again in the fall, when maple and ninebark leaves turn brilliant red.

Start: Mount Galbraith Park Trailhead

Distance: 4.25-mile lollipop

Hiking time: 1.5 to 2.25 hours

Difficulty: Moderate due to elevation gain

Elevation gain: 970 feet

Trail surface: Natural surface and rocky trail

Seasons: Best Apr through Nov. Avoid hot summer days—visit in the evening or early morning.

Other trail users: Hikers only

Canine compatibility: Dogs must be on leash

Land status: Jefferson County Open Space

Fees and permits: Large groups and unique activities require special permits. Please check jeffco.us/open-space/parks or call 303-271-5925.

Schedule: Open year-round, 1 hour before sunrise to 1 hour after sunset

Maps: USGS Ralston Buttes, Golden; National Geographic Trails Illustrated 100 Boulder/Golden

Trail contact: Jefferson County Open Space, 700 Jefferson County Parkway, Golden; 303-271-5925; jeffco.us/open-space

Other: Camping is prohibited in Mount Galbraith Park.

Special considerations: Bring water—there is none in the park. Bears and mountain lions live in this area. Come prepared for an outdoor experience. Please leave valuables at home.

Finding the trailhead: In Golden, from the mouth of Clear Creek Canyon at the junction of SH 93, SH 58, and US 6, drive north on SH 93 heading toward Boulder. In 1.3 miles turn left onto Golden Gate Canyon Road. Drive 1.4 miles up Golden Gate Canyon Road just past mile marker 17 to Mount Galbraith Park. Turn left into the parking lot, where vault toilets are available.

When John H. Gregory discovered lode gold in 1859 in the vicinity of today's Black Hawk and Central City, miners rushed to the boom area. Clear Creek Canyon was rough and difficult, its other name being Toughcuss Canyon. The miners needed food and a way to transport ore, so entrepreneurs Dan McCleery and Tom Golden used black powder (dynamite wasn't invented until 1866) to create a toll road up the gulch to the north of Mount Galbraith. Golden Gate City sprang up in 1859 at the canyon's mouth, where distinctive stone formations resembled a gate. The "Golden" part probably came from Tom Golden. By 1860, the town included log houses, a few stores, a pottery kiln, hotels, and other businesses. People called it "Baled Hay City" because every house sold hay.

The Golden Gate and Gregory Road Company received its charter in 1862 from the territorial government. Anyone wanting to travel to the gold fields paid 75 cents per wagon to pass through the tollgate in Golden Gate City. When the toll road was moved out of the creek bed and slightly higher up the mountain, the gate-like formation was destroyed. The toll road operated from 1860 to 1871.

Nearby Golden City started out with tents and a few farms. George West and W. A. H. Loveland saw promise in its location and began to build a "real" town. Congress created the Colorado Territory in February 1861, and the following year Golden City became the capital. The town held that honor until 1867, when the territorial government moved to Denver. The town continued to grow, and by 1872 trains whistled through on their way to and from Denver and Central City/

The Cedar Gulch Trail heading to the Mount Galbraith Loop.

View of Mount Evans from the Mount Galbraith Loop trail.

Black Hawk. That year, "City" was deleted from its name, and Golden became a one-word town. Farming, clay pits from which building bricks were produced, and nearby coal and oil assured the town's existence and future growth.

Mount Galbraith is the highest hill near Golden. The Cedar Gulch Trail climbs and traverses along the peak's northeast side. Cottonwoods grow along inter-mittent streams, and Rocky Mountain junipers and ponderosa pines are inter-spersed with a wide variety of shrubs, grasses, and flowers. Douglas firs grow on the cooler north slopes. Spring brings not only wildflowers, but also flower-filled bushes. Chokecherries develop hanging clusters of white flowers, while balls of little yellow flowers bloom on skunkbush (a type of sumac). Mountain mahoganies sport white "trumpets" edged in yellow sepals. Later, this bush is quite noticeable with its fuzzy spiral tails extending from tiny fruits. Ninebark, like Douglas fir, grows in shadier spots and displays its pretty flowers: five petals of white with yellow centers. A member of the rose family, ninebark sheds its bark in layers, thus its name. Big white flowers decorate thimbleberry (Boulder raspberry) bushes.

Mount Galbraith's north side is covered in thick forest and rocky areas. The trail climbs up some nice stone steps. Look for pretty white sand lilies along the trail. As the trail curves south then east, the forest thins. Mount Galbraith's sum-mit rises to the left, and scenic vistas open up over short bushes and grasses. Lookout Mountain, with its radio towers, rises across Clear Creek Canyon. Green Mountain appears to the southeast, and downtown Denver skyscrapers reach for

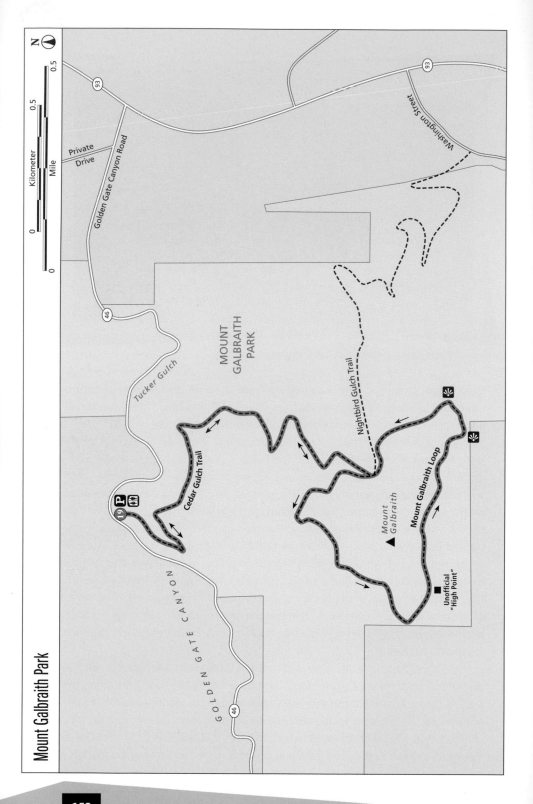

Mount Galbraith Park

N

Kilometer
0   0.5

Mile
0   0.5

93
Private Drive
Golden Gate Canyon Road
46
Tucker Gulch
MOUNT GALBRAITH PARK
Nightbird Gulch Trail
93
Washington Street
GOLDEN GATE CANYON
46
Cedar Gulch Trail
19 P
Mount Galbraith
Mount Galbraith Loop
Unofficial "High Point"

the sky to the east. Coors Brewery and South Table Mountain pop into view near a side trail to an overlook. You're higher than both Table Mountains, and you get a bird's-eye view of their tops.

Mount Galbraith provides a great hike close to home with views of Golden, the Denver metro area, and mountains to the west.

MILES AND DIRECTIONS

0.0 Start from the Mount Galbraith Park Trailhead. Elevation: 6,240 feet. GPS: N39 46.41'/W105 15.24'. The hike starts on Cedar Gulch Trail, which follows along the stream for a while then makes a sharp left switchback to begin ascending the slope.

1.3 Junction with Mount Galbraith Loop. There is no sign at this intersection; if you reach the sign for the Nightbird Gulch Trail, you've gone too far and need to come back to this junction. Turn right onto the loop.

1.6 The trail climbs up several stone steps.

2.1 The high point of the hike, below Mount Galbraith's summit. Nice views to the south and east. Elevation: 7,210 feet. GPS: N39 45.77'/W105 15.44'. Two spur trails at 2.6 and 2.7 miles lead to overlooks.

3.0 Junction with the Nightbird Gulch Trail on the right. Continue to the left on the Mount Galbraith Loop. In about 50 feet is the junction with the Cedar Gulch Trail (where you turned right at mile 1.3). This completes the loop. Turn right and return the way you came.

4.25 Arrive back at the trailhead.

Mount Galbraith was named for Den Galbraith (1918–1974), who was a professor at the Colorado School of Mines in Golden and an area historian.

19

HIKE INFORMATION

Local Information: Greater Golden Chamber of Commerce, Golden; 303-279-3113; goldencochamber.org

Local Events/Attractions: American Mountaineering Center, Golden; 303-996-2747; americanmountaineeringcenter.org

Colorado Railroad Museum, Golden; 303-279-4591, 800-365-6263; coloradorailroadmuseum.org

Organizations: Colorado Mountain Club, Golden; 303-279-3080, 800-633-4417; cmc.org

Jefferson County Open Space Volunteers, Golden; 303-271-5922; jeffco.us/open-space/volunteer

---

🍃 **Green Tip:**
Stay on the trail. Cutting through from one part of a switchback to another can destroy fragile plant life, disturb wildlife, and cause erosion.

White Ranch Park Northwest Loop

Beautiful meadows, flower-filled drainages, views of the plains, and forested areas pro-vide variety on this loop in the northwest section of White Ranch Park. The ranch house and buildings still remain and, along with an interpretive display of old farm imple-ments, create the feeling of being on a real-life ranch. While cattle no longer graze, a herd of mule deer live in the park. Many trails give hikers numerous loop options. Two backcountry campgrounds make it easy to escape the city for a quick overnight. This "remote" area is a pleasant place to hike and explore some Colorado history.

Start: Trailhead at the northwest corner of the main west parking lot

Distance: 4.6-mile loop

Hiking time: 1.75 to 2.5 hours

Difficulty: Moderate due to eleva-tion gains and losses

Elevation gain: 400-foot loss, 340-foot gain, 240-foot loss, then 300-foot gain

Trail surface: Natural surface and rocky trail, and old ranch roads (closed to the motorized public)

Seasons: Best May through Nov

Other trail users: Equestrians and mountain bikers

Canine compatibility: Dogs must be on leash

Land status: Jefferson County Open Space

Fees and permits: Camping per-mits are required. Large groups and unique activities require special permits. Please check jeffco.us/open-space or call 303-271-5925.

Schedule: Open year-round, 1 hour before sunrise to 1 hour after sunset

Maps: USGS Ralston Buttes; National Geographic Trails Illus-trated 100 Boulder/Golden; Lati-tude 40°: Colorado Front Range

Trail contact: Jefferson County Open Space, 700 Jefferson County Parkway, Golden; 303-271-5925; jeffco.us/open-space

Other: You can camp by permit only in the Sawmill Hiker Camp-ground or Sourdough Springs Campground. Advance camping permits are available at the Open Space office in Golden only. Per-mits are free. Each campground has an outhouse, free firewood, and bear-proof trash can and food storage poles.

Special considerations: Bring water—only a little is available along the trail. Come prepared for an outdoor experience. Please leave valuables at home.

THE HIKE

In late May and early June, before summer's sun turns the grass golden, "Green" Ranch seems a more appropriate name for the northwest part of White Ranch Park. Little shrubs and ponderosa pines punctuate the meadows. The former ranch buildings sit below the west parking lot, encompassed by undulating grasslands. Rounded humps of hills or rocky ridges surround this upper area.

The Rawhide Trail starts off on an old ranch road, now used by Jefferson County personnel for park management. Wrangler's Run is a narrow single-track, descending one of five little drainages that indent the landscape and nourish riparian areas thick with narrow-leaf cottonwood trees and willows. Rocky

Approaching the Wrangler's Run Trail from the Rawhide Trail.

20

Looking west from the Rawhide Trail on a late-summer morning.

Mountain junipers grow in drier spots, while aspens have taken over moister places. Blue lupine, pink Wood's rose, white yarrow, green sage, purple spiderwort, and various yellow sunflowers brighten the trail. Connecting with the Rawhide Trail, now a single-track, the loop climbs through a thick ponderosa forest.

This hike then turns onto the Longhorn Trail, passing the junction to the picnic area and toilets. Grasses and flowers bloom in the open ponderosa forest. As the trail heads downhill, you may get the impression you're going to drop off the end of the earth. The ranch meadows span a "flat" area above the steep upslope, where the foothills rise from the high plains around Denver. North Table Mountain's summit at 6,550 feet looks small from 7,200 feet, and Arvada Reservoir and Tucker Lake are dots on the plains.

A rocky viewpoint looks down onto Ralston Reservoir, built in 1936 by the City of Denver as part of their water-supply system. Denver diverts water from the Fraser River and Williams Fork River in Grand County on the western slope through the Moffat Tunnel. The water flows into South Boulder Creek, where it is stored in Gross Reservoir. It is released again into South Boulder Creek, where some of the flow travels through a series of canals and pipelines to Ralston Creek and Ralston Reservoir. The water then goes to Arvada, where the City contracts with Denver for it.

The Maverick Trail undulates along the edge of steeper terrain. Ponderosa pines, occasional rock outcroppings, flowers, and meadows line the trail. The Belcher Hill Trail is an old road along the southeast ridge of Belcher Hill. The Sawmill Trail to the left (optional) takes you to ten backcountry campsites nestled in an open ponderosa pine forest.

As you traverse Belcher Hill, ranch buildings appear. You'll also see the Ralston Buttes jut up to the northeast. These upturned rocks are the Fountain Formation, so prevalent along the Front Range and typically found in the Flatirons near Boulder and the tilted red rocks of Red Rocks Park, South Valley Park, and Roxborough State Park. From Golden, the Buttes resemble a reclining human head, earning them the name "Old Indian Head."

Paul and Anna Lee White operated a cattle ranch here, starting in 1913. Kenneth Green, whose family owned a ranch near today's Centennial Cone Park and another where Golden Gate Canyon State Park is now, married Lela White, Paul and Anna's daughter. After rounding up their cattle in the fall, the Greens chose which ones to send to market and then drove them from their ranch near Centennial Cone to the White Ranch. From there the two families herded the cattle out of the foothills, over dirt roads through Denver to the stockyards near today's Denver Coliseum along I-70 just east of I-25. Eventually trucks hauled the cattle on better roads to Denver, ending the tedious trail drives.

MILES AND DIRECTIONS

0.0   Start from the trailhead at the northwest corner of the main west parking lot. Elevation: 7,500 feet. GPS: N39 49.13' / W105 17.21'. Head to the left, down the Rawhide Trail, which is a double-track old ranch road.

0.3   Belcher Hill Trail comes in from the left. Continue straight ahead and downhill on the Rawhide Trail.

1.1   Junction with Wrangler's Run. Turn right and follow the single-track Wrangler's above the little stream.

1.4   T-intersection with the Rawhide Trail. Elevation: 7,180 feet. Turn right and head uphill on Rawhide.

2.2   Junction with the Longhorn Trail. Elevation: 7,450 feet. GPS: N39 49.23' / W105 17.10'. Turn left onto Longhorn.

2.5   Junction with a trail that goes to picnic tables to the right. Stay left to continue on Longhorn.

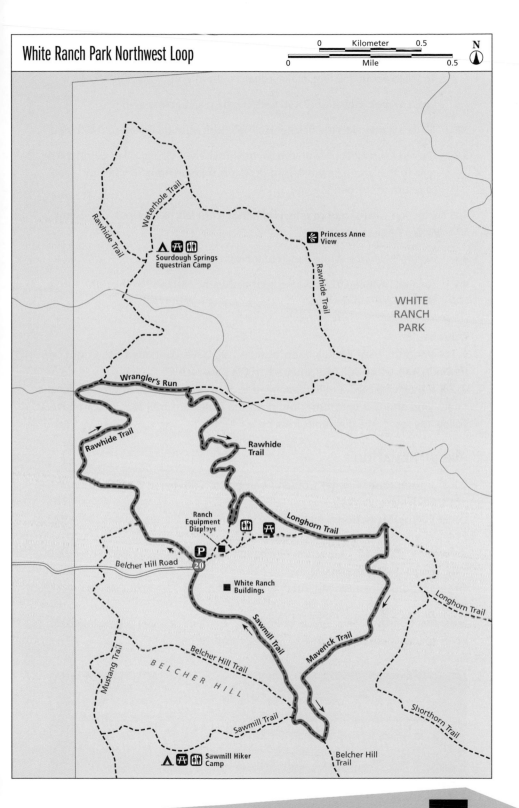

White Ranch Park Northwest Loop

2.8 Nice view of Ralston Reservoir and points east. GPS: N39 49.19' / W105 16.59'. In about 250 feet, make a sharp right turn onto Maverick Trail.

3.0 Cross a creek. Elevation: 7,190 feet. Head up and across a ridge.

3.8 T-intersection with the Belcher Hill Trail. Turn right on Belcher, an old road.

3.9 Curved T-intersection with the Sawmill Trail. The Sawmill Hiker Camp is 0.4 mile to the left on Sawmill. Turn right (north) here onto Sawmill (old road) to return to the parking lot.

4.15 Junction with a road to ranch buildings. Turn left to continue on Sawmill, now a single-track trail.

4.3 Good view of the White Ranch buildings to the right.

4.6 Sawmill Trailhead. The parking lot is across the road and to the right. Arrive back where you started.

Options

1. For a shorter, easy 2.4-mile loop, at mile 2.2 above, continue to the right on Rawhide Trail, which will take you back to the parking lot.
2. For a shorter, easy 2.3-mile loop, head toward the outhouse, then the picnic tables, and after 0.2 mile, turn right onto the Longhorn Trail at mile 2.5 above. Follow the rest of the directions from here.

HIKE INFORMATION

Local Information: Greater Golden Chamber of Commerce, Golden; 303-279-3113; goldenchamber.org

Local Events/Attractions: American Mountaineering Center, Golden; 303-996-2747; americanmountaineeringcenter.org

Colorado Railroad Museum, Golden; 303-279-4591, 800-365-6263; coloradorailrroadmuseum.org

Organizations: Colorado Mountain Club, Golden; 303-279-3080, 800-633-4417; cmc.org

Jefferson County Open Space Volunteers, Golden; 303-271-5922; jeffco.us/open-space/volunteer

> 🌱 Green Tip:
> *Never feed wild animals under any circumstances. You may damage their health and expose yourself (and them) to danger. Wild animals that become used to handouts become pests to hikers and campers.*

Travois Trail—Centennial Cone Park

Enjoy this upside-down hike across grassland and knolls to an overlook into Clear Creek Canyon. The trail loses elevation to the overlook, with one climb up to a rocky outlook on the way. Aptly named, Centennial Cone has long been a landmark on the way to hunting grounds and mining camps. Native Americans held celebrations here, and later ranchers grazed their cattle during winter. Jefferson County now preserves and manages the land for elk habitat and human recreation.

Start: Centennial Cone Park's north trailhead

Distance: 7.0 miles out and back

Hiking time: 2.75 to 3.5 hours

Difficulty: Moderate due to length

Elevation gain: 710-foot gain and 240-foot loss from turnaround point

Trail surface: Natural surface and rocky trail

Seasons: Best Apr through Nov. Elk Range Trail is closed seasonally (typically Feb through mid-June) for elk calving.

Other trail users: Equestrians all week; multiuse weekdays but weekends alternate hiking and mountain biking; see Schedule below.

Canine compatibility: Dogs must be on leash

Land status: Jefferson County Open Space

Fees and permits: Large groups and unique activities require special permits. Please check jeffco.us/open-space or call 303-271-5925.

Schedule: Open Feb through Nov, 1 hour before sunrise to 1 hour after sunset (closed Dec and Jan for hunting). Centennial Cone Park has a unique ranger-enforced system on weekends, where mountain bikers use the trails on even-numbered days (no hikers), and hikers use the trails on-odd numbered days (no mountain bikers). See jeffco.us/open-space for the exact schedule. During spring closure of the Elk Range Trail for elk calving, park hours are 8 a.m. to 4 p.m.

Maps: USGS Evergreen, Ralston Buttes; National Geographic Trails Illustrated 100 Boulder/Golden

Trail contact: Jefferson County Open Space, 700 Jefferson County Parkway, Golden; 303-271-5925; jeffco.us/open-space

Other: Camping and fires are prohibited at Centennial Cone Park.

Special considerations: Bring water—there is none in the park. Bears and mountain lions live in the area. Come prepared for an outdoor experience. Please leave valuables at home.

THE HIKE

Travois Trail is named for the historic Arapaho Travois Trail that crossed the ridges of the foothills from Golden to the North Fork of Clear Creek. Native Americans hauled their goods using a travois (sled) pulled by dogs, and later by horses. Two long poles were crossed at one end and secured in a V-shape, and the other ends were smoothed flat for easier drag. A rectangular platform of sticks was built across the wide end to which belongings were secured. The pointed end went near the animal's head. The Arapaho originally lived in the Great Lakes area, but as white settlers advanced into their territory, they moved west to the eastern edge of the Rocky Mountains around 1750. The Southern Arapaho settled in eastern Colorado, while the Northern tribe moved into Wyoming.

The historic trail crosses the new Travois Trail close to its north junction with the Evening Sun Loop trail. Starting in Golden, the old trail headed west up a drainage between Clear Creek Canyon and Mount Galbraith. Settlers called this drainage "Indian Gulch," but the US Geological Survey incorrectly used the name for a gulch draining into Clear Creek Canyon. From Centennial Cone, the Arapaho followed Elk Creek along present-day Robinson Hill Road, then dropped down to today's Smith Hill Road. The historic trail arrived at the North Fork of Clear Creek near the junction of Smith Hill Road and SH 119 southeast of Black Hawk. Ruts created by the travois can still be seen in some areas today.

As homesteaders arrived in Colorado, they tried their luck at farming and ranching. Homesteads consisted of 160 acres, but in the short, dry Colorado summers, 160 mountain acres just weren't enough to support a family, so homesteaders often sold their acreage to others. One family, George and Edna Green and their two young sons, moved from their homestead near Trinidad to 900 acres along Smith Hill Road in 1917. They built a successful cattle business on the Green Ranch, but winters were harsh and they looked for better winter pasture. In 1920, they purchased a 1,000-acre ranch on Robinson Hill Road. They summered at Green Ranch and drove their cattle along Robinson Hill Road between

Crossing Elk Creek on the Travois Trail below Centennial Cone.

their ranches in the spring and fall. Their son Kenneth studied veterinary medicine at Colorado State University in Fort Collins and in 1931 became the second veterinarian registered in Jefferson County. Kenneth married Lela White, whose family's ranch on Belcher Hill is now Jefferson County's White Ranch Park.

After driving their cattle from Robinson Hill to the Green Ranch in the spring, the Greens branded new calves. In early July, they herded about 250 cattle onto nearby national forest lands to graze for the summer. In the fall, the Greens rounded up their cattle, chose which ones to send to market, and drove them from their Robinson Hill spread to the White Ranch. From there, the two families herded the cattle out of the foothills, over dirt roads through Denver to the stockyards near today's Denver Coliseum along I-70 just east of I-25. Eventually trucks hauled the cattle on better roads to Denver, ending the tiresome trail drives. The Greens continued ranching until the 1990s. Much of their two ranches are preserved in Golden Gate State Park (Green Ranch) and Centennial Cone Park (their ranch on Robinson Hill).

Today you can enjoy hiking among these grassy fields and wooded knolls. Near the trail's start, look for old equipment rusting away in a field. An interesting outcropping of bright white rock stands out along this pleasant foothills hike.

MILES AND DIRECTIONS

0.0   Start from Centennial Cone Park's north trailhead. Start your hike to the right of the bulletin board. Elevation: 7,750 feet. GPS: N39 46.30' / W105 20.81'.

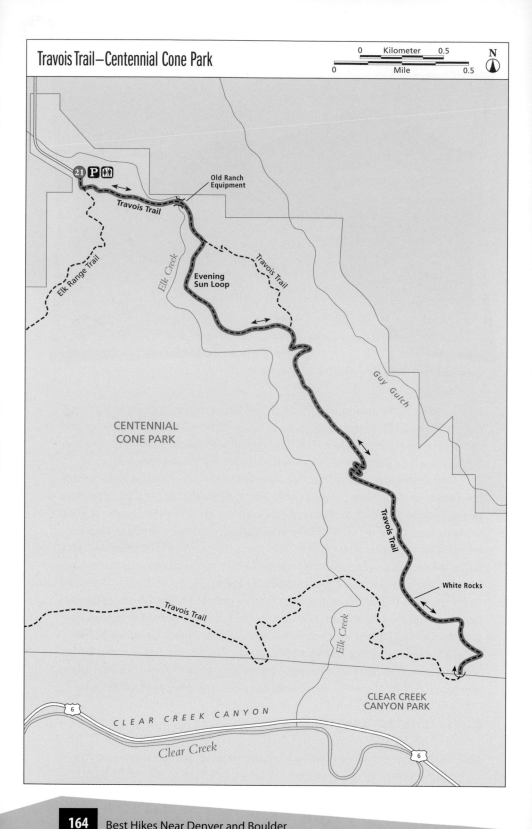

Travois Trail–Centennial Cone Park

Old Ranch Equipment

Travois Trail

Elk Range Trail

Elk Creek

Evening Sun Loop

Travois Trail

Guy Gulch

CENTENNIAL CONE PARK

Travois Trail

White Rocks

Travois Trail

Elk Creek

CLEAR CREEK CANYON PARK

CLEAR CREEK CANYON

Clear Creek

200 feet Junction with the Elk Range Trail. Turn left onto the Travois Trail.

0.6 Junction with Evening Sun Loop. Turn right onto the Evening Sun Loop trail.

1.3 Junction with the Travois Trail. Turn right onto Travois, which heads uphill toward a little ridge.

2.1 Reach the top of a lumpy cone with standing rocks. Elevation: 7,680 feet. GPS: N39 45.36' / W105 19.61' The trail switchbacks downhill. You can see parts of US 6 in Clear Creek Canyon, and at 2.25 miles you can see a piece of I-70.

2.9 Big white quartz boulders with yellow and green lichen stand out on the right side of the trail.

3.5 Saddle and viewpoint down into Clear Creek Canyon. Trail drops from here into Elk Creek. Turn around here and return the way you came. Elevation: 7,280 feet. GPS: N39 44.63' / W105 19.18'.

7.0 Arrive back at the trailhead.

Option

For a shorter, moderate 4.2-mile out-and-back hike, turn around at the top of the lumpy cone at mile 2.1 above and return the way you came.

View of Centennial Cone from the highpoint of the Travois Trail, at 7,680 feet.

21

HIKE INFORMATION

Local Information: Greater Golden Chamber of Commerce, Golden; 303-279-3113; goldenchamber.org

Local Events/Attractions: American Mountaineering Center, Golden; 303-996-2747; americanmountaineeringcenter.org

Colorado Railroad Museum, Golden; 303-279-4591, 800-365-6263; coloradorailroadmuseum.org

Organizations: Jefferson County Open Space Volunteers, Golden; 303-271-5922; jeffco.us/open-space

8,679-foot Centennial Cone was originally called Sheep Mountain, but confusion ensued with two other hills named Sheep Mountain in Jefferson County. The cone-shaped hill was renamed Centennial Cone after the Centennial Ranch, located on Golden Gate Canyon Road west of Robinson Hill Road.

Elk Management at Centennial Cone Park

As many as 400 elk have been sighted at one time at Centennial Cone Park. The Clear Creek herd numbers around 1,500 and ranges from I-70 to Left Hand Canyon in northwest Boulder. Hunting had been allowed when the land was in private ownership. The Colorado Division of Wildlife continues to use hunting for population management, helping to maintain a healthy herd and historic migratory patterns. Large herds can overgraze and damage vegetation. Hunters who hold valid elk and deer licenses for the Jefferson County (Jeffco) portion of Game Management Unit 38 may apply to Jeffco Open Space in September for a special permit to hunt at Centennial Cone Park in December and January. The number of permits issued is determined by herd populations.

Typically from February to mid-June, the Elk Range Trail and most of the interior part of the park are closed to human use to protect critical elk winter range and calving areas. Once the elk move to higher country, the trail and interior parts are reopened. The closures do not affect the Travois Trail and Evening Sun Loop trail. Check jeffco.us/open-space for information on seasonal closures.

Beaver Brook Trail

The Beaver Brook Trail travels like a roller coaster through a variety of ecosystems and interesting rocky sections. Starting in Genesee Park on the west, the trail drops 840 feet to Beaver Brook in a wild, primitive area close to Denver. It then climbs 1,200 feet until leveling out, before descending 880 feet to Windy Saddle above Golden. Viewpoints look down into Clear Creek Canyon, where semitrailer trucks look like ants. Although sections are open and dry, little oases and a small waterfall provide surprises along this trail through the first Denver Mountain Park and two Jefferson County Open Space parks.

Start: West Beaver Brook Trailhead

Distance: 9.8 miles point to point

Hiking time: 4 to 6 hours

Difficulty: Most Difficult due to length, many elevation gains and losses, and rocky areas

Elevation gain: 1,400-foot gain and 1,920 foot loss

Trail surface: Natural surface and rocky trail

Seasons: Best May through Nov

Other trail users: Hikers only; mountain bikers allowed on the easternmost 0.2 mile, which is Lookout Mountain Trail in Windy Saddle Park

Canine compatibility: Dogs must be on leash

Land status: Denver Mountain Parks, private land on easements, Jefferson County Open Space

Fees and permits: None required

Schedule: Open year-round, 1 hour before sunrise to 1 hour after sunset.

Maps: USGS Evergreen, Morrison; National Geographic Trails Illustrated 100 Boulder/Golden; Latitude 40°: Colorado Front Range

Trail contacts: Denver Mountain Parks, Denver; 303-697-4545; denvergov.org; Jefferson County Open Space, 700 Jefferson County Parkway, Golden; 303-271-5925; jeffco.us/open-space

Other: Stay on the trail when passing through private property. Camping, fires, and hunting are prohibited. Observe Leave No Trace ethics of land use. Half-mile markers are posted beginning at the east entrance at Windy Saddle. Take note of the mile marker information as you hike so rescue personnel can decide the closest access point if emergency assistance is needed. On some parts of this trail, neither GPS nor cell phones may work.

Special considerations: Potable water is not available along this trail, so be sure to bring plenty. North-facing slopes may be icy at times in winter.

Finding the trailhead: For the point-to-point hike, park one car at the east trailhead at Windy Saddle, then drive a second car to the west trailhead on Stapleton Drive to start the hike. Some people prefer to hike east to west, so at the end of the hike they lose elevation then regain it. If you'd prefer to hike east to west, leave a car at the west trailhead and start hiking from Windy Saddle.

East trailhead at Windy Saddle: From I-70 exit 256, Lookout Mountain, turn right then turn immediately left onto Mount Vernon Canyon Road. In 1.5 miles turn right onto Lookout Mountain Road. Follow the twisty road up past Buffalo Bill's Museum and Grave, then downhill on a twistier Lariat Loop Road for 5.9 miles total from Mount Vernon Canyon Road to the Windy Saddle parking lot on the left. You can also get there by heading west on 19th Street from US 6 in Golden. The parking lot is on the right 0.9 mile from the brick pillars at the base of Lookout Mountain Road. A port-a-potty is available at the trailhead.

West trailhead: From I-70 exit 253, Chief Hosa, turn right then immediately right onto Stapleton Drive, a broad dirt road. Drive down Stapleton for 0.7 mile to the trailhead parking area. The trail starts from the new trailhead on Stapleton. At the time of this update, a new parking area and toilets are under construction. This parking area also serves as winter parking for trail access in that area of Genesee Park.

THE HIKE

Imagine back in time when I-70 didn't exist, and trains transported people and goods in a roadless Clear Creek Canyon. In 1871, the Colorado Central Railroad began its journey from Golden to the mines in Central City and Black Hawk. Gilpin County residents approved a bond issue with the stipulation that the rails had to reach Central City by June 1, 1872. Stations were built at frequent intervals along the way to load coal, lumber, and hay and to provide water for the steam engines. The railroad company built a dancing and picnic pavilion where Beaver Brook flowed into Clear Creek (near today's Tunnel 2). A sixty-step staircase led up to the structure, where Denver residents made merry on many a summer night. The Beaver Brook Depot was removed in 1893.

Fast-forward a few years to 1910, when John Brisben Walker approached Denver's Chamber of Commerce and the Denver Real Estate Exchange with his idea for a system of roads and parks in the mountains west of Denver that would be accessible to tourists. Frederick Law Olmstead Jr., a landscape architect, was hired to study and report on possible lands and routes. Plans were discussed for a road up Lookout Mountain near Golden—the Lariat Trail. Denver citizens approved

View down into Clear Creek Canyon from the east trailhead at Windy Saddle.

a mill levy and purchased Genesee Park in 1912. The Lariat Trail Road was completed in 1914. Denver purchased Lookout Mountain Park in 1916 and buried Buffalo Bill Cody there the following year. Chief Hosa Lodge and campground were built near Genesee Park to provide meals and lodging. The complete 68.2-mile loop went from Denver to Golden to Genesee to Bergen Park, then through Evergreen, down Bear Creek Canyon to Morrison, and back to Denver.

Hiking and mountaineering enthusiasts established the Colorado Mountain Club (CMC) in 1912. A CMC committee encouraged the Denver Mountain Parks Commission to build trails as well as roads. In 1917, the Commission accepted their trails plan and appropriated money. CMC members designed the Beaver Brook Trail and worked with Denver to build it. The intrepid hikers also convinced the Colorado & Southern (C&S) Railroad to build a station platform at the old Beaver Brook stop. The trail started at the train stop and climbed out of Clear Creek Canyon. In about 0.5 mile it forked, with the right branch leading to Chief Hosa Lodge/campground and the left branch (perhaps originally named Colorow Trail) heading toward Golden. By fall 1919, the trail had been completed to Windy Saddle.

A typical Beaver Brook Trail outing for CMC members in 1921 included taking the interurban trolley to Golden for 52 cents round-trip. The hikers then caught the C&S train to Beaver Brook for 42 cents one-way. With lunch and a cup in hand to gather water from springs and creeks, the hikers walked the 11 miles of the Beaver Brook Trail to Windy Saddle, then down Chimney Gulch Trail to Golden, where they caught the interurban back to Denver.

A rocky outcrop on the trail with a view of North Table Mountain in Golden.

The last train up Clear Creek Canyon ran in May 1941. Three years later, a flash flood down Bear Gulch washed out the lower portion of the Beaver Brook Trail to Clear Creek Canyon.

Hiking this trail is an adventure. After it reaches Beaver Brook, an interesting but easy rock scramble presents itself. As you head up an unnamed gulch, the trail gets a little confusing over rock slabs—look for yellow diamonds or fleurdelis-shaped markers. The trail follows ridges and meadows, with several overlooks along the way providing good views into Clear Creek Canyon. Near Windy Saddle, several rocky ledges require some scrambling with good handholds and footholds, completing the adventure.

MILES AND DIRECTIONS

0.0 Start from the trailhead at the west end of this hike, on Stapleton Drive by the bulletin board. Elevation: 7,400 feet. GPS: N39 42.89′ / W105 18.52′. Start hiking on the Beaver Brook Trail, to the left of the trailhead sign, and head slightly downhill into the forest.

0.4 Junction with a connector to the Chavez Trail on the right. Stay left.

0.6 Cross a drainage.

1.1 Junction with an old road on the right. Turn left onto it. GPS: N39 43.11′ / W105 19.28′.

Beaver Brook Trail

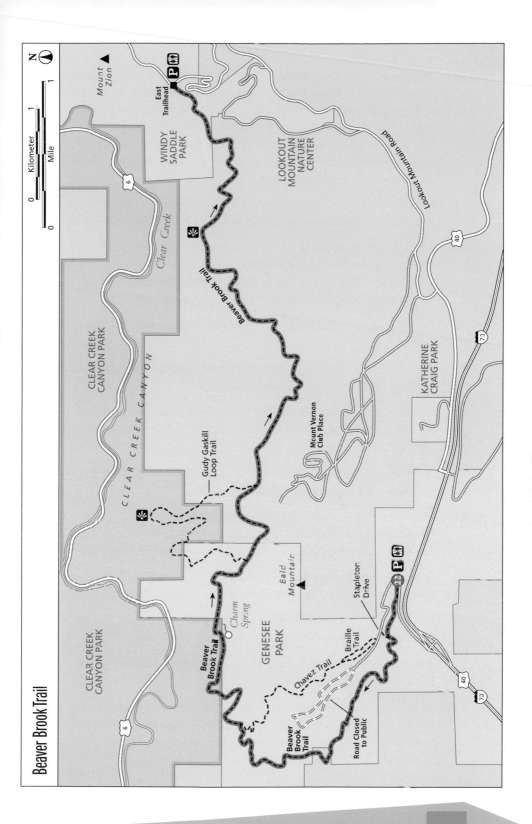

2.8 Junction with the Chavez Trail. GPS: N39 43.88' / W105 19.59'. Head downhill on the Beaver Brook Trail. The trail crosses some interesting rock slabs, which require a bit of hand and foot work (scrambling). The trail makes a right U-turn up a drainage just past B/B 7.0. This point is the lowest on the hike. After crossing the little creek, you may lose the trail in the rock slabs. Look for red and white B/B signs or yellow diamonds to find the trail. The trail then climbs quite steeply.

3.1 A blocked trail comes in from the right. Continue uphill. The trail turns left over a creek, then crosses an open grassy area as it continues to climb.

3.4 A rock outcropping to the left offers a view of Clear Creek below and Travois Trail in Centennial Cone Park above and to the north. GPS: N39 44.01' / W105 19.31'. This part of Beaver Brook Trail is in Jefferson County's Clear Creek Canyon Park. The trail keeps climbing steadily.

3.7 The trail is in thick forest and curves left by Charm Spring. The spring may be dry.

3.9 The trail climbs up through some rock outcroppings and goes back into Genesee Park.

4.3 Junction with the trail around Bald Mountain. Continue to the left on Beaver Brook Trail. In about 250 feet is a viewpoint to the left near the B/B 5.5 sign. GPS: N39 43.96' / W105 18.53'.

4.7 Junction with west end of Gudy Gaskill Loop. GPS: N39 43.82' / W105 18.35'. See Option 2 for information on this side trail.

4.9 Junction with a double-track trail (Mount Vernon Access) and Bald Mountain Loop. Make a right turn onto the double-track and hike down it a few feet. The Beaver Brook Trail then turns left and becomes a single-track again.

5.5 Junction with the east end of the Gudy Gaskill Loop. GPS: N39 43.69' / W105 17.74'. Continue straight ahead on the Beaver Brook Trail.

7.3 A PRIVATE PROPERTY ON EITHER SIDE OF TRAIL sign. For the next 1.4 miles, the trail is on an easement. Please stay on the trail.

7.7 The trail curves left over a creek, which when it has water in it, tumbles in a pretty little waterfall on the right.

8.2 A rocky outcrop with a good view down into Clear Creek Canyon is on the left. GPS: N39 44.07' / W105 15.89'. Take a few minutes to walk out there for both the view and the interesting rocks forming the overlook.

8.7 The trail climbs up a rock (good hand- and footholds), passes another PRIVATE PROPERTY ON EITHER SIDE OF TRAIL sign, then enters Jefferson County's Windy Saddle Park. The trail goes over a series of various rocks and ledges for the next 0.4 mile.

9.2 The trail appears to split around a large boulder. Take either branch.

9.4 The trail crosses two boulder fields.

9.5 Junction with the Lookout Mountain Trail, which is multiuse so be aware of bikers. Continue to the left to Windy Saddle.

9.8 Arrive at the east trailhead at Windy Saddle parking lot. Elevation: 6,880 feet. GPS: N39 44.20' / W105 14.73'.

Options

1. If you'd prefer to hike the recommended route east to west, starting at Windy Saddle, read the directions above backwards.

2. For a 11.4-mile hike, at mile 4.7 above, turn left onto the Gudy Gaskill Loop. This 2.4-mile trail loses about 200 feet of elevation as it winds its way at the edge of the forest to an overlook into Clear Creek Canyon. It then climbs about 200 feet to join the Beaver Brook Trail at mile 5.5 above. Turn left and continue following the above directions to the east trailhead.

3. If you can't do a car shuttle, you can hike from either trailhead for whatever distance that time allows. Some suggestions:

   3a. From the east end, hike to the overlook at mile 8.2 above for a 3.2-mile out-and-back hike.

   3b. For a 12.6-mile round-trip, from the west end, hike down the Beaver Brook Trail to the Gudy Gaskill Loop at mile 4.7 above. Turn left, hike the loop, then turn right onto the Beaver Brook Trail at mile 5.5 above. Hike 0.8 mile to the west end of Gudy Gaskill Loop and return the way you came.

   3c. From the west end, hike down the Beaver Brook Trail to the junction with the Chavez Trail. Turn right onto the Chavez Trail and follow it back to the Beaver Brook Trail and then the trailhead. This loop is about 4.5 miles and has an 840-foot gain.

HIKE INFORMATION

Local Information: Greater Golden Chamber of Commerce, Golden; 303-279-3113; goldencochamber.org

Evergreen Chamber of Commerce and Visitor Information Center; 303-674-3412; evergreenchamber.org

Local Events/Attractions: Lariat Loop National Scenic and Historic Byway, Morrison; 720-971-9649; lariatloop.org

Buffalo Bill Museum and Grave, Golden; 303-526-0747; buffalobill.org

American Mountaineering Center, Golden; 303-996-2747; americanmountaineeringcenter.org

Colorado Railroad Museum, Golden; 303-279-4591, 800-365-6263; coloradorailroadmuseum.org

Hike Tours: Colorado Mountain Club, Golden; 303-279-3080, 800-633-4417; cmc.org

Organizations: Denver Mountain Parks Foundation; mountainparksfoundation .org

In the May 1926 issue of the Colorado Mountain Club's Trail & Timberline, *Alice Hale described designing the Beaver Brook Trail: "[I]t took time and thought . . . to make it the best way, . . . with the finest views, with the spring just where it is needed, and the charming dips into the steep cool ravines coming as a sharp contrast to the long stretches on the very edge of the hills."*

Gudy Gaskill Loop

In many places, the Beaver Brook Trail between Genesee Park and Windy Saddle Park had been built on narrow easements through private property, obtained from the Lookout Mountain Realty and Investment Company. It crosses Jefferson County's (Jeffco) Clear Creek Canyon Park in places, providing a wider trail easement. You'll pass Jeffco Open Space signs along the trail. Clear Creek Canyon Park encompasses both sides of the canyon, with an eye toward preserving view corridors and wildlife habitat while providing for non-motorized recreation, such as kayaking and rock climbing.

In 1999, Jeffco purchased a little peninsula along the ridge south of Clear Creek and constructed a U-shaped trail from the Beaver Brook Trail across grassy meadows to a rocky outcropping overlooking Clear Creek Canyon. The 2.4-mile Gudy Gaskill Loop honors former Golden resident Gudy Gaskill, whose tireless efforts assured the creation and completion of the Colorado Trail, among her many conservation contributions. Gudy is a past president of the Colorado Mountain Club. She passed away in July of 2016 at the age of eighty-nine.

Sisters/Bearberry Loop—Alderfer/Three Sisters Park

Twist your way up and across the Three Sisters ridge, then descend through ponderosa pine forest. Rocky Mountain junipers grow in sunny spots, while Douglas firs enjoy northern exposures. The Bearberry Trail takes you into the Blair Ranch parcel, past an old caretaker's house with interesting outbuildings. The meadows between Eddie's Rocks and the Alderfer ranch house nurture purple wild irises in the spring. The Three Sisters tower over the eastern meadow. Scramble up to Brother's Lookout for lunch and a beautiful view of the Evergreen area and Mount Evans.

Start: Trailhead at the east parking lot

Distance: 3.7-mile loop with a spur

Hiking time: 1.5 to 2 hours

Difficulty: Moderate due to some steep sections

Elevation gain: 580 feet total between Sisters and Brother, with a 260-foot loss in between

Trail surface: Natural surface and rocky trail, and old dirt road (closed to the motorized public)

Seasons: Best Apr through Nov

Other trail users: Equestrians and mountain bikers

Canine compatibility: Dogs must be on leash

Land status: Jefferson County Open Space

Fees and permits: Large groups and unique activities require special permits. Please check jeffco.us/open-space or call 303-271-5925.

Schedule: Open year-round, 1 hour before sunrise to 1 hour after sunset

Maps: USGS Evergreen, Conifer; National Geographic Trails Illustrated 100 Boulder/Golden; Latitude 40°: Colorado Front Range

Trail contact: Jefferson County Open Space, 700 Jefferson County Parkway, Golden; 303-271-5925; jeffco.us/open-space

Other: Camping is prohibited. Fires allowed only in designated areas.

Special considerations: Bring water because none is available on the trail. Come prepared for an outdoor experience. Leave valuables at home.

Finding the trailhead: From I-70 exit 252, Evergreen Parkway, drive southwest on Evergreen Parkway (SH 74) through Evergreen to its junction with Jefferson CR 73 near the Evergreen Lake dam. Turn right (south) onto JCR 73 and drive 0.5 mile to Buffalo Park Road. Turn right (west) and drive 1.4 miles on Buffalo Park Road to the east parking lot for Alderfer/Three Sisters Park. A vault toilet is available at the trailhead, but no water.

THE HIKE

The Three Sisters rock formation has long been a landmark for Evergreen settlers and residents. Magma gathered under an ancient Colorado about 1.4 billion years ago and cooled before ever reaching the surface. Over time, the land rose, was buried in sediment, and then rose again numerous times. This hardened rock, called quartz monzonite (a type of granite), repeatedly emerged and eroded. The rocky ridge of Alderfer/Three Sisters Park is the result of this geologic history. The three highest humps became known as the Three Sisters. The smaller granitic outcrop at the ridge's south end was named "The Brother" by Hank Alderfer, who once owned the core of this wonderful park.

E. J. Alderfer made a down payment on the ranch house (at today's west parking lot) on Christmas Eve 1945. The 245 acres was about to be advertised for sale, but E. J. had arranged for a sneak preview. Without consulting his wife, he purchased the open meadow before anyone else could buy it. Luckily his wife, Arleta, loved their new home.

In the late 1940s, many people living in the mountains raised silver foxes, and the Alderfers were no exception. Movie stars paid highly for silver fox fur coats—one fox fur sold for $1,000. The family raised foxes until 1962. Pelts had dropped to $7 each, which didn't cover the $25 tab to feed the little animals.

The Alderfers also raised three children, Black Angus cattle, and hay on their ranch. E. J. owned the first mechanical haying equipment around, and cut hay for neighbors as well as for himself. Eventually, as ranches were sold to nonranchers

Eddie's Rocks on the Homestead Trail.

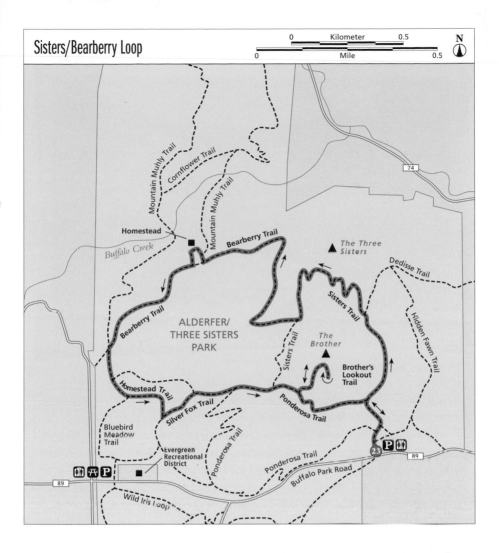

or for housing developments, neighbors frequently complained that the Alderfers' bovines were grazing on their petunias. Boarding horses and raising thoroughbreds replaced the cattle business, and E. J. worked other jobs, including superintendent of the Bergen Park School District. He and Arleta helped establish the Evergreen Recreation Association.

After E. J. died in 1972, the family decided to sell and donate 280 acres of land to Jefferson County (Jeffco) over nine years, starting in 1977. They wanted their land preserved instead of developed. Jeffco also obtained 57 acres, including Three Sisters, from the Spencer Wyatt family. Land that the Alderfers had leased from the State Land Board became Jeffco property in 2005.

In 2002, Jeffco purchased the Blair Ranch to the north. Hank Alderfer and the Mountain Area Land Trust he helped establish were key in the purchase. Local citizens pledged donations large and small to assure the deal happened. With the Blair

Mount Evans view from the Ponderosa Trail.

Ranch addition and adjoining Elephant Butte and Dedisse Park (Denver Mountain Parks), Evergreen now has 2,000 acres of unbroken open space in its backyard.

Several trails in Alderfer/Three Sisters Park reflect the ranching heritage or natural features, such as Silver Fox, Sisters, and Brother's Lookout. The Homestead Trail loops around Eddie's Rocks, named for Hank's deceased older brother, and passes the site of the original homestead of James T. Hester. The Evergreen Naturalists Audubon Society installed the bluebird boxes along the meadow in 1975 (Bluebird Meadow Trail). Wild irises grow in the wetter meadow areas in the spring (Wild Iris Loop), and the Ponderosa Trail ambles through a ponderosa pine forest.

When you turn down the Bearberry Trail, look for low-growing bearberry, or kinnikinnick, with its small, dark green, waxy-looking leaves. Little heather-like white flowers with a dash of pink become bright red fruits on these woody shrubs. Similar plants with small bush-like leaves are whortleberry, or mountain blueberry. By looking closely, you can tell the difference.

Preserving open space takes hard work, money, and community. Alderfer/Three Sisters Park provides a great example of the outcome of such efforts.

MILES AND DIRECTIONS

0.0　Start from the trailhead at the east parking lot. Elevation: 7,480 feet. GPS: N39 37.40′ / W105 20.79′. Start on the trail to the left of the bulletin board. Turn right, between the vault toilet and the large trail-map sign.

View of Mount Evans from the summit of The Brother.

225 feet   Four-way junction of the Sisters, Ponderosa, Hidden Fawn, and Evergreen Mountain East Trails. Go basically straight ahead (slightly right) on Sisters Trail.

0.2   T-intersection with the Ponderosa Trail. Turn right to continue on Sisters Trail.

0.4   Junction with the Hidden Fawn Trail. Turn left and head uphill on Sisters Trail.

0.75   Top of the ridge between two of the Sisters. Elevation: 7,740 feet.

1.0   Junction with the Bearberry Trail. Turn right onto Bearberry.

1.5   A dirt service road comes in from the right. Bearberry becomes a double-track trail here as it curves to the left. Stay to the left.

1.7   Junction with Mountain Muhly Trail. An old homestead is just ahead to the right. Turn right onto Mountain Muhly, then in about 160 feet turn left onto the road that goes into the homestead. Take a little time to look around and imagine life here.

1.8   Junction with the Bearberry Trail. GPS: N39 37.84′ / W105 21.34′. Turn right to continue the loop.

2.0   An old dirt road (closed) comes in from the left. Continue curving to the right on Bearberry.

2.2 Four-way intersection of the Bearberry Trail with a service road and the Mountain Muhly Trail. Turn left onto the single-track to continue on Bearberry.

2.3 Junction with the Homestead Trail. Turn right and head across the meadows to the west of Eddie's Rocks.

2.4 Junction with the Bluebird Meadow Trail. GPS: N39 37.52' / W105 21.55'. Turn left to continue on the Homestead Trail.

2.5 T-intersection with the Silver Fox Trail. Turn left onto Silver Fox.

2.6 Junction with the Homestead Trail. Turn right and continue on the Silver Fox Trail.

2.7 T-intersection with the Ponderosa Trail. Turn left onto Ponderosa.

2.8 Junction with the Sisters Trail. Continue straight ahead on Ponderosa.

2.9 Junction with Brother's Lookout. Turn left to go up The Brother for a beautiful view.

3.1 Trail-end marker. From here, scramble up the rocks ahead of you for a great view. An easy way up is to walk around to the left side just past some lodgepole pines. Walk up the rocks here, then across the top to the west end for a nice place to sit and enjoy the view. Elevation: 7,800 feet. Return the way you came to the Ponderosa Trail.

3.3 Back at the junction with the Ponderosa Trail. Turn left and head downhill.

3.6 Junction of Sisters Trail and Ponderosa Trail; same as mile 0.2 above. Turn right and head downhill to the parking lot.

3.7 Arrive back at the trailhead.

Options

Alderfer/Three Sisters Park's many trails provide opportunities for loop hikes of various distances.

HIKE INFORMATION

Local Information: Evergreen Area Chamber of Commerce; 303-674-3412; evergreenchamber.org

Local Events/Attractions: Lariat Loop National Scenic Byway, Golden; 720-971-9649; lariatloop.org

Annual Big Chili Cook-Off, Music and Arts Festival, Evergreen; 303-973-1209; bigchili.org

Hiwan Homestead Museum, Evergreen; 720-497-7650; jeffco.us/open-space.

Organizations: Jefferson County Open Space Volunteers, Golden; 303-271-5922; jeffco.us/open-space/volunteer

Hank Alderfer attended college in Los Angeles, but he returned to Colorado for the summers. He noted, "It was always a culture shock to return to California, especially when I saw tract homes springing up where orange groves once stood. Those California developments fueled my dedication to land conservation."

🌱 **Green Tip:**
Be considerate of others. Many people visit natural areas for quiet, peace, and solitude, so avoid making loud noises, playing music, or otherwise intruding on others' privacy.

Shadow Pine Loop—Flying J Ranch Park

Flying J Ranch Park is an excellent place for a family outing. With nice picnic gaze-bos and easy trails, everyone from the youngest child to grandparents can enjoy a day in the mountains. Foothills zone meets montane zone here, and a riparian area borders a little stream. The variety of trees and flowers offers opportunities for eco-logical education. The park provides habitat for deer and elk, so keep an eye out for these ungulates. Kid-size granitic boulders provide great scrambling for prospective mountain climbers. The trail loop winds through two parcels belonging to Denver Mountain Parks.

Start: Trailhead bulletin board
Distance: 2.8-mile loop
Hiking time: 1 to 2 hours
Difficulty: Easy due to length and minor elevation gain
Elevation gain: 220 feet
Trail surface: Natural surface trail
Seasons: Best May through Nov
Other trail users: Equestrians and mountain bikers
Canine compatibility: Dogs must be on leash
Land status: Jefferson County Open Space, Denver Mountain Parks
Fees and permits: Large groups and unique activities require spe-cial permits. Please check jeffco.us/open-space or call 303-271-5925.
Schedule: Open year-round, 1 hour before sunrise to 1 hour after sunset

Maps: USGS Conifer; National Geographic Trails Illustrated 100 Boulder/Golden
Trail contact: Jefferson County Open Space, 700 Jefferson County Parkway, Golden; 303-271-5925; jeffco.us/open-space
Other: Camping is prohibited. Fires are allowed only in provided grills—use only charcoal. You can cross-country ski or snowshoe on the trails in the winter when there's enough snow.
Special considerations: Bring water, as very little is available along the trail. Bears and moun-tain lions live in the area. Come prepared for an outdoor experience. Leave valuables at home.

Finding the trailhead: From I-70 exit 252, Evergreen Parkway, drive on Evergreen Parkway (SH 74) through Evergreen to its junction with Jefferson County Road 73 near the Evergreen Lake dam. Turn right onto JCR 73 and drive 7.1 miles south to the entrance to Flying J Ranch Park. Turn right into the park and drive 0.6 mile to the parking lot. Flush toilets, picnic tables and gazebos are available at the trailhead.

THE HIKE

A tipi ring and artifacts found at Flying J Ranch Park indicate Native Americans used the area for many years during their annual loop from the hogback valleys west of Denver over the Continental Divide to North Park, Middle Park, and South Park then back over the Continental Divide before winter arrived.

Years later, in 1948, John and Marguerite Schoonhoven purchased about 500 acres near Conifer and started a small cattle ranch they called Flying J. John loved to fly and worked for United Airlines as a pilot for thirty-five years, while his wife and three daughters did most of the ranch work in his absence. The family built a small runway on the east side of the property so John could land his biplane. John continued to fly after he retired. On one contract job, he delivered a Boeing 747 to King Hussein of Jordan. He even flew his plane over Greenland when he was eighty years old. The family sold 322 acres of their ranch to Jefferson County Open Space, starting in 1995, to "keep it the way it was." Their house and other buildings are on the property to the north of the access road.

While you hike, notice the different trees. The bigger ones with long needles growing in packets of two or three are ponderosa pines. Some people say the bark smells like butterscotch. Ponderosas live in dry, warm places between 5,500 and 9,000 feet elevation. These trees can grow 150 feet tall and 3 to 4 feet in diameter. Bigger trees may live 300 to 500 years. A healthy ponderosa forest is open and park-like, with good spacing between trees. Low-intensity fires every

A nice rest spot on the Shadow Pine Loop.

five to forty-five years are necessary to keep appropriate spacing. The bark of a mature ponderosa is fairly thick and fire-resistant, but if the fire reaches the crown, the tree will burn.

You'll often find Douglas firs growing with ponderosa pine. Its cones hang down, so it is not a true fir (whose cones point up). The needles are flat and friendly, and the cones have a little bract between the scales, which together look like a mouse's two hind feet and tail. It prefers cooler, moister areas than the ponderosa, but often lives in the same vicinity, between 5,500 and 9,000 feet elevation. The Douglas fir also has a thick bark that is fairly fire-resistant but, with their lower-growing branches, fire often burns into the crown.

The skinnier pine trees are lodgepole pines, used by Native Americans for tipi poles, hence the name. Lodgepole forests are the forests of fire. Most trees produce serotinous cones (sealed shut by resin) until a very hot fire opens them and releases the seeds. Some lodgepoles have non-serotinous cones, so they can also regenerate without fire. Here's an interesting statistic from studies after the 1988 Yellowstone National Park fire: 50,000 to 970,000 lodgepole seeds per acre covered burned areas. You'll pass a couple of very crowded "dog-eared" stands of lodgepole pines along your hike. As lodgepoles age, they become more susceptible to fires and pine beetles, probably nature's way of making room for new tree life. Their needles grow in packets of two.

Aspens also grow in Flying J Ranch Park. In winter, elk scrape the bark off with their teeth to eat the nutritious cambium layer just under the surface. Since

On the east side of the Shadow Pine Loop.

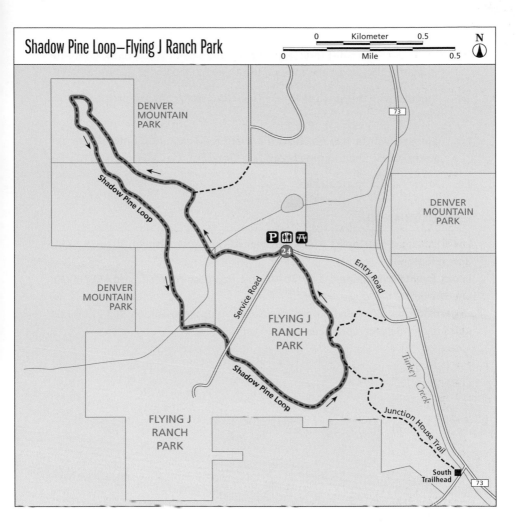

aspens sprout from rhizomes (root-like stems that grow underground), they are the first to sprout after a fire and usually develop within about ten years. One stand of aspens may actually consist of clones, all growing from one set of roots.

MILES AND DIRECTIONS

0.0 Start from the trailhead bulletin board. Hike to the right (west) on Shadow Pine Loop. Elevation: 8,060 feet. GPS: N39 32.70′ / W105 19.33′.

0.2 The trail appears to Y, but it really curves to the right and crosses a little creek.

0.5 Junction with a neighborhood access trail. Turn left to continue on the Shadow Pine Loop.

1.9 The trail crosses a dirt service road. GPS: N39 32.44'/W105 19.51'. Continue straight ahead across the road on the Shadow Pine Loop.

2.4 Junction with the Junction House Trail. Turn left to continue on the Shadow Pine Loop.

2.5 Junction with a trail down to the main road, JCR 73. Continue straight ahead on the Shadow Pine Loop.

2.8 Arrive back at the trailhead.

HIKE INFORMATION

Local Information: Conifer Area Chamber of Commerce, Conifer; 303-838-5711; goconifer.com

Local Events/Attractions: Tiny Town and Railroad, Morrison; 303-697-6829; tinytownrailroad.com

Organizations: Jefferson County Open Space Volunteers, Golden; 303-271-5922; jeffco.us/open-space/volunteer

O'Fallon Park Loop

This popular gem in the Denver Mountain Parks system offers hikers-only trails close to Denver. About a fourth of the main loop is multiuse trail, shared by hikers, mountain bikers, and equestrians. Hike through a ponderosa pine, Douglas fir, and Rocky Mountain juniper forest, then across flower-filled meadows. The trail drops into a peaceful and lush section along a little stream that runs through a Colorado blue spruce forest. A stand of aspens shimmers beautiful gold colors in autumn. With fishing in Bear Creek, picnic grounds, trails for those who love to hike, and grassy areas for games, bring the whole family for an outing that all will enjoy.

Start: Beginning of the West Ridge Trail at the west edge of the upper (west) parking lot (on busy summer weekends and holidays, you can start from the Pence Park trailhead on Meyers Gulch Road and head up the Bear Creek Trail to the main loop.)

Distance: 3.7-mile loop (4.9-mile lollipop from Pence Park)

Hiking time: 1.5 to 3 hours

Difficulty: Moderate due to some steep trail sections

Elevation gain: 390 feet

Trail surface: Natural surface trail and old dirt road (closed to the motorized public.)

Seasons: Best Apr through Nov

Other trail users: Hikers only, except on the Bear Creek Trail section with equestrians and mountain bikers

Canine compatibility: Dogs must be on leash

Land status: Denver Mountain Parks

Fees and permits: None required

Schedule: Open year-round from 5 a.m. to 11 p.m.

Maps: USGS Evergreen; National Geographic Trails Illustrated 100 Boulder/Golden; Latitude 40°: Colorado Front Range

Trail contact: Denver Mountain Parks, Denver; 720-865-0900; denvergov.org/content/denvergov/en/denver-parks-and-recreation/parks/Mountain-Parks.html

Other: Please start your hike from the Pence Park trailhead (directions below) on crowded summer weekends and holidays. Camping and hunting are prohibited. No fires except in grills provided in picnic areas. Glass bottles or containers may not be used. Consumption of wine and liquor is prohibited; 3.2 percent beer in cans or paper cups is allowed.

Special considerations: Bring water with you, as little to no potable water is available along the trail.

Finding the trailhead: West Ridge Loop Trail: From C470, exit at Morrison Road (SH 8) and head west 0.7 mile through Morrison to the junction of SH 8 and SH 74. Continue straight ahead on SH 74 for 7.3 miles to the O'Fallon Park entrance, which is just after a curve and easy to miss. The entrance is right before a REDUCED SPEED AHEAD sign for Kittredge. Turn left and drive 0.1 mile; turn right and cross a stone bridge to reach the upper parking area. Two parking areas are available below this one. There are picnic tables and an outhouse, but no water.

Pence Park trailhead: From C470, exit at Morrison Road (SH 8) and head west 0.7 mile through Morrison to the junction of SH 8 and SH 74. Continue straight ahead on SH 74 for 7.7 miles to Myers Gulch Road and turn left. Drive 1.8 miles to the Pence Park trailhead on the right side of the road. Restrooms are available, but no water.

THE HIKE

O'Fallon Park is a late addition to the Denver Mountain Parks system. Tucked between Corwina Park and Pence Park, it preserves the old George Bancroft Ranch and provides fishing access along a quiet bend of Bear Creek. East of Corwina Park is Jefferson County's Lair o' the Bear Park, which lies on the western border of Denver's Little Park. The multiuse Bear Creek Trail starts in Pence Park and crosses the other three parks to end in Little Park.

When Denver decided to create a system of mountain parks, its stated purpose in 1913 was "to assure perpetually to the residents of Denver the sublime scenery of the Rockies, the preservation of native forests, and having a pleasure ground in the mountains for the thousands of annual visitors to the city accessible."

Building roads for a circle tour was a high priority back then. A variety of parks with picnic shelters and other amenities, including springs or creeks from which to obtain water for auto radiators, would be located along the highways. The first mountain circle tour included Bear Creek Canyon, already popular with campers and picnickers. Between 1912 and 1916, Denver purchased properties along the scenic loop to create Lookout Mountain Park, Genesee Park, Fillius Park, Bergen Park, Corwina Park, and Little Park. Dedisse Park in Evergreen was procured to build a dam for flood control on Bear Creek. Evergreen Dam was completed in 1927, and that same year Denver obtained Bear Creek Canyon Park, an undeveloped strip of land between Morrison and Idledale, which provides fishing access.

Martin J. O'Fallon came to the United States in 1880 from Roscommon County, Ireland, when he was seventeen years old. Nine years later he moved to Denver and landed a job as a salesman for a plumbing supply company. After marrying his sweetheart back in Ireland, on his return he made a promise that if he succeeded in business, he would share any wealth he earned. Back in Denver,

View to the west from the West Ridge Loop trail.

he represented six eastern companies, traveling to mining camps in a horse and buggy selling everything from raincoats to bar iron. A year later, he opened a small plumbing supply company in Denver. His company succeeded and, in 1925, he merged with the Crane Company of Chicago, becoming Chairman of the Board.

O'Fallon loved the mountains, and he wanted to do something to preserve the land he so enjoyed. For three years, he searched the mountains looking for a tract to buy. Denver's Mayor Stapleton encouraged O'Fallon to buy the Bancroft Ranch along Bear Creek between Corwina and Pence Parks. After careful consideration, he purchased the property. He deeded the 860 acres to the Denver Mountain Parks system in September 1938 while he was still alive to see it developed, which he indicated was important to him.

Tucked behind a little ridge, it's easy to miss O'Fallon Park when driving up Bear Creek Canyon. Once you've arrived, you'll find a large grassy area and picnic tables along sparkling Bear Creek. Hiking up a narrow gully on the single-track West Ridge Trail, a wilderness feeling surrounds you. Colorful wildflowers line the trail. Much of the West Ridge Loop is probably an old ranch road. The West Ridge Trail leads you to the Bear Creek Trail, but be sure to stay on the West Ridge Loop. The multiuse Bear Creek Trail starts in nearby Pence Park and joins the West Ridge Loop for about 1.2 miles. It passes below a subdivision of homes, then heads down to its intersection with the Meadow View Trail. Once the trails separate, you'll again be in "wilderness" and on hikers-only trails wandering through more meadows and a lush gully back to the east trailhead.

The Bear Creek Trail on the east side of the loop.

MILES AND DIRECTIONS

0.0 Start from the West Ridge Trail trailhead on the west edge of the west parking lot. Elevation: 6,800 feet. GPS: 39 39.31′ / W105 17.31′. The bulletin board is about 60 feet up the trail. Head straight up to the left of it, into the small gully. (*Note:* On crowded summer weekends, please consider starting at the Pence Park trailhead. See Option 1 below.)

0.6 Junction with a shorter section of the West Ridge Trail. Turning left will shortcut the loop and get you back to the parking lot sooner. To hike the full loop, continue straight ahead.

0.9 The trail crosses an old road that has been blocked off for restoration. Continue heading straight. GPS: N39 38.84′ / W105 17.30′. Head uphill to the right.

1.6 Old road comes in from the right. Head straight.

1.7 Junction of the West Ridge Loop Trail and the Bear Creek Trail. Turn left onto the Bear Creek Trail portion of the loop. This section of trail is multiple use.

1.9 A trail comes in from the left. This segment is CLOSED and blocked off. Continue heading right on the main loop.

2.3 Junction of the West Ridge Trail (the other end of the shortcut trail from mile 0.6 above) with the Bear Creek Trail. Continue straight ahead on the Bear Creek Trail. GPS: N39 38.60′ / W105 16.75′.

O'Fallon Park Loop

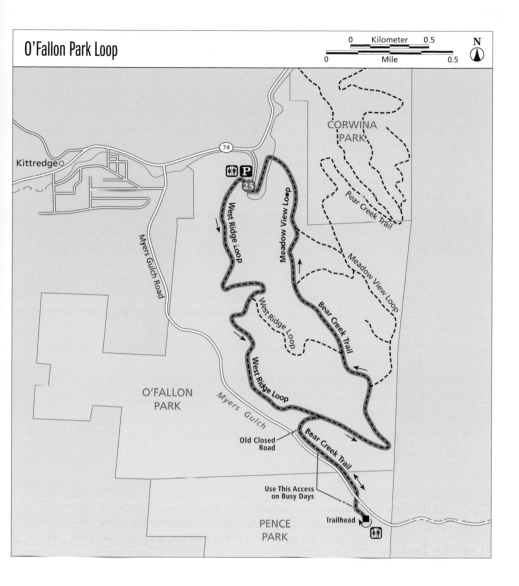

0 Kilometer 0.5

0 Mile 0.5

N

Kittredge

CORWINA PARK

74

25

West Ridge Loop

Meadow View Loop

Myers Gulch Road

Bear Creek Trail

Meadow View Loop

West Ridge Loop

West Ridge Loop

Bear Creek Trail

O'FALLON PARK

Myers Gulch

Old Closed Road

Bear Creek Trail

Use This Access on Busy Days

PENCE PARK

Trailhead

2.8   Junction with the Meadow View Loop. GPS: N39 38.94′ / W105 17.09′. The Bear Creek Trail continues to the right and heads uphill. Turn left onto the Meadow View Loop and head down to a small stream.

3.1   Start/end of the Meadow View Loop. GPS: N39 39.10′ / W105 17.07′. Turn left onto the Meadow View Trail.

3.4   Cross the bridge over Bear Creek. Turn left and walk on the dirt road along the creek to the picnic area and through the east parking lot to the road.

3.7   Turn left and cross over the stone bridge that you drove over to get to the west parking lot. You are back at the trailhead.

Options

1. From the Pence Park trailhead on Myers Gulch Road: To the right of the bulletin board is a post with a BCT (BEAR CREEK TRAIL) 5.0 sign. GPS: N39 38.12' / W105 16.76'. Start here and turn right onto the trail along the edge of the parking lot. Follow this multiuse trail to the HIKER CROSSING sign on Myers Gulch Road and cross the road to the continuation of BCT on the other side. In a little over 0.5 mile from the trailhead, just past the BCT 4.5 sign, a trail crosses BCT at an angle. To the left is an open area. Continue to the right, where the West Ridge Loop joins the BCT. This junction is mile 1.7 above. Follow the directions from there. When you return to this location, turn right onto BCT to return to the Pence Park trailhead.

2. As noted above at mile 0.6, you can take this shortcut and make the loop smaller. Pick up the route description at mile 2.3 (the other end of the shortcut).

HIKE INFORMATION

Local Information: Evergreen Chamber of Commerce and Visitor Information Center; 303-674-3412; evergreenchamber.org

Local Events/Attractions: Lariat Loop National Scenic and Historic Byway, Morrison; 720-971-9649; lariatloop.org

Annual Big Chili Cook-Off, Music and Arts Festival, Evergreen; bigchili.org

Hiwan Homestead Museum, Evergreen; 720-497-7650; jeffco.us/open-space/parks/hiwan-homestead-museum

Organizations: Denver Mountain Parks Foundation; mountainparksfoundation.org

The Denver mountain parks immediately became extremely popular, due in part to people staying close to home because of World War I. In the summer of 1917, 66,507 cars were counted entering the scenic loop at Lookout Mountain and at Morrison. The following summer, 116,292 cars were counted in the same time period.

Denver Mountain Parks Foundation

Denver citizens voted a mill levy to create the Mountain Parks system in 1912. The system consists of over 14,000 acres in four counties, including Red Rocks Amphitheater, the Winter Park Ski Area, and Echo and Summit Lakes below Mount Evans. Bison and elk herds live at Genesee Park. The Mountain Parks Commission was dissolved in the late 1940s and the mill levy terminated in 1955. Since then the mountain parks have received only a small portion of Denver's Parks and Recreation budget. Several million dollars are now needed for restoration and repair.

In 2004, the nonprofit Denver Mountain Parks Foundation (DMPF) was incorporated and established as a donor-advised fund under the Denver Foundation. The mission of the DMPF is "to restore the historical integrity, relevance, quality and appreciation for Denver's Mountain Parks system; to advocate for it and ensure its future as a recreational, educational and open space resource for the city of Denver: its citizens, neighbors and visitors." Tax-deductible donations to the DMPF are used in addition to existing city funding to care for and maintain structures and trails and to implement various plans for the Mountain Parks system. Visit mountainparksfoundation.org for more information.

26

Mount Falcon Park Upper Loop

Mount Falcon Park provides not only pleasant hiking country, with rolling meadows and shady forests on small hills, but also a walk back in history. Once owned by visionary John Brisben Walker, the remains of his mansion and the start of a futile dream lie ready for exploration. A former summer cabin has been remodeled into a viewpoint and picnic pavilion. This lollipop hike visits these sites on a tour of the western part of the park. Excellent interpretive displays explain the human and natural history. The park protects wildlife habitat and offers recreational trails near the cultural features.

Start: Edge of the west parking lot and the start of the dirt road (Castle Trail)

Distance: 4.3 miles, with loop in middle

Hiking time: 2 to 3 hours

Difficulty: Moderate due to length and one steep section

Elevation gain: 210-foot loss and 355-foot gain

Trail surface: Natural surface and rocky trail, and old roads (closed to the motorized public)

Seasons: Best May through Nov

Other trail users: Mountain bikers and equestrians

Canine compatibility: Dogs must be on leash

Land status: Jefferson County Open Space

Fees and permits: Large groups and unique activities require special permits. Please check jeffco.us/open-space or call 303-271-5925.

Schedule: Open year-round, 1 hour before sunrise to 1 hour after sunset

Maps: USGS Morrison; National Geographic Trails Illustrated 100 Boulder/Golden; Latitude 40°: Colorado Front Range

Trail contact: Jefferson County Open Space, 700 Jefferson County Parkway, Golden; 303-271-5925; jeffco.us/open-space

Other: During spring snowmelt, trails in the eastern section of the park, including Castle Trail, may be closed to protect them from deterioration. Call the trails hotline at 303-271-5975 for up-to-date information.

Special considerations: Bring water, as none is available along the trail. Come prepared for an outdoor experience. Leave valuables at home.

Finding the trailhead: From C470, take the US 285 South exit and head southwest. In 4.5 miles turn right (north) onto Parmalee Gulch Road. In 2.7 miles turn right at the MOUNT FALCON sign onto Picutis Road, then immediately turn left onto Comanche Road. Turn right onto Oh Kay Road, then right onto Picutis Road. You'll find yourself driving on Nambe Road. This circuitous route is well-signed, so just follow the signs. The Mount Falcon Park information sign is 1.8 miles from Parmalee Gulch Road. Turn right into the upper parking lot 0.1 mile past the information sign. There are picnic tables near the parking lot, but no water is available. Vault toilets are located about 0.1 mile down the trail past the bulletin board.

THE HIKE

John Brisben Walker and his wife named Mount Falcon while watching one of the beautiful birds circling overhead as they were visiting the site of their new home. Walker, a visionary and entrepreneur, lobbied for a system of mountain parks for Denver and envisioned concerts at the Red Rocks Amphitheater, which he once owned. He built an incline railroad up Mount Morrison, manufactured Stanley Steamers, owned *Cosmopolitan* magazine, and dreamt of creating a Summer White House for US presidents. Interpretive displays give a detailed history of the man and his pursuits.

Walker's second wife, Ethel, died in 1916; his Mount Falcon home burned in 1918; and World War I took a toll on his finances. He died penniless in 1931; however, a number of his dreams came true. Denver created a system of mountain parks and built an amphitheater in Red Rocks Park, popular for summer concerts. Walker donated Inspiration Point near I-70 and Sheridan Boulevard to Denver for a park, and Regis University sits on land he gave to the Jesuits.

In 1914 when Frederick Law Olmstead Jr. recommended lands for Denver to obtain for its Mountain Parks system, Mount Falcon made his list. Although Denver did not buy Mount Falcon, in 1974 the Mount Falcon Association approached Jefferson County (Jeffco) to see if they wanted to purchase 1,490 acres. With the help of the Colorado Open Lands Foundation, Jeffco procured Walker's old property—very appropriate because of his vision to acquire mountain lands for preservation of forests and for people to enjoy.

Numerous overlooks on this hike offer views of the eastern plains and the Continental Divide, one of the reasons Walker enjoyed Mount Falcon. From the scenic view spur trail near the Summer White House, you'll find a good view of Red Rocks Park and its amphitheater, the hogback running north, Green Mountain, and Mount Morrison. Castle Trail drops steeply below you—it's hard to believe people raced cars up this old road during Walker's time.

View across the valley to Mount Evans in early summer.

A lookout tower stands on Mount Falcon's summit along Tower Trail. Besides views to the plains and the Continental Divide, the tower puts you at eye level with cones on nearby Douglas fir trees. Look closely at the cones, and you'll see three-pronged bracts sticking out. The story goes that a fox was chasing a little mouse one day. A kindly Douglas fir looked down and invited the mouse to jump into its branches for safety. As a result, you can see the mouse's hind feet and tail as they disappear into the cone. Douglas firs are not true firs, because their cones hang down. Cones point up on true firs, such as the subalpine firs found at higher elevations. When the bracts fall off the cones, they look like small candles in the tree tops. Douglas firs typically grow on shady, cooler northern exposures in the foothills.

After you descend from the tower, look for the fancy old steps with white, black, and red stones. Perhaps people once walked this decorative path to Mount Falcon's summit. The trail leads next to Eagle Eye Shelter, a 1930s-style former summer home. Jeffco Open Space's crew built a nice picnic pavilion and observation deck here. Views include Turkey Creek Canyon, Indian Hills, and the Continental Divide. Near the walk leading to the shelter, look for an old well. An arch over the well reads AM BRUNNEN VOR DEM THORE [TORE] ("By the well at the town gate"), the first line of Franz Schubert's song "Der Lindenbaum (The Linden Tree)"—a touch of culture in the foothills.

A place to rest and enjoy the views.

MILES AND DIRECTIONS

0.0 Start from the southeast edge of the parking lot where the dirt road (Castle Trail) starts. Elevation: 7,720 feet. N39 38.17' / W105 14.34'. Walk down Castle Trail.

0.1 The Parmalee Trail crosses the road. Continue straight ahead on Castle Trail. Vault toilets are to the left.

0.25 Interpretive sign about fire. The Castle Trail starts to climb slightly.

0.4 Junction of Castle Trail and Meadow Trail. Turn left onto Castle Trail (still a dirt road). There's a bench here and, to the right, a little trail to an overlook.

0.8 Junction of Castle Trail, Meadow Trail, and a trail to the Walker Home ruins. Turn left here to check out the remains of the Walker Mansion. GPS: N39 38.12' / W105 13.62'. Out-and-back distance to the interpretive display in the courtyard is about 500 feet. When you return, turn left onto Castle Trail. You'll soon come to a gate that is closed when the trails beyond are muddy.

1.3 Junction with the Two Dog Trail. Continue straight ahead on the road.

1.4 Junction with Walker's Dream Trail. Turn left and head uphill to Walker's proposed location of the Summer White House. (**Option:** At mile 1.7, turn

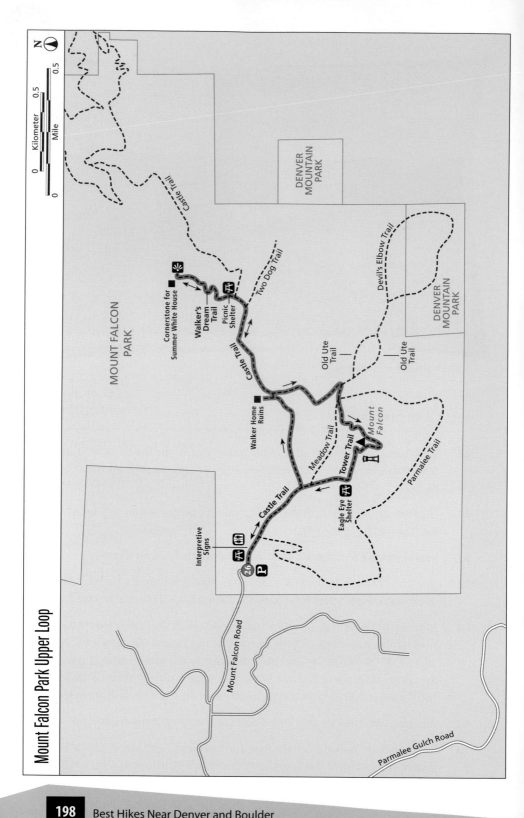

Mount Falcon Park Upper Loop

- **MOUNT FALCON PARK**
- Cornerstone for Summer White House
- Walker's Dream Trail
- Picnic Shelter
- Castle Trail
- Two Dog Trail
- Walker Home Ruins
- Old Ute Trail
- Old Ute Trail
- Devil's Elbow Trail
- **DENVER MOUNTAIN PARK**
- **DENVER MOUNTAIN PARK**
- Meadow Trail
- Tower Trail
- *Mount Falcon*
- Parmalee Trail
- Eagle Eye Shelter
- Castle Trail
- Interpretive Signs
- 26
- Mount Falcon Road
- Parmalee Gulch Road

Kilometer
Mile

right to walk to an overlook with a good view to the east and south [about 350 feet out and back]. Return the way you came, then turn right and continue uphill on Walker's Dream Trail.)

1.8 Interpretive display and cornerstone for the Summer White House. Elevation: 7,613 feet. GPS: N39 38.43' / W105 13.10'. Return down Walker's Dream Trail.

2.2 Junction with Castle Trail. Turn right.

2.7 Junction of Castle Trail, Meadow Trail, and a trail to the Walker Home ruins. Turn left onto the Meadow Trail.

3.0 Junction of Meadow Trail and Old Ute Trail. Turn right to continue on Meadow Trail.

3.1 Junction of Meadow Trail, Tower Trail, and Parmalee Trail. Go about 45 degrees to the left onto the Tower Trail.

3.5 The trail splits, with equestrians going to the left. Just beyond the split is the tower. You can walk up the stairs for nice views. Elevation: 7,851 feet. GPS: N39 37.78' / W105 13.82'.

3.7 White stone path to the Eagle Eye Shelter. Turn left onto the stone path to check out the observation deck, with nice views, and have a bite to eat (about 0.1 mile out and back). Picnic tables are in the shelter. GPS: N39 37.83' / W105 13.99'. When you return to the trail, turn left onto the Tower Trail.

3.9 Junction of Tower Trail and Meadow Trail. Turn left.

4.0 Junction of Meadow Trail and Castle Trail. Turn left and return the way you came.

4.3 Arrive back at the trailhead.

Option

For a shorter, easy 3.5-mile out-and-back, hike to the Summer White House then return the way you came, instead of hiking the middle loop.

> 🌿 **Green Tip:**
> *Even if it says it's biodegradable, don't use soap in streams or lakes. If you need to use soap, only use biodegradable and bring the water to you, at least 200 feet away from the water source.*

HIKE INFORMATION

Local Information: Town of Morrison; 303-697-8749; town.morrison.co.us

Local Events/Attractions: Morrison Natural History Museum; 303-697-1873; mnhm.org

Red Rocks Park and Amphitheater, Morrison; 303-697-4939; redrocksonline.com. Tours available May through Oct or by appointment, 303-697-6910.

Organizations: Jefferson County Open Space Volunteers, Golden; 303-271-5922; jeffco.us/open-space/volunteer

John Brisben Walker believed that reason could bring about world peace. In 1914, he invited President Woodrow Wilson to a meeting of 500 of the most capable men in the United States, at the Camp of the Red Rocks, to promote better understanding, broader ideas, and more tolerance for the nation.

Part of the Walker Home ruins.

Bill Couch Mountain—Deer Creek Canyon Park

Deer Creek Canyon Park is a close-to-home escape for residents of the south Denver metro area. With Plymouth Mountain and Bill Couch Mountain separated by Plymouth Creek, the hike winds through both open meadows and a cool narrow canyon. This out-and-back journey climbs up to a rocky point where views of South Valley Park's flatirons and hogback contrast with Denver's skyscrapers beyond. Over half of the hike is on hikers-only trails. Colorful wildflowers and shrubs burst forth in spring. Deer Creek Canyon Park is a great place for a hike and picnic.

Start: Deer Creek Canyon Park trailhead

Distance: 7.0 miles out and back

Hiking time: 2.8 to 4 hours

Difficulty: Difficult due to 10 percent grade on Meadowlark Trail and gains/losses

Elevation gain: 1,187-foot gain and 180-foot loss to top of Bill Couch Mountain

Trail surface: Natural surface and rocky trail

Seasons: Best Apr through Nov. Avoid hot summer days—visit in the evenings or early mornings.

Other trail users: Mountain bikers and equestrians on some sections

Canine compatibility: Dogs must be on leash

Land status: Jefferson County Open Space

Fees and permits: Large groups and unique activities require special permits. Please check jeffco.us/open-space or call 303-271-5925.

Schedule: Open year-round, 1 hour before sunrise to 1 hour past sunset

Maps: USGS Indian Hills; National Geographic Trails Illustrated 100 Boulder/Golden; Latitude 40°: Colorado Front Range

Trail contact: Jefferson County Open Space, 700 Jefferson County Parkway, Golden; 303-271-5925; jeffco.us/open-space

Other: Camping is prohibited. Fires allowed only in designated areas.

Special considerations: Bring water. Beware of rattlesnakes. Mountain lions and bears are also in the area. Come prepared for an outdoor experience. Leave valuables at home.

Finding the trailhead: From C470, Kipling exit, head south on Kipling Parkway 0.5 mile to West Ute Avenue. Turn right (west) onto Ute—stay in the left lane—and drive 2.8 miles to Grizzly Drive. (*Note:* Ute curves left onto South Owens Street, which curves right onto Deer Creek Canyon Road.) Turn left onto Grizzly Drive and travel 0.4 mile to a right curve in the road, where you'll make a right turn into the Deer Creek Canyon Park parking lot. There are restrooms and water at the trailhead.

Hunter-gatherers lived in the Deer Creek Canyon area as long as 12,000 years ago. East of Deer Creek Canyon Park, archaeologists have unearthed one of the largest mammoth kill sites that has been discovered so far in the United States. Members of the Ute, Arapaho, and Cheyenne tribes were later drawn to the canyon's plentiful resources.

Suffering from tuberculosis, John Williamson, along with his wife Annie, son John, and Annie's niece Esther arrived in Denver in April 1872 from Plymouth, England. John had been given only three months to live unless he moved to a dry climate, like Colorado. While walking around to find a place to settle, he came upon Deer Creek on the west side of a hogback. The south side attracted him, but a squatter had laid claim to the place. John purchased the rights from the squatter for $500. That summer he built an interesting six-room house using no wood. Instead he used foot-high forms and poured concrete in between.

The family named their new home Glen Plym (Glen is Scottish for "valley") for their old Plymouth home. The mountain to the west became Plymouth Mountain and the creek Plym Creek. They grew 50 acres of wheat, 25 to 30 acres of corn, a large vegetable garden, and 350 tons of hay using water from Plym Creek for irrigation.

In 1882, John added a large dining room and kitchen to the house. For the next twenty-five years, he and Annie hosted people with tuberculosis, especially

Looking north from the Meadowlark Trail.

from the eastern states. Guests stayed in tent houses and ate meals in the large dining room. On Sundays, 100 to 150 people arrived from Denver to enjoy the clean air and eat a good dinner. Many caught the train that traveled along the South Platte River, disembarked at Chatfield Ranch, and then walked to Glen Plym. Others came by stagecoach or bicycle.

Niece Esther married Sam Couch, who owned a ranch to the north of the current Lockheed-Martin facility near South Valley Park. The other mountain on Glen Plym was named after their son, Bill.

John and Annie both died in 1911. The Colorado air must have been good to John, since back in 1872 his English doctor had predicted he'd only live another year if he moved to Colorado. Their son, John William, and his wife, Olive, operated the property as a cattle ranch. After their daughter-in-law died in 1956, Frank Murcrays purchased the ranch house and 10 acres. The rest of the property had been sold and some of it subdivided. Today, Deer Creek Canyon Park contains parts of the Williamson, Couch, and Clark homesteads.

Hiking up the Meadowlark Trail, you'll pass Gambel oaks (oakbrush), prickly pear cactus, yucca, cup-like white mariposa lilies, yellow sulphur flowers, and Rocky Mountain junipers. Oakbrush produces little acorns, about 1 inch long. Native Americans ground the nuts and soaked them in water to release the bitter tannic acid. The acorn meal became mush, bread, and pancakes. Deer enjoy browsing oakbrush, while birds and bears eat the acorns.

Ascending a steep section of the Plymouth Creek Trail.

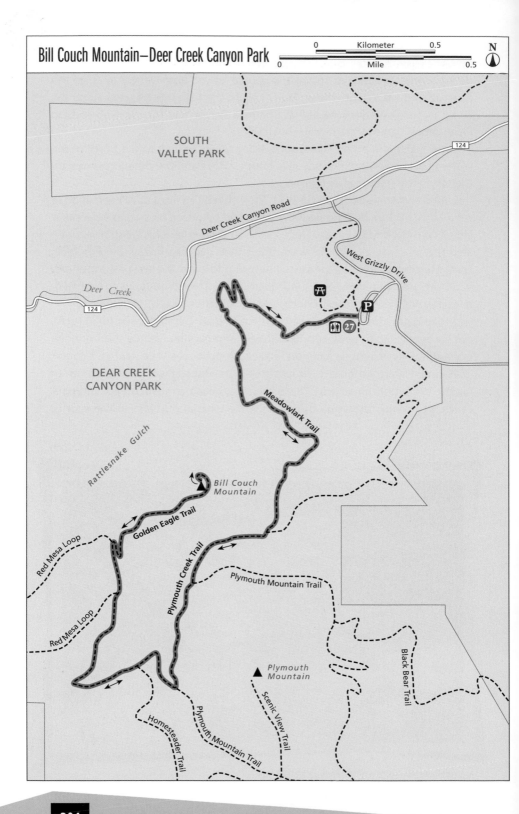

0   Kilometer   0.5
0   Mile   0.5

N

SOUTH
VALLEY PARK

124

Deer Creek Canyon Road

West Grizzly Drive

Deer   Creek

124

P

27

DEAR CREEK
CANYON PARK

Meadowlark Trail

Rattlesnake Gulch

Bill Couch
Mountain

Golden Eagle Trail

Red Mesa Loop

Plymouth Creek Trail

Plymouth Mountain Trail

Red Mesa Loop

Plymouth
Mountain

Black Bear Trail

Homesteader Trail

Plymouth Mountain Trail

Scenic View Trail

On the eastern slope of Colorado, oakbrush only grows roughly south of Morrison (SH 74), but on the western slope it grows in most locations between 5,500 to 10,000 feet.

Hiking along Plymouth Creek is a pleasant change from the hotter, open slopes of the other trails. Douglas firs grow in this cool, moist drainage along with ponderosa pines and various shrubs. Plymouth Creek becomes a trickle the higher you climb. The final ascent up Bill Couch Mountain is across open grassy areas with intermittent ponderosa pines and Rocky Mountain junipers. The rocky top makes a nice lunch spot with great views in all directions.

MILES AND DIRECTIONS

0.0   Start from the Deer Creek Canyon Park trailhead on the Meadowlark Trail, to the right of the bulletin board. This trail is hikers-only. Elevation: 6,080 feet. GPS: N39 32.59′ / W105 09.13′.

0.7   Trail appears to split. Left branch goes to a little viewpoint. Continue straight ahead on the trail.

1.6   Walk over a small creek and reach a T-intersection with the Plymouth Creek Trail. Turn right onto Plymouth Creek. This trail is multiuse, so be aware of mountain bikers. GPS: N39 32.11′ / W105 09.39′. In another 100 feet, some wooden stairs take you up a steep section.

View of Bill Couch Mountain and the hogback, with downtown Denver on the horizon, from the Golden Eagle Trail.

2.0 Junction with the north end of the Plymouth Mountain Trail. Continue straight ahead on Plymouth Creek Trail.

2.1 Junction with the south end of the Plymouth Mountain Trail. Turn to the right to continue on Plymouth Creek Trail.

2.4 Homesteader Trail comes in sharply from the left. Continue straight ahead on Plymouth Creek Trail.

2.8 Plymouth Creek Trail ends and the Red Mesa Loop starts. Turn right onto Red Mesa Loop.

3.0 Junction with the Golden Eagle Trail. Turn right and head downhill on Golden Eagle Trail, which is hikers-only. GPS: N39 32.09' / W105 09.83'.

3.5 Rocky top of Bill Couch Mountain. Elevation: 7,087 feet. GPS: N39 32.22' / W105 09.59'. Nice views and a good lunch spot. Return the way you came.

7.0 Arrive back at the trailhead.

HIKE INFORMATION

Local Information: South Metro Denver Chamber of Commerce, Centennial; 303-795-0142; bestchamber.com

Local Events/Attractions: Chatfield State Park, Littleton; 303-791-7275; cpw.state.co.us/placestogo/parks/chatfield

Organizations: Jefferson County Open Space Volunteers, Golden; 303-271-5922; jeffco.us/open-space/volunteer

Around Golden and at Willow Springs, oil seeped up with water from natural springs. The Williamsons and their neighbors lubricated their farm machinery with oil that they obtained from Willow Springs.

Alferd Packer

Alferd Packer, Colorado's famous cannibal, lived the last years of his life just west of the Williamsons' ranch in Phillipsburg. Packer had been hired to guide a group of miners from Salt Lake City to Breckenridge in 1874. He led them into the high mountains near Lake City during severe winter weather. Only Packer survived. When the miners' bodies were found in summer, it was determined that all had been shot and parts of their bodies had been removed— Packer had eaten them.

Packer was found guilty of premeditated murder and sentenced to execution on May 19, 1883, in Lake City, but the conviction was overturned because the murders occurred in Ute Territory. He was tried again in Gunnison in 1886, found guilty of five counts of murder, and sentenced to forty years in the state penitentiary at Cañon City. In 1900, the Denver Post decided to request parole for Packer. After several interesting incidents, he was paroled by Governor Thomas in 1901. He worked on different ranches and mines along Deer Creek and often ate dinner with the Williamsons. Local families found him kind and fatherly. Packer died in 1907 and is buried in Littleton Cemetery.

Spruce Mountain Loop

Spruce Mountain is a forested island in the sky rimmed with rock ledges. Views include Pikes Peak, Cheyenne Mountain, the old Greenland Ranch, thousands of acres of protected Douglas County Open Space, and points north to Longs Peak. Numerous view opportunities lie along the south rim, culminating at Windy Point on the southwest end. You can circle the top of Spruce Mountain or drop down and finish the hike around the north end of this pleasant mesa between the prairie and the foothills.

Start: Spruce Mountain Trailhead on Spruce Mountain Road
Distance: 5.6-mile lollipop
Hiking time: 2 to 3 hours
Difficulty: Moderate due to distance
Elevation gain: 505 feet
Trail surface: Natural surface trail and service road (closed to the motorized public)
Seasons: Best May through Nov
Other trail users: Equestrians and mountain bikers
Canine compatibility: Dogs must be on leash
Land status: Douglas County Open Space
Fees and permits: None required

Schedule: Open year-round, 1 hour before sunrise to 1 hour after sunset
Maps: USGS Larkspur, Greenland
Trail contact: Douglas County Open Space, 100 Third Street, Castle Rock; 303-660-7495; douglas.co.us/government/departments/open-space
Other: Please stay on designated trails. You can snowshoe the north side in the winter if there's enough snow. Trails can be icy in winter, and the trailhead might not always be plowed.
Special considerations: Bring water as none is available along the trail.

Finding the trailhead: From I-25, take exit 173, Larkspur, which puts you on Spruce Mountain Road (DCR 53). Drive 5.8 miles and turn right into the parking lot for the Spruce Mountain Trail. You'll pass through the town of Larkspur on the way. A portable toilet is available at the trailhead

THE HIKE

Believe it or not, no spruce trees grow on Spruce Mountain! Douglas firs, ponderosa pines, and Gambel oaks (oakbrush) cover its slopes and top. Some early settlers called Douglas fir "yellow spruce," hence the name of the mountain.

The trail starts in grassland along the mountain's base, then gradually switchbacks its way to the sizable flat top. As you round one right curve along a slope of oakbrush, a whitish rock outcrop above catches your eye. This Dawson Arkose geologic formation edges Spruce Mountain, creating many overlook opportunities.

About 70 million years ago, the Rocky Mountains started slowly rising and Pikes Peak, a huge block of granite, emerged. While the mountains rose, erosion wore them down, creating large alluvial fans at their base. The coarse sandstone eroded from Pikes Peak became the white and buff rock we call Dawson Arkose. Some layers erode very easily, leaving behind the many buttes along I-25, such as Castle Rock, and hoodoos (rock columns weathered into interesting shapes) that may be seen on Spruce Mountain.

From the south rim you see Greenland Open Space across Spruce Mountain Road. More than 4,700 acres with trails and a picnic shelter are preserved on the west side of I-25. East across I-25 another 17,000 acres are protected in private conservation easements (closed to the public).

Fred Soloman platted a 20-acre town named Greenland in 1875 along the Denver & Rio Grande railroad. One year in the early 1900s, the farmers around Greenland reportedly shipped 400 railcars of potatoes. Settlers also shipped lumber, grain, cattle, clay, milk, and building stones from the Greenland station. I. J. Noe ranched the Spruce Mountain area back in the 1800s, and his descendants still ranch nearby.

After the right switchback that takes you close to the rim, look to your left for a tiny window in the rock along the edge. Farther along, a split in the trail indicates equestrians go left to avoid a rock outcropping about horse belly high. On the hikers' section lies Paddock's Point, with a small sign in memory of Craig Paddock, who loved this mountain and worked on the Spruce Mountain Forest Management Plan. To the north is a nice view of Eagle Mountain, now preserved in a conservation easement. On a clear day you can see all the way north to Longs Peak in Rocky Mountain National Park. When you reach the junction with Mountain Top Loop, head left for some great southern views at various places. At Windy Point, where the loop curves to the right, the rocky outcrop is a great place to eat lunch and enjoy the sun and the views—if it's not windy. Private Spruce Mountain Ranch, with its little ponds and twisting roads, lies below.

A developer once eyed Spruce Mountain as a resort, complete with a tram to a large hotel on top, a golf course, and about 180 homes. Spruce Mountain Open Space was purchased in several phases over nine years starting in 2000. The

Eagle Mountain from the Eagle Pass Trail.

Conservation Fund (TCF) orchestrated the purchase of Spruce Mountain from the developer and held the land until Douglas County Open Space had enough cash on hand. Great Outdoors Colorado and the USDA Forest Service's Forest Legacy Program provided partial funding. Spruce Mountain had been a key parcel identified in TCF's I-25 Conservation Corridor Initiative, initiated in 1996 to protect 25,000 acres along a 12-mile corridor between Denver and Colorado Springs.

Douglas County Open Space continues to enhance Spruce Mountain amenities, so check the website and visit often to enjoy this special piece of Colorado.

MILES AND DIRECTIONS

0.0 Start from the Spruce Mountain Trailhead on Spruce Mountain Road (DCR 53). Elevation: 7,100 feet. GPS: N39 10.07' / W104 52.48'.

370 feet Four-way junction with Spruce Meadows Trail. Continue straight ahead on the Spruce Mountain Trail.

0.4 Junction with the Eagle Pass Trail. Turn left to stay on Spruce Mountain Trail.

0.7 Junction with Oak Shortcut. Turn right to continue on Spruce Mountain Trail. There's a bench here.

0.8 Switchback with whitish rock outcrop above.

Spruce Mountain Loop

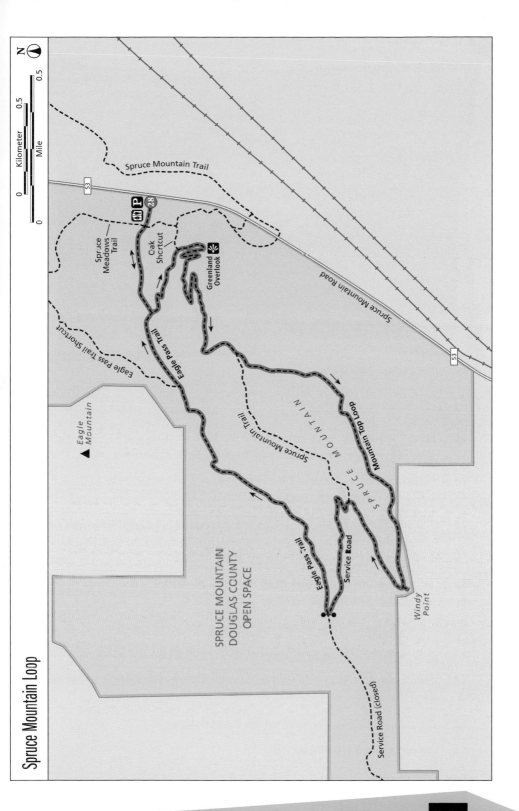

Spruce Mountain Trail

53

Spruce Meadows Trail

Oak Shortcut

Greenland Overlook

Eagle Pass Trail Shortcut

Eagle Mountain

Eagle Pass Trail

Spruce Mountain Trail

SPRUCE MOUNTAIN
DOUGLAS COUNTY
OPEN SPACE

Eagle Pass Trail

Service Road

Spruce Mountain Road

S P R U C E   M O U N T A I N

Mountain Top Loop

Windy Point

Service Road (closed)

53

N

0   Kilometer   0.5

0   Mile   0.5

A collection of buttes northeast of the Eagle Pass Trail.

1.6 Equestrian bypass goes left. Stay to the right past Paddock's Point. Nice view of Eagle Mountain. Equestrian bypass comes in from the left.

1.7 Mountain Top Loop starts. GPS: N39 09.82' / W104 53.03'. Hike to the left. You're now on a double-track trail.

2.9 Trail junction to Windy Point. Turn left for a good lunch and view spot on the rocks (if it's not too windy). Elevation: 7,605 feet. GPS: N39 09.30' / W104 53.93'. Return to Mountain Top Loop and turn left.

3.3 Junction with service road (closed to the motorized public) that heads down to Eagle Pass Trail. Turn left onto the road.

3.7 Maintenance gate that should be open except in emergencies.

3.8 Turn right onto the Eagle Pass Trail. GPS: N39 09.54' / W104 53.99'.

4.9 Junction with the Eagle Pass Trail Shortcut. Continue straight ahead on Eagle Pass Trail.

5.2 Junction with Spruce Mountain Trail. Turn left here.

5.6 Arrive back at the trailhead.

Option

For a slightly shorter, 5.3-mile loop hike, at the junction with the service road that heads down to the Eagle Pass Trail (mile 3.3 above), turn right and return to the junction of Mountain Top Loop and Spruce Mountain Trail. Turn left at that junction and return the way you came, to the trailhead.

HIKE INFORMATION

Local Information: Tri-Lakes Chamber of Commerce, Monument; 719-481-3282; trilakeschamber.com
Castle Rock Chamber of Commerce; 303-688-4597; castlerock.org
Local Events/Attractions: Colorado Renaissance Festival and Artisan Marketplace, Larkspur; 303-688-6010; coloradorenaissance.com
Lucretia Vaile Library and Museum, Palmer Lake; palmerdividehistory.org/museum.html
Castle Rock Wine Fest; 303-688-4597; castlerockculture.com/castle-rock-winefest
Hike Tours: Douglas County Open Space, Castle Rock; 303-660-7495; douglas.co.us/openspace
Organizations: Volunteer Program, Douglas County Open Space, Castle Rock; 303-660-7495; douglas.co.us/openspace

The Conservation Fund, according to its website (conservationfund.org), "enables conservationists, government agencies, community leaders and land trusts to swiftly protect properties for wildlife, recreation and/or historic significance. . . We've helped permanently protect over 7.5 million acres in all fifty states."

Ancient Castle Rock Rainforest

Some 63 million years ago, palm, fig, magnolia, poplar, and oak trees thrived in Colorado's warm and temperate climate. In 2008, during construction of the Plum Creek interchange on I-25 near Castle Rock, workers discovered a palm frond 4 feet wide by 5 feet long. In previous years, other rainforest plant fossils had been discovered in the area. The Castle Rock rainforest is the oldest documented rainforest in the world, according to a September 20, 2008, article in the Castle Rock/Douglas County News Press. Paleontologists removed about 750 plant specimens from the construction zone.

The article quoted Steve Wallace, CDOT's staff paleontologist: "The Castle Rock rainforest also disclosed that recovery from the 'extinction event' was much shorter than earlier believed. For years, popular theory was that the rainforests took 10 million years to recover from the catastrophic event that wiped dinosaurs from the face of the earth. This site discloses the plant species recovered in about 1.7 million years."

Honorable Mentions

C. Meyer Ranch Park Loops

Meyer Ranch Park offers numerous loop trails appropriate for hikers of all abilities. Mountain bikers, joggers, and equestrians also enjoy the park. Typical of the Front Range foothills, various grasses, lodgepole and ponderosa pines, aspens, Douglas firs, and a few spruces cover the hills. Picnic tables are available along Owl's Perch Trail and under a shelter where Old Ski Run Trail heads uphill. This hike follows west-side trails to the top of the park and back along east-side trails. Near the top you can get a nice view of Mount Evans to the west.

Hike up the service road to the vault toilet, follow the sign to the picnic tables (not the service road), and turn right onto Owl's Perch Trail. Continue taking right turns onto Lodgepole Loop and Sunny Aspen Trail to reach Old Ski Run Trail. Turn right near the picnic shelter onto Old Ski Run Trail, which is a lollipop. When you return to this junction at the picnic shelter, turn right onto Sunny Aspen Trail, then right again onto Lodgepole Loop to Owl's Perch Trail. Turn right here to return to the trailhead for a moderate 4.5-mile loop with a 900-foot elevation gain. Dogs must be on leash. You can make shorter loops by just doing Lodgepole Loop (2.5 miles) or Lodgepole Loop and Sunny Aspen Trail (2.9 miles).

Finding the trailhead: From the intersection of C470 and US 285, drive about 11.2 miles west up Turkey Creek Canyon (US 285). Just past mile marker 239, take the South Turkey Creek exit. The exit loops around and under the overpass. In 0.1 mile turn right onto South Turkey Creek Road, then take an immediate left into the trailhead entrance. Elevation: 7,840 feet. GPS: N39 32.77' / W105 16.35'. There are no facilities at the trailhead, but a composting toilet is located 0.2 mile up the trail.

D. Eagle's View Outlook—Reynolds Park

Hike up a pretty little drainage on the Oxen Draw Trail to the Eagle's View viewpoint. Pikes Peak, the Rampart Range, and lots of rock-topped mini-peaks fill the southern view. The drainage is lush with riparian-area bushes, trees, and flowers, while some huge Douglas firs live on the higher ridge just before the viewpoint. Rocky Mountain junipers and ponderosa pines grow on the drier slopes. Reynolds Park is open to hikers and equestrians only on the west side of South Foxton Road; the east side is multiuse.

Start at the Reynolds Park bulletin board. Elevation: 7,200 feet. GPS: N39 28.00' / W105 14.35'. At the first junction of Oxen Draw Trail and Elkhorn Trail, go a little left on Oxen Draw. At the next junction of Oxen Draw and Elkhorn, turn right onto Oxen Draw. At the last junction of Oxen Draw and Elkhorn, head left and uphill on Oxen Draw. When you reach the junction of Oxen Draw Trail,

Raven's Roost Trail, and Eagle's View Trail, turn left and switchback up Eagle's View to a ridge with a good view south. Elevation: 8,120 feet. GPS: N39 27.60' / W105 15.05'. Some logs make convenient benches for lunch. Return the way you came for a 3.2-mile out-and-back and 920-foot elevation gain. Dogs must be on leash.

Finding the trailhead: From C470, take the US 285 exit and head southwest. In 14.9 miles (past Conifer), exit US 285 at FOXTON ROAD and REYNOLDS PARK signs. In 0.2 mile turn left onto Foxton Road, then drive 4.9 miles and turn right into the Reynolds Park trailhead parking lot. A vault toilet is available a few feet up the trail. Bring water with you, as no potable water is available.

Wild iris.

The Mountains

The Arapaho Glacier Trail in the Indian Peaks.

These twelve hikes in the high mountains take you to beautiful lakes, lofty peaks, alpine tundra, former ranches, and abandoned mines. These hikes probably represent most people's vision of Colorado. Views seem to reach out forever, and the majestic scenery is hard to beat.

Roughly speaking, this mountain "strip" lies west of the north–south line formed by SH 119, SH 72, and SH 7 and east of the Continental Divide. It ranges from Mount Evans on the south to Estes Park on the north. These hikes start as low as 7,870 feet, while the high point is 13,132-foot Mount Flora above Berthoud Pass. Trails vary in length from 3.5 to 10 miles. Five hikes take you above treeline, where the wind usually blows (at least a little) and lightning can kill. Summer temperatures may reach no more than 50°F. In winter, winds howl over 100 miles per hour and avalanches pose a danger to skiers and snowshoers. The land is beautiful, but learn its idiosyncrasies to assure a safe journey at any time of year.

The Front Range is generally composed of Precambrian granite cooled from magma that gathered under an ancient Colorado about 1.4 billion years ago. When the magma intruded into cooler rocks, the heat changed them. These metamorphic rocks are somewhat easily identified as gneiss, schist, and quartzite. Gneiss has light and dark layers (think "nice" lines). Schist is usually dark-colored with lots of shiny mica imbedded. When sandstone (composed of mostly quartz grains) was heated to very high temperatures, the quartz grains grew into larger crystals that interlocked, creating the rock called quartzite.

Between 750,000 and 12,000 years ago, a series of ice ages gripped Colorado. The east slopes of the Rockies filled with snow blown by west winds. Snow remained year-round and grew deeper with each season, creating glaciers. As the glaciers crept forward, they eroded the land underneath, pushing the sediments to their sides and creating ridges known as lateral moraines. Valleys left behind are typically U-shaped. Cirques created at the heads of glaciers harbor today's beautiful lakes.

Prehistoric peoples passed through this area but didn't stay. Ranchers and miners lived in the high valleys, but only a few hardy animals can live year-round on the highest peaks and valleys. One is the little pika, a member of the rabbit family, which gathers grass and flowers in summer and stores them between boulders for winter. Mountain goats live around treeline all year, while bighorn sheep move from alpine tundra to lower climes in winter. A good place to see bighorns is along I-70 around Georgetown.

Lodgepole pines populate forests between 8,500 and 10,500 feet. Aspens often intersperse with lodgepoles. Limber and bristlecone pines grow above 7,500 feet in windy and rocky places. Englemann spruces and subalpine firs start around 9,000 feet and mainly live between 10,000 and 11,000 feet. Alpine tundra is the "land above the trees," a rough terrain composed of micro-communities of delicate plants.

Enjoy hiking in these spectacular areas while being gentle on the land so that future generations may also enjoy them.

Gem Lake

At 8,830 feet and surrounded by granitic boulders, ledges, and cliffs, Gem Lake is a small gem of a rain-filled lake with no inlet or outlet. The trail travels along south- and east-facing slopes, wandering in and out of a couple of narrow canyons between granitic outcroppings. Interesting rock formations inspire the imagination, and several sections offer spectacular views of Estes Park, Twin Sisters, Longs Peak, and the Continental Divide in Rocky Mountain National Park. Colorful wildflowers grace the trail from mid-June to early July. This trail is a good early and late season hike in Rocky Mountain National Park.

Start: Lumpy Ridge Trailhead at the bulletin board

Distance: 3.5 miles out and back

Hiking time: 1.5 to 3 hours

Difficulty: Difficult due to elevation gain and some steep sections

Elevation gain: 960 feet

Trail surface: Natural surface trail with some steeper sections with log or stone steps

Seasons: Best May through Oct. Avoid hot summer days or hike early morning or evening.

Other trail users: Equestrians

Canine compatibility: Dogs not permitted

Land status: National park wilderness and easement through private property

Fees and permits: None required for day use. Backcountry camping permit (fee charged) required for overnight camping. Food canisters are required for backcountry camping below treeline from May 1 through Oct 31. For information about backcountry camping permits, call 970-586-1242 or go to nps.gov/romo/planyourvisit/wild_guide.htm

Schedule: Open year-round

Maps: USGS Estes Park; National Geographic Trails Illustrated 200 Rocky Mountain National Park; Latitude 40°: Colorado Front Range Trails

Trail contact: Rocky Mountain National Park, 1000 Highway 36, Estes Park; 970-586-1206, 970-586-1333 (24-hour recorded message); nps.gov/romo

Other: An outhouse is located just below Gem Lake.

Special considerations: The trail is neither marked nor maintained for winter use. Bring water because none is available along the trail.

Finding the trailhead: In Boulder, from 28th Street (US 36) and Canyon Boulevard (SH 119), head north on US 36 to its junction with SH 66. Turn left on SH 66 and drive through Lyons to the yield sign at the T-intersection (US 36 and SH 7). Turn right onto US 36 and drive 21 miles to Estes Park. At the intersection of US 34 and US 36 in Estes Park, drive straight ahead onto US 34 west (bypasses downtown) and continue 0.4 mile to MacGregor Avenue, Larimer County Road 43 (also called Devil's Gulch Road). Turn right onto LCR 43 and drive 1.3 miles, just past mile marker 1, to the Lumpy Ridge Trailhead sign. Turn left onto Lumpy Ridge Road and drive another 500 yards to the trailhead parking lot. Vault toilets, but no water, are available at the trailhead.

THE HIKE

When people think of Rocky Mountain National Park, visions of craggy peaks, shimmering lakes, tumbling streams, and alpine tundra come to mind. However, the eastern part of the park offers a very different landscape called Lumpy Ridge, where large granitic domes of various shapes and forms extend above the surrounding hills. The glaciers that carved the high peaks to the west did not reach this area.

The trail wanders through a forest of ponderosa pine, Douglas fir, and aspen, climbing with water bars and long steps. After turning right on the trail at the intersection with the Twin Owls View Trail, you arrive at several big granitic boulders. Look northwest for a good view of Twin Owls.

Eons ago, a sea covered this area. As sediments washed into the sea and accumulated, they compacted into sandstones and shales. Later, under great pressure, they were heated and transformed into gneiss and schist. Then about 300 million years ago, the Ancestral Rocky Mountains rose from a shallow sea. Molten magma oozed into cracks and cooled into granitic rocks.

The present Rocky Mountains were uplifted between 60 and 70 million years ago. Erosion wore the mountains down to a sloping arch. By about 5 million years ago, the entire area had been uplifted about 5,000 feet. Steeper streams quickened erosion, exposing old metamorphic rocks and granitic intrusions such as those on Lumpy Ridge. When erosion uncovers granite, the rock expands, and joints or fractures form along large exposed surfaces. Freeze-thaw cycles take over, causing joints to expand, and eventually rock surfaces break off, much like peeling layers off an onion. The granite then erodes into interesting shapes.

As the trail continues to climb, flat horizontal rocks on the left and then on the right offer great views of the Estes Park area. Human history in this area starts about 11,000 years ago. Native Americans found abundant game here in summer, but left during the long, cold winters. Various explorers came through the area, but none stayed. In 1859, while searching for gold, Joel Estes entered a grassy area surrounded by mountains (called a "park" in Colorado). A year later he moved his family to the area and claimed some land. Estes decided to harvest the abundant elk and deer to sell meat to the growing Denver market. In 1864, William N. Byers, founder of Denver's *Rocky Mountain News,* hiked up the primitive path that Estes had created for a visit, and named the area Estes Park.

Some early settlers realized that they could make more money by entertaining tourists than by ranching, and they built tourist lodges. By 1875, a toll road operated up North Saint Vrain Canyon, with a road up Big Thompson Canyon completed in 1904. Three years later, F. O. Stanley, of Stanley Steamer fame, and B. D. Sanborn built the Stanley Hotel, which you passed on your way to the trailhead, complete with the first electricity in Estes Park. At the urging of residents, such as Enos Mills and F. O. Stanley, Congress created Rocky Mountain National Park in 1915.

The trail enters a narrow canyon between granitic outcroppings, where it climbs numerous short switchbacks supported by rock retaining walls. There's a great place to stop and catch your breath by an interesting rock formation called Paul Bunyan's Boot. The trail proceeds up a series of water bar steps. The cliff on the left looks like a badly assembled LEGO structure.

In a few more steps, you reach Gem Lake. Explore all sides of the lake, especially the view to the south from the north end. Many of the trees around the lake are limber pine, with five needles per bunch.

View of Mount Meeker and Longs Peak from the Gem Lake Trail.

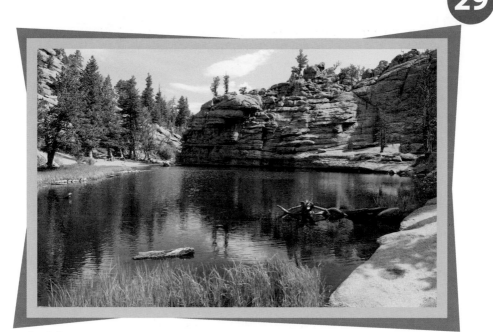

Gem Lake.

MILES AND DIRECTIONS

0.0 Start at the Lumpy Ridge Trailhead at the bulletin board. Elevation: 7,870 feet. GPS: N40 23.79' / W105 30.79'. Take the trail to the right of the vault toilets. A little way up is the Gem Lake bulletin board. The trail on the right goes to the horse trailer parking area.

0.5 Enter Rocky Mountain National Park; beyond here is also the Rocky Mountain National Park Wilderness Area. The junction with Twin Owls View Trail is just a little farther. At the junction, turn right on the trail to go to Gem Lake.

0.6 Big granitic boulders on your right provide great views and a nice place to stop. The trail stays to the left.

0.8 Views of Longs Peak with its diamond-shaped east face, Mount Meeker, Estes Park, Twin Sisters, and the Continental Divide open up to the west and south along this area. GPS: N40 24.23' / W105 30.61'. The trail enters a nice aspen grove.

1.4 Several interesting rock formations, including Paul Bunyan's Boot, provide a good place to rest before the next steep section. GPS: N40 24.52' / W105 30.35'.

1.6 The outhouse ("Privy") spur. Please use the outhouse instead of the area around Gem Lake.

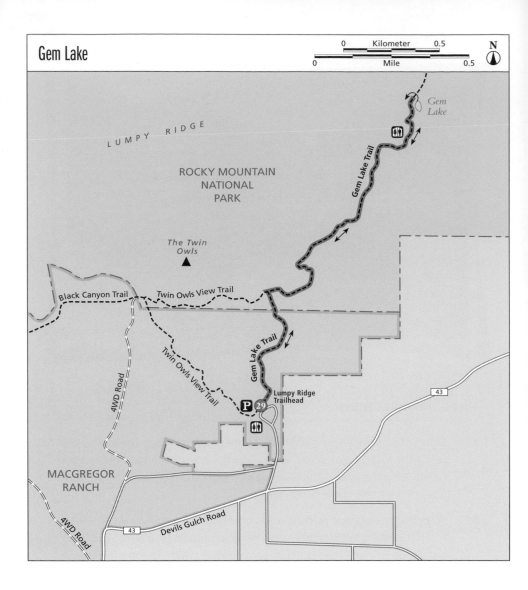

Gem Lake

Gem Lake

LUMPY RIDGE

ROCKY MOUNTAIN NATIONAL PARK

The Twin Owls

Gem Lake Trail

Black Canyon Trail

Twin Owls View Trail

Gem Lake Trail

43

Twin Owls View Trail

4WD Road

Lumpy Ridge Trailhead

Gem Lake Trail

P 29

MACGREGOR RANCH

4WD Road

43 Devils Gulch Road

1.75   Gem Lake. Elevation: 8,830 feet. GPS: N40 24.64' / W105 30.22'. Return the way you came.

3.5   Arrive back at the trailhead.

Option

On the way back, continue straight ahead on the Twin Owls View Trail (mile 3.0 on the return). You'll hike an extra 0.6 mile (4.1 miles total) for a close-up look at the Twin Owls. In 0.3 mile is the right turn to the climbers' access to Upper Twin Owls. In another 0.2 mile is the junction with the right turn to the climbers' access to Lower Twin Owls, followed in a few steps with the junction with Black Canyon Trail. Turn left here to return to the Lumpy Ridge Trailhead parking lot in another 0.6 mile. The trail goes up initially, then starts to drop with some undulations back to the trailhead.

HIKE INFORMATION

Local Information: Estes Park Visitor Center; 800-443-7837, 970-577-9900; visitestespark.com

Local Events/Attractions: MacGregor Ranch, Estes Park; 970-586-3749; macgregorranch.org

Longs Peak Scottish-Irish Highland Festival, Estes Park; 800-903-7837, 970-586-6308; scotfest.com

Scandinavian Midsummer Festival, Estes Park; estesmidsummer.com

Hike Tours: Rocky Mountain National Park Ranger-Led Programs, Estes Park; 970-586-1206; nps.gov/romo/planyourvisit/ranger_led_activities.htm

Organizations: Rocky Mountain Conservancy, Estes Park; 970-586-0108; rmconservancy.org

Geology Babble

Erosion: The process of losing material, most often due to water, wind, or glacial ice.

Freeze-thaw cycle: When water freezes in a rock crack, it expands; when the ice thaws, the water takes less space. The result is similar to a crowbar that eventually cracks a rock open.

Glacier: A flowing, compacted mass of ice that moves because of its own weight on a sloping surface.

Gneiss: A metamorphic rock with light and dark layers.

Granite: A light-colored igneous rock formed when magma cooled under the earth's surface, usually in underground rock cracks, often with pink minerals and quartz imbedded.

Igneous rock: A rock formed when magma (molten rock) cooled underground.

Joint: A fracture or crack in rock.

Metamorphic rock: A rock formed when high heat and/or intense pressure caused one type of rock to be transformed into another type of rock.

Schist: A metamorphic rock, usually dark-colored, with lots of mica (a shiny mineral).

Since June 1974, various pieces of legislation have been introduced to Congress to designate much of Rocky Mountain National Park as wilderness. Finally, The Omnibus Public Lands Management Act of 2009 designated almost 250,000 acres (of approximately 265,770 acres) of Rocky Mountain National Park as wilderness. President Obama signed the Act on March 30, 2009.

Purple fringe.

Sandbeach Lake

Tucked away in the Wild Basin area of Rocky Mountain National Park (RMNP) at an altitude of over 10,000 feet above sea level, Sandbeach Lake is a unique gem with a lovely sandy beach wrapped around crystal-clear alpine waters, sitting below lofty mountain peaks. The sandy shore seems a bit out of place in this high, wild setting but it's a welcome surprise on hot summer days when you need to go higher to escape the summer heat. To the north/northwest, you'll get impressive views of Pagoda Peak and Mount Meeker, and a small sliver of Longs Peak in between them. To the south/southwest, a long string of mountains unfolds before you. Take a map with you and see if you can identify some of this stunning geography.

Start: Sandbeach Lake Trailhead near the Wild Basin entrance station

Distance: 9.0 miles out and back

Hiking time: 3 to 5 hours

Difficulty: Difficult due to distance and elevation gain

Elevation gain: 1,970 feet

Trail surface: Natural surface and rocky trail

Seasons: Best mid-June through mid-Oct

Other trail users: Equestrians

Canine compatibility: Dogs not permitted

Land status: National park wilderness

Fees and permits: Entry fee required. The entrance station is at the start of the road into Wild Basin. Backcountry camping permit (fee charged) required for overnight camping. Food canisters are required for backcountry camping below treeline from May 1 through Oct 31. For information about backcountry camping permits, call 970-586-1242 or go to nps.gov/romo/planyourvisit/wild_guide.htm.

Schedule: Open year-round

Maps: USGS Allenspark; National Geographic Trails Illustrated 301 Longs Peak/Bear Lake/Wild Basin or 200 Rocky Mountain National Park; Latitude 40°: Colorado Front Range Trails

Trail contact: Rocky Mountain National Park, 1000 Highway 36, Estes Park; 970-586-1206, 970-586-1333 (24-hour recorded message); nps.gov/romo

Other: Some areas of this trail have easy access to water but others do not; water from these sources must be filtered/treated before consuming. It's best to bring your own.

Special considerations: Avoid the possibility of attracting bears and having your vehicle damaged. If you leave any food items or garbage in your car, it must be stored in the trunk or as low in the passenger compartment as possible and covered from sight, with the vehicle windows and doors closed and locked. If parking overnight in the Wild Basin area, you are required to use the food storage locker that is provided at the trailhead. It is prohibited to leave food items or garbage within a vehicle when parking overnight here.

Finding the trailhead: In Boulder, from 28th Street (US 36) and Canyon Boulevard (SH 119), head north on US 36 to its junction with SH 66. Turn left on SH 66 and drive through Lyons to the yield sign at the T-intersection (US 36 and SH 7). Turn left onto SH 7 and drive 23.4 miles to the junction with the road to Wild Basin, Boulder County Road 84W. Turn left onto BCR 84W and drive 0.4 mile to the road to Wild Basin/Copeland Lake. Turn right and pay the fee at the entrance station. The parking lot for the Sandbeach Lake Trailhead is immediately past the entrance station on the right. Vault toilets are available.

THE HIKE

Before Rocky Mountain National Park was established in 1915, several lakes in the Wild Basin area of what is now the Park were used as reservoirs to gather water for Front Range towns. Sandbeach Lake provided drinking water for Longmont, out on the plains northeast of Boulder. The original dam at the lake wasn't structurally reinforced and failed in 1903, sending a wall of water down the North Saint Vrain Creek. The floodwaters destroyed a bridge near Copeland Lake and caused significant damage to the area. Three years later, a new dam was constructed of masonry but this one lasted for only five years and was replaced in 1911 by a concrete structure. Eventually, the Park Service bought the water rights for the Sandbeach watershed and the dam was permanently removed. The trail to Sandbeach Lake was originally built to enable the construction of the dam, and the route has not changed much since then.

The hike to Sandbeach Lake ascends through the forest, steeply at times, with both smooth and rocky sections of trail. Hiking poles might be a good idea to help stabilize your footing in the rocky terrain and on the log bridges. After a couple of switchbacks, you'll pass the trail intersection with a trail to Meeker Park to the north. The trail passes below granite cliffs, ascends a drainage under Lookout Mountain to the north, and then traverses below Meeker Ridge. You'll pass the access trails to four backcountry campsites before crossing Hunters' Creek (camping in these sites is by permit only—see contact information above). The trail then climbs the final steep section to the lake. You'll pass the access to a group campsite and then suddenly the vista opens wide before you, and you're standing on the sandy north shore of Sandbeach Lake. It was well worth the effort!

To the north of the lake, Mount Meeker looms large while hiding most of its more-famous sibling, Longs Peak. Immediately west is Mount Orton, with the

To the north, Mount Meeker stands guard over Sandbeach Lake.

very rugged Pagoda Peak peeking out to the north of it. To the south are Mount Copeland, St. Vrain Mountain, and a chain of peaks along the Continental Divide.

Along the trail and while at the lake, you might encounter chipmunks, golden-mantled ground squirrels, chickarees ("red squirrels"), or marmots that are curious about the food you've brought along with you. **Please, never feed wildlife!** Feeding them food that they don't normally eat will do them more harm than good.

If you're an angler, please note that Hunters' Creek is closed to all fishing. The Greenback cutthroat trout is now on the Federal Threatened Species List. The Park is participating in a program to restore this trout species to its native range in the Arkansas and South Platte Rivers. The Park Service reports that it will take several years to establish a stable population but, once that has been accomplished, Hunters' Creek will reopen to catch-and-release fishing. Violations face stiff penalties, so please observe this closing and help reestablish a healthy trout population to its native habitat.

MILES AND DIRECTIONS

0.0 Start at the Sandbeach Lake Trailhead, to the left of the bulletin board. Elevation: 8,330 feet. GPS: N40 13.19' / W105 32.06'. Head up and stay right at the first trail intersection.

1.4 Junction with a trail to Meeker Park on the right. GPS: N40 13.03' / W105 33.20'. Stay left.

Mount Copeland leads a string of peaks south of Sandbeach Lake.

1.6 Trail starts traversing below Lookout Mountain, up the right side of a drainage.

1.9 Junction with a trail to the Hole-in-the-Wall backcountry campsite on the left. GPS: N40 12.98′ / W105 33.70′. Stay right.

2.1 Junction with a trail to the Campers' Creek backcountry campsite on the left. GPS: N40 12.99′ / W105 33.93′. Stay right.

3.0 Junction with a trail to the Beaver Mill backcountry campsite on the left. GPS: N40 12.98′ / W105 34.77′. Stay right.

3.3 Junction with a trail to the Hunters' Creek backcountry campsite on the left. GPS: N40 13.02′ / W105 35.01′. Stay right.

3.6 Cross Hunters' Creek on two long log bridges. GPS: N40 13.14′ / W105 35.28′. Hunters' Creek is completely closed to fishing.

4.5 Reach the sandy north shore of Sandbeach Lake. Elevation: 10,300 feet. GPS: N40 13.24′ / W105 36.07′. Just before the lake, there is a group campsite. The Sandbeach campsite is at the lake. Return to the trailhead the way you came.

9.0 Arrive back at the trailhead.

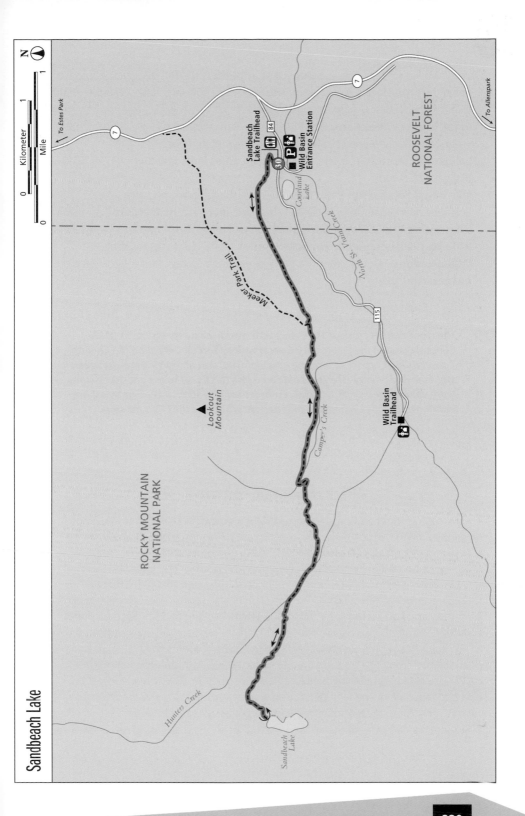

Sandbeach Lake

HIKE INFORMATION

Local Information: Estes Park Visitor Center; 800-443-7837, 970-577-9900; visitestespark.com

Local Events/Attractions: Elk Fest, Estes Park; 800-443-7837, 970-577-9900; visitestespark.com/events-calendar/special-events/elk-fest

Longs Peak Scottish-Irish Highland Festival, Estes Park; 800-903-7837, 970-586-6308; scotfest.com

MacGregor Ranch, Estes Park; 970-586-3749; macgregorranch.org

Scandinavian Midsummer Festival, Estes Park; estesmidsummer.com

Hike Tours: Rocky Mountain National Park Ranger-Led Programs, Estes Park; 970-586-1206; nps.gov/romo/planyourvisit/ranger_led_activities.htm

Organizations: Rocky Mountain Conservancy, Estes Park; 970-586-0108; rmconservancy.org

The stock market crash of 1929 created a world-wide depression. In 1933, Congress passed the Emergency Conservation Work Act, creating the Civilian Conservation Corps (CCC). Young, unemployed, and unmarried men between eighteen and twenty-five years old could join this Corps to get good work and learn valuable job skills. Natural resources conservation, including forest fire fighting and trail building and maintenance, became the CCC's mission.

Rocky Mountain Conservancy

The Rocky Mountain Conservancy (RMC) is a nonprofit 501(c)(3) organization formed in 1931 to partner with Rocky Mountain National Park (RMNP). Its purpose is "to support research, interpretive and other educational programs of the National Park Service and allied public agencies." RMC publishes and sells books and other interpretive materials in the bookstores in RMNP and in several National Forest Visitor Centers. Seminars on topics such as the human history and natural history of RMNP, along with writing and photography workshops, are offered each year. RMC and RMNP co-sponsor the Rocky Mountain Research Fellowship, awarded yearly to graduate students to conduct research in the park. RMC also collects donations for the Rocky Mountain National Park Fund, which helps RMNP finance capital construction, historical preservation, visitor education, and land protection acquisitions. For more information about RMC or to join, check out rmconservancy.org or call 970-586-0108.

Buchanan Pass Trail 910

The nonmotorized Buchanan Pass Trail 910 takes you gently uphill through thick forest north of Middle Saint Vrain Creek and into high meadows with beautiful vistas of the Continental Divide. This hike is featured as access to explore the area. Past the 4.5-mile turnaround, you can hike any of several different trails to the Saint Vrain Glaciers—Red Deer Lake, Saint Vrain Mountain, Beaver Creek Trail, or Buchanan Pass—that traverse the Divide. As a day hike, you can enjoy big rock outcroppings at mile 2.1 and the broad meadows and creekside stops just before the Indian Peaks Wilderness boundary.

Start: Buchanan Pass Trailhead at the far end of the parking lot west of Camp Dick campground
Distance: 9.0 miles out and back
Hiking time: 3 to 4.5 hours
Difficulty: Difficult due to distance
Elevation gain: 1,080 feet
Trail surface: Natural surface and rocky trail
Seasons: June through early Oct. The forested section of the trail is marked with blue diamonds for snowshoeing and cross-country skiing in winter.
Other trail users: Equestrians and mountain bikers; mountain bikers not allowed in wilderness area.
Canine compatibility: Dogs permitted May through Nov and must be under voice control. They must be on leash in the Indian Peaks Wilderness.
Land status: National forest
Fees and permits: None required for day hikes. Permits are required for overnight stays inside the Indian Peaks Wilderness from June 1 to Sept 15. Permits can be obtained from the Boulder Ranger District office in Boulder and the Sulphur Ranger District office in Granby. A permit form is downloadable from www.fs.usda.gov/recmain/arp/recreation, but it must be mailed in or brought in person to either ranger district office. This trail is surrounded by and leads into the Middle Saint Vrain Backcountry Zone.
Schedule: Open year-round, but the access road is closed 1.2 miles from the trailhead in winter.
Maps: USGS Allenspark and Isolation Peak; National Geographic Trails Illustrated 102 Indian Peaks/Gold Hill, Latitude 40°: Boulder County Trails
Trail contact: Roosevelt National Forest, Boulder Ranger District, 2140 Yarmouth Avenue, Boulder; 303-541-2500; www.fs.usda.gov/recmain/arp/recreation
Other: The first 0.5 mile of the trail is day-use only. The next 4.0 miles are open to dispersed camping following Leave No Trace principles. If you hike or backpack into the

wilderness area, observe Wilderness Regulations. For example: Permit required from June 1 to Sept 15. Group size is limited to twelve people and pack stock combined. No campfires are allowed east of the Continental Divide.

Special considerations: The road is closed in winter near SH 72, about 1.2 miles from the trailhead. Hunters use this area during hunting season. The first few feet of the trail are shared with four-wheel-drive vehicles.

Finding the trailhead: In Boulder, from 28th Street (US 36) and Canyon Boulevard (SH 119), head north on US 36 to its junction with SH 66. Turn left on SH 66 and drive through Lyons to the stop sign at the T-intersection. Turn left onto SH 7 and drive 14.3 miles to the junction with SH 72 (Peak-to-Peak Highway). Turn left (south) onto SH 72 and drive 4.1 miles just past a big left switchback at mile marker 50. Make a sharp right onto the road to Peaceful Valley and Camp Dick campgrounds and drive 1.3 miles through both of them to the trailhead parking area. This paved road is a little more than a car-width wide and has speed bumps. Water and vault toilets are available in the campgrounds.

THE HIKE

The nonmotorized Buchanan Pass Trail takes you along the north side of Middle Saint Vrain Creek, gently undulating through a thick forest of lodgepole and limber pines, spruce, fir, aspen, and common juniper. Several rock ledges provide a sunny picnic spot at 2.1 miles. Beautiful views open up at 3.4 miles, when you cross a little boulder field. About 0.25 mile farther, the trail crosses a meadow with a huge boulder, perhaps deposited by a glacier long ago.

The beautiful, rugged peaks along the Continental Divide west of Boulder, known as the Indian Peaks, received names honoring different tribes of Native Americans: Arapaho, Arikaree, Kiowa, Navajo, Apache, Pawnee, and Paiute. Crystal-clear streams and alpine lakes have drawn people to this area for many years. Native Americans crossed the passes, following game and other food. Bighorn sheep were one high-altitude source of food and materials. On lofty ridges, hunters built low rock-wall blinds. Others drove the sheep toward the walls, where the hunters could ambush them. Hunting sites have been dated back 7,500 years.

In the late 1800s, people came to the Indian Peaks to recreate, fish, hunt, and harvest the plentiful water for the growing cities on the plains and the area's mines. Arthur Carhart, a landscape architect with the USDA Forest Service (USFS) and one of the founders of the wilderness movement, successfully recommended that the Indian Peaks become a special management area of 47,000 acres in 1927. The region held the largest concentration of glaciers in Colorado

Sawtooth Mountain from the Buchanan Pass Trail.

(ten), over a hundred miles of hiking and horse trails, and more than forty lakes. The USFS expanded the management area to 55,000 acres in 1965 and closed it to motorized vehicles. Because the USFS managed the Indian Peaks as wilderness, it remained reasonably undeveloped, wild, and pristine.

By 1968, citizens developed a preliminary recommendation for an 80,000 acre Indian Peaks Wilderness, starting at the southern end of Rocky Mountain National Park and extending south of Arapaho Pass on both sides of the Continental Divide. Three years later, several members of Colorado's congressional delegation introduced bills to start the process to establish a wilderness area. Wilderness designation would continue watershed protection, protect rare and endangered species, and provide the growing Front Range population of 1.5 million people (in 1970) an opportunity for quality recreation.

By 1976, the USFS had completed its study of the proposed Indian Peaks Wilderness and proposed 16,270 acres as the Saint Vrain Glaciers Wilderness. The proposal included six options, the largest containing 82,125 acres on both sides of the Divide, including the Arapaho Pass area. After two more years of negotiations, Congress created the Indian Peaks Wilderness, with approximately 70,000 acres, and the 36,235-acre Arapaho National Recreation Area. President Jimmy Carter signed the legislation, Public Law 95-450, on October 11, 1978. Subsequent legislation increased the Indian Peaks Wilderness to 76,711 acres.

Approaching the Indian Peaks Wilderness boundary on the Buchanan Pass Trail.

Because of its location near the Denver/Boulder metro area, the Indian Peaks Wilderness is one of the most popular and heavily used wilderness areas in the country.

MILES AND DIRECTIONS

0.0   Start from the Middle Saint Vrain 4WD Trailhead bulletin board and walk down the dirt road. Elevation: 8,720 feet. GPS: N40 07.80′ / W105 31.45′.

400 feet   Turn right onto the trail at the BUCHANAN PASS TRAIL sign. Please read the information on the bulletin board before crossing the creek on the sturdy bridge.

2.2   Several rock outcroppings provide a nice rest stop.

3.1   A wooden post on the right side of the trail indicates 3 miles.

3.5   Forest opens for views of Sawtooth Mountain (12,304 feet).

3.8   The trail reaches a T-intersection at a dirt road (nonmotorized). Turn right onto the dirt road, which is the Buchanan Pass Trail. Elevation: 9,600 feet. GPS: N40 08.26′ / W105 35.16′.

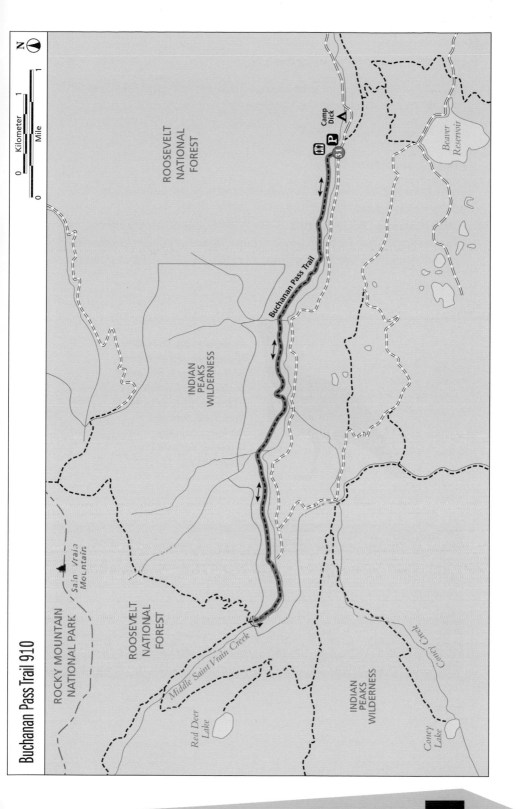

4.2 Great view of Elk Tooth (12,848 feet).

4.5 Indian Peaks Wilderness boundary. Elevation: 9,800 feet. GPS: N40 08.41' / W105 35.69'. Return the way you came.

9.0 Arrive back at the trailhead.

HIKE INFORMATION

Local Information: Boulder Convention and Visitors Bureau; 303-442-2911; bouldercoloradousa.com
Boulder Chamber of Commerce; 303-442-1044; boulderchamber.com
Organizations: Indian Peaks Wilderness Alliance, Boulder; indianpeakswilderness.org
Colorado Mountain Club Boulder Group, Boulder; 303-554-7688; cmcboulder.org

Around 1908, Enos Mills recommended inclusion of the Indian Peaks area in the initial boundaries of the proposed Rocky Mountain National Park, but mining interests defeated the proposal.

🍂 **Green Tip:**
Even if fires are permitted, try to avoid making one at all. If you must, then minimize the use and impact of the fire. Use designated fire spots or existing fire rings. When building fires, use small sticks (less than 1.5 inches in diameter) that you find on the ground. Keep your fire small, burn it to ash, put it out completely, and scatter the cool ashes. Always be aware of current fire restrictions—they can change quickly!

31

Indian Peaks Wilderness Alliance

Before the Indian Peaks were designated as a wilderness area, local citizens were concerned that the area was already eroded and denuded of vegetation from heavy use. In 1980, three women, Dr. Anne Forrest Ketchin, Anne Vickery, and Jan Robertson, organized a citizens' forum to discuss how to deal with increasing use and protect the wilderness resource. Attendees included people from diverse groups. They developed twenty-seven management recommendations, most of which the USDA Forest Service (USFS) agreed to implement.

A nonprofit called the Indian Peaks Working Group incorporated in 1985 to help the USFS care for and maintain the Indian Peaks Wilderness. The group is committed to "providing quality education to the public on all aspects of the Indian Peaks Wilderness Area; providing a forum for exchanging information and for discussing wilderness and area-related management solutions; supporting research on the natural sciences in the Indian Peaks Wilderness; and, instilling in society a sense of respect and stewardship for public lands." The group changed its name to Indian Peaks Wilderness Alliance, Inc. (IPWA) in 1999. IPWA adopted the neighboring James Peak Wilderness when it was designated in 2002.

For more information about IPWA or to find out about membership, donations, and volunteer opportunities, visit indianpeakswilderness.org.

Ouzel Falls and Lake

Wild Basin is a wonderful and somewhat hidden part of Rocky Mountain National Park. You'll hike along the sparkling, fast-flowing North Saint Vrain Creek and then pass beautiful Calypso Cascades and thundering Ouzel Falls. Beyond Calypso Cascades, nature is doing an excellent job of regenerating the forest that burned in the 1978 fire, which started near Ouzel Lake. The trail offers beautiful views of Longs Peak, Mount Meeker, and the rugged Continental Divide, especially along a ridge lined with healthy new growth. Pretty Ouzel Lake lies on a bench not far below treeline. Back-country campsites are located along or near the trail, with one at Ouzel Lake.

Start: Trailhead near the Wild Basin Ranger Station

Distance: 10 miles out and back

Hiking time: 5 hours

Difficulty: Moderate to Ouzel Falls, then Difficult to Ouzel Lake due to distance and elevation gain

Elevation gain: 880 feet to Ouzel Falls; 1,510 feet to Ouzel Lake

Trail surface: Natural surface and rocky trail

Seasons: Best mid-June through mid-Oct

Other trail users: Equestrians

Canine compatibility: Dogs not permitted

Land status: National park wilderness

Fees and permits: Entry fee required. The entrance station is at the start of the road into Wild Basin. Backcountry camping permit (fee charged) required for overnight camping. Food canisters are required for backcountry camping below treeline from May 1 through Oct 31. For information about backcountry camping permits, call 970-586-1242 or go to nps.gov/romo/planyourvisit/wild_guide.htm.

Schedule: Open year-round

Maps: USGS Isolation Peak, Allenspark; National Geographic Trails Illustrated 301 Longs Peak/Bear Lake/Wild Basin or 200 Rocky Mountain National Park; Latitude 40°: Colorado Front Range Trails or Boulder County Trails

Trail contact: Rocky Mountain National Park, 1000 Highway 36, Estes Park; 970-586-1206, 970-586-1333 (24-hour recorded message); nps.gov/romo

Other: Park only in designated places along Wild Basin Road and in the parking lot.

Special considerations: Some areas of this trail have easy access to water; others do not. The road is closed 1.2 miles from the trailhead in winter. Park in the winter parking lot and cross-country ski or snowshoe to the trailhead. The trail is neither marked nor maintained for winter use.

THE HIKE

As you walk along North Saint Vrain Creek and around Calypso Cascades and Ouzel Falls, keep an eye open for a robin-size bird bobbing up and down on a rock in the water. Hopefully you'll see it dive into the quickly flowing stream to feed. This dark gray bird is the American dipper, or water ouzel. It feeds on aquatic larvae and insects while walking along stream bottoms or dipping its head into the water to catch an unsuspecting yummy tidbit. The bird prefers rushing water, including cascades and waterfalls. Scales cover its nostrils so it doesn't drown. Ouzel Falls, Ouzel Lake, and Ouzel Peak are named after this interesting bird.

The hike to Ouzel Falls climbs through a typical subalpine forest of Engelmann spruce, subalpine fir, lodgepole pine, low-growing common juniper, the occasional aspen, and many wildflowers. In damper areas, ferns grow along the trail. Limber pines join the mix a little higher up, when lodgepole pines reach their elevation limit.

A few hints on tree identification: Spruces have sharp and square needles— you can roll one between your fingers. Fir needles are flat and friendly, and don't roll. Pine needles are prickly and come in packets. Two lodgepole needles are in each packet. Limber needles come in packets of four or five. Limber pinecones are much larger (3 to 10 inches long) than lodgepole pinecones (less than 2 inches long).

After Calypso Cascades, you'll find an open hillside with a few dead trees still standing, while smaller lodgepoles, spruces, aspens, and wildflowers are thriving where the Ouzel Fire swept through almost forty years ago. After the junction with the Thunder Lake Trail, the Bluebird Lake Trail switchbacks up to the ridge that the fire blazed down. Beautiful views of Ouzel Peak, Mahana Peak, Tanima Peak, and Pilot Mountain can be seen through old and new trees. Most of the forest recovers slowly at this elevation, but aspens shoot up relatively quickly,

32

Ouzel Falls.

benefitting from the increased sunlight on fire-ravaged slopes; their root systems are typically below the heat of the fire, so new growth begins soon after the fire is gone. Grasses and wildflowers grow profusely between the small trees. Little spruce trees will one day be over a hundred feet tall, blocking the view of the mountains like they did before the fire.

On August 13, 1978, a ranger smelled smoke and discovered a small fire burning in duff near a tree obviously struck by lightning. Park personnel considered the location a low-risk zone and let it burn. Fire is part of the natural process, and park policy was to let nature-caused fires burn unless they threatened property. Ten days later the fire was creeping along between Ouzel Lake and Chickadee Pond. Park personnel constantly monitored it. By September 1, high winds caused the fire to take off and firefighters arrived to contain it. The winds died down, but then unpredicted winds gusted through the area on September 15, sending the fire toward Ouzel Falls and Allenspark to the east. The fire was finally contained within Rocky Mountain National Park at the beginning of October.

One year after the blaze, ferns, grasses, fireweed, and other flowers had reappeared. The second year, lodgepole seedlings popped up. Serotinous lodgepole cones are covered with a resin that melts in the heat of a forest fire, releasing seeds. Fires, therefore, renew lodgepole forests. At higher elevations, limber pines often are the first pioneers. Aspen shoots grow quickly from roots underground. Within ten years after the fire, flowers had returned nitrogen to the soil.

Aspen sprouts had grown over 12 feet. Dead trees fell, their slowly decaying trunks returning nutrients to the soil. The area now supports a greater variety of vegetation than it did before the fire. Nature recovers.

MILES AND DIRECTIONS

0.0 Start from the Wild Basin Trailhead. Elevation: 8,500 feet. GPS: N40 12.46' / W105 33.99'. In about 200 feet, you enter the Rocky Mountain National Park Wilderness Area.

0.4 Spur trail to the left to Copeland Falls.

1.1 Sunny rock slab along North Saint Vrain Creek. A nice place to sit.

1.3 Junction with a trail to several campsites. Continue on the main trail to the left.

1.8 T-intersection with a trail to Allenspark. GPS: N40 11.74' / W105 35.42'. Turn right here and continue a few feet to Calypso Cascades.

2.7 Ouzel Falls. Elevation: 9,380 feet. (Elevation gain from trailhead: 880 feet.) GPS: N40 11.92' / W105 35.98'. (**Option:** For a 5.4-mile out-and-back hike, turn around here and return the way you came.) To reach Ouzel Lake in another 2.3 miles, continue up the trail.

Ouzel Lake below Ouzel Peak.

Ouzel Falls and Lake

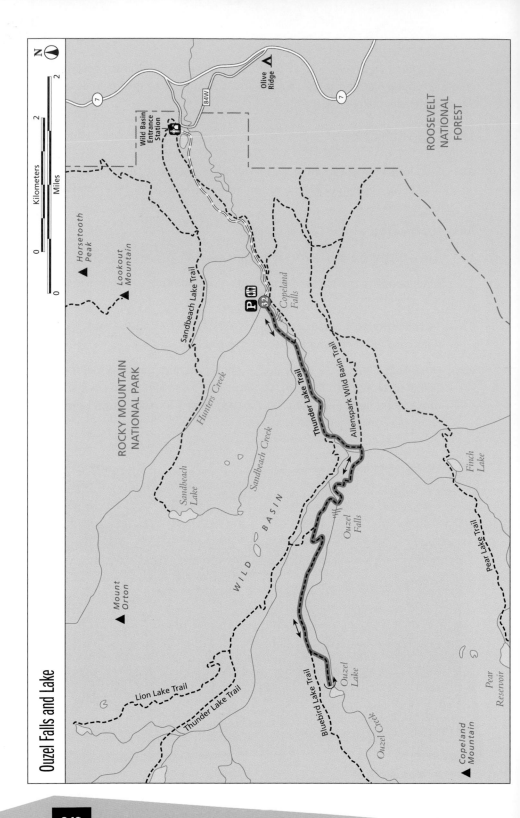

3.0   Trail reaches a Y with the Bluebird Lake Trail. Take the left branch to continue to Ouzel Lake. GPS: N40 12.09′ / W105 36.21′.

3.4   Trail travels above Ouzel Creek along a ridge that was badly burned in the Ouzel Fire but has recovered nicely.

4.5   Junction of Ouzel Lake and Bluebird Lake Trails. Turn left here as the trail descends a tad toward Ouzel Creek. GPS: N40 12.14′ / W105 37.52′.

5.0   Ouzel Lake. Walk past the designated Ouzel Lake campsite to a set of rocks that are a nice lunch spot. Elevation: 10,010 feet. GPS: N40 11.97′ / W105 37.91′. Return the way you came.

10.0   Arrive back at the trailhead.

Option

You can hike to Bluebird Lake, which is 1.8 miles beyond the junction of the trail to Ouzel Lake (mile 4.5 above). Elevation: 10,978 feet. GPS: N40 11.32′ / W105 39.09′. Strenuous due to 12-mile out-and-back length and 2,478-foot elevation gain.

HIKE INFORMATION

Local Information: Estes Park Visitor Center; 800-443-7837, 970-577-9900; visitestespark.com

Local Events/Attractions: MacGregor Ranch, Estes Park; 970-586-3749; macgregorranch.org

Longs Peak Scottish-Irish Highland Festival, Estes Park; 800-903-7837, 970-586-6308; scotfest.com

Scandinavian Midsummer Festival, Estes Park; estesmidsummer.com

Hike Tours: Rocky Mountain National Park Ranger-Led Programs, Estes Park; 970-586-1206; nps.gov/romo

Organizations: Rocky Mountain Conservancy, Estes Park; 970-586-0108; rmconservancy.org

In early June, keep an eye open for the delicate Calypso orchids, or fairy slippers (Calypso bulbosa), near Calypso Cascades. These delicate pink to purple flowers with one basal leaf grow in moist, shady places and only in soil where a certain fungus grows.

What Is Wilderness?

Wilderness areas are very special places. The American people, through acts of Congress, designate certain pristine and primitive sections of undeveloped Federal land as Wilderness. The Wilderness Act of 1964, which created a National Wilderness Preservation System (NWPS), gives Congress the authority to designate lands as Wilderness.

Back in the 1870s, people became alarmed at the rapid rate of development in America and the overuse of natural resources on public lands. Efforts were made to conserve and preserve certain areas in their pristine condition.

The purpose of the NWPS is to assure that Americans now and in the future have the benefits of a wilderness resource. Those benefits include "outstanding opportunities for solitude or a primitive and unconfined type of recreation" and "the public purposes of recreational, scenic, scientific, educational, conservation, and historical use." The Wilderness Act specifically states "A wilderness, in contrast with those areas where man and his works dominate the landscape, is hereby recognized as an area where the earth and its community of life are untrammeled by man, where man himself is a visitor who does not remain . . . an area of undeveloped Federal land retaining its primeval character and influence, without permanent improvements or human habitation, which is protected and managed so as to preserve its natural conditions and which . . . generally appears to have been affected primarily by the forces of nature . . ."

Chasm Lake

"Wow!!" comes to mind as a fitting description for this popular hike! The trail winds up through lodgepole pine forest, then climbs through limber pines and krummholz *to the alpine tundra. On clear days, you can see for miles across the eastern plains. Longs Peak, Mount Meeker, and Mount Lady Washington loom to the southwest. Along the shelf trail, Peacock Pool, Columbine Falls, and colorful wildflowers captivate your eyes. Chasm Lake, snuggled beneath the shear East Face of Longs Peak, can't be beat for scenic beauty. Glaciers quarried and sculpted this gorgeous land through which you hike.*

Start: Longs Peak Trailhead

Distance: 8.6 miles out and back

Hiking time: 4 to 7 hours

Difficulty: Most Difficult due to elevation gain and high altitude

Elevation gain: 2,360 feet, plus a few undulations

Trail surface: Natural surface and rocky trail, with one rock band scramble

Seasons: Best late June through early Oct

Other trail users: Equestrians (to mile 3.4)

Canine compatibility: Dogs not permitted

Land status: National park wilderness

Fees and permits: None required for day use. Backcountry camping permit (fee charged) required for overnight camping. Food canisters are required for backcountry camping below treeline from May 1 through Oct 31. For information about backcountry camping permits, call 970-586-1242 or go to nps.gov/romo/planyourvisit/wild_guide.htm.

Schedule: Open year-round

Maps: USGS Longs Peak; National Geographic Trails Illustrated 301 Longs Peak/Bear Lake/Wild Basin or 200 Rocky Mountain National Park; Latitude 40°: Colorado Front Range Trails or Boulder County Trails

Trail contact: Rocky Mountain National Park, 1000 Highway 36, Estes Park; 970-586-1206, 970-586-1333 (24-hour recorded message); nps.gov/romo

Other: Because many people start the popular climb of Longs Peak by 3 a.m., the parking lot fills quickly. You can park along the right side of the road going downhill. Please follow any current posted parking directions. Two privies are located above treeline. One is just above the junction of the trails to Chasm Lake and the Boulderfield; the other is in the meadow below Chasm Lake. Please use these privies instead of digging a cathole in the fragile tundra. Bring binoculars to look for climbers tackling the vertical rock of the East Face.

Special considerations: Make sure to get an early start and be back below treeline before thunderstorms develop. Storms often sneak up quickly from behind Longs Peak. Once above treeline, very little water is available until just below Chasm Lake (and this needs to be treated). Bring extra warm clothes, including gloves. The ever-present wind gets mighty chilly above treeline, even in summer. In the last 0.25 mile to the lake, you'll climb up a short sloping rock band with good handholds and little ledges. At the ridge, head down to the lake through a field of boulders (no defined trail). The trail is neither marked nor maintained for winter use.

Finding the trailhead: In Boulder, from 28th Street (US 36) and Canyon Boulevard (SH 119), head north on US 36 to its junction with SH 66. Turn left on SH 66 and drive through Lyons to the stop sign at the T-intersection (US 36 and SH 7). Turn left onto SH 7 and drive 24.6 miles to the junction with the Longs Peak Area road at mile marker 9. Turn left onto the road to Longs Peak and drive 1.1 miles to the parking lot at the Longs Peak Ranger Station. If the parking lot is full, park along the right side of the road heading downhill or follow the current posted parking directions. The trailhead is to the left (south) of the ranger station, and several vault toilets are to the right of it.

THE HIKE

Longs Peak Trail to its junction with the Chasm Lake Trail is one of many steps—steps created by logs or stones to prevent erosion on the steadily climbing trail. Hiking poles are highly recommended for the downward trek.

The hike starts in a typical "sterile" lodgepole pine forest. After the first mile, Englemann spruces and subalpine firs intersperse among the lodgepoles. Farther up the trail, limber pines make an appearance. This trail is great for watching changes in vegetation the higher you hike (or lower on the way back). An alpine tundra interpretive sign reminds you that the land above the trees is a delicate place. Plants at and above treeline take years to grow—and to recover from thoughtless human acts.

By 2.3 miles and 10,800 feet, the limber pines grow smaller and are stunted. The growing season is so short that these trees propagate through a root system. These tree islands are called *krummholz,* German for "crooked wood." Growing close together helps them survive the fierce winter winds that race down the mountain slopes. Some trees shoot up skinny trunks known as flag trees.

The Ships Prow, Longs Peak, and the southern flanks of Mount Lady Washington along the Chasm Lake Trail.

Often they are stripped bare on one side by blowing ice crystals. Yellow alpine avens and purple harebell wildflowers add color to the woodland. Here the tops of Longs Peak, Mount Meeker, and Mount Lady Washington emerge above the *krummholz*. Glaciers sculpted the sharp ridges and jagged rocks between Longs Peak and Mount Meeker.

The present Rocky Mountains were uplifted starting about 70 million years ago. A regional uplift occurred between 5 and 2 million years ago, raising the Rockies as much as 5,000 feet. Between 150,000 and 12,000 years ago, the climate changed and snow remained year-round, growing deeper with each season. The east slopes of the Rockies, filled with snow blown by west winds, developed glaciers. As the glaciers crept forward, they eroded the land underneath and pushed the resulting sediments out of the way, creating ridges known as lateral moraines.

In 3.4 miles, the trail reaches the top of the Mills Moraine, created by the Mills Glacier. Here the trail splits. To the right, climbers continue on to the Boulderfield, the Keyhole, and up Longs Peak. A not-so-private privy is off to the left, beyond the main trail. The Chasm Lake Trail heads left and contours along Mount Lady Washington's steep east flank. Along this shelf trail, bushes, subalpine firs, and limber pines find rootholds among rocks and boulders. Clumps of beautiful blue columbine, the Colorado state flower, dance in the breeze. In the glacier-gouged valley below, Peacock Pool lies serenely below the plunging waters of Columbine Falls. The trail drops slightly to an alpine meadow with a tiny sparkling creek

33

Chasm Lake below the East Face of Longs Peak.

flowing past pink rose crown and ruby-red king's crown. Greenish-white arctic gentians signal fall's approach in early August.

At the west end of the meadow, you'll reach a small sign pointing the way to Chasm Lake; the trail ascends a shallow gully and rocky ridge to arrive at the lake. Carefully follow the cairns (rock piles) to climb up a rock slab with good hand-holds and ledges. This high lake is nestled in a glacial cirque below what remains of Mills Glacier, and Longs Peak's massive East Face which rises more than 2,400 vertical feet. Binoculars come in handy to scan the East Face for climbers, who look like tiny bugs as they make their way to the top. The Diamond challenges climbers from all over the world.

Jagged gendarmes, sharp arêtes, sheer rock walls, and piles of boulders sur-round Chasm Lake. These features were created when glacial ice stripped away rock and dirt. Freeze-thaw cycles continue to add artistic touches, whittling away at the rocks little by little.

MILES AND DIRECTIONS

0.0   Start from the Longs Peak Trailhead. Elevation: 9,400 feet. GPS: N40 16.33′ / W105 33.41′. Please sign in at the trail register a few feet up the trail. A short distance up the trail, you enter the Rocky Mountain National Park Wilder-ness Area.

Chasm Lake

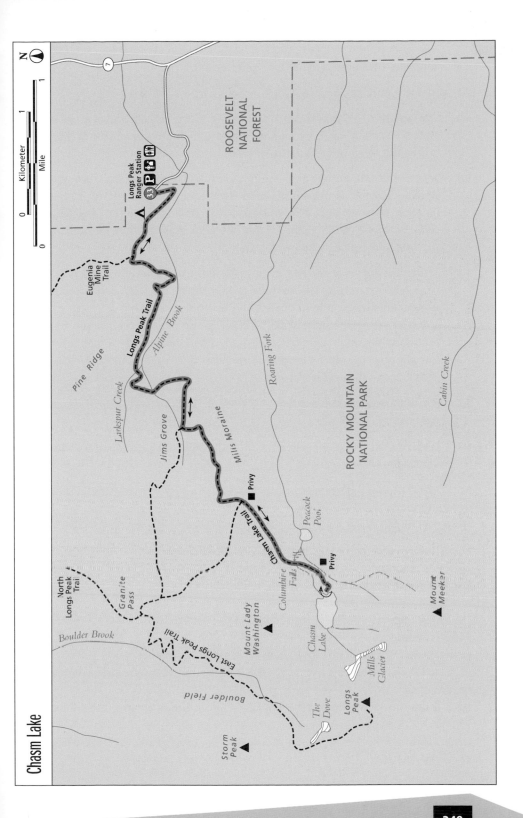

0.5   Junction with Eugenia Mine Trail. Continue left up Longs Peak Trail.

2.0   Alpine tundra interpretive sign.

2.6   Trail junction to Battle Mountain campsite. Continue left up Longs Peak Trail. If you need water, try the little creek to the right (remember to treat any water). Next water source is 1.5 miles.

3.4   Junction of Chasm Lake Trail and Boulderfield/Longs Peak Trail. Turn left onto the trail to Chasm Lake. The privy is to the east (further left) of the trail junction. Horses are not allowed beyond this point. Elevation: 11,560 feet. GPS: N40 15.94' / W105 35.55'. The trail descends slightly before heading up to a beautiful alpine meadow.

4.1   Trail to the privy is on the left. To the right, look up to find cairns (rock piles) marking the route up a shallow gully in a broken rock face. When you reach a rock band, stay a little to the left and scramble up the big stone "steps" along a notch in the stone slab. The cairns are sometimes hard to see, but the route is easier than it looks, with good handholds and footholds. On the way down, if walking is uncomfortable, sitting while moving from one little ledge to the next works well.

4.2   Top of the rock band. Elevation: 11,800+ feet. Find your way down through the boulders to the lake.

4.3   Edge of Chasm Lake. Elevation: 11,760 feet. GPS: N40 15.52' / W105 36.18'. Return the way you came.

8.6   Arrive back at the trailhead.

HIKE INFORMATION

Local Information: Estes Park Visitor Center; 800-443-7837, 970-577-9900; visitestespark.com

Local Events/Attractions: MacGregor Ranch, Estes Park; 970-586-3749; macgregorranch.org

Longs Peak Scottish-Irish Highland Festival, Estes Park; 800-903-7837, 970-586-6308; scotfest.com

Scandinavian Midsummer Festival, Estes Park; estesmidsummer.com

Peak to Peak Scenic Byway; codot.gov/travel/scenic-byways/north-central/peak-to-peak

Hike Tours: Rocky Mountain National Park Ranger-Led Programs, Estes Park; 970-586-1206; nps.gov/romo

Organizations: Rocky Mountain Conservancy, Estes Park; 970-586-0108; rmconservancy.org

Chasm Meadows Patrol Cabin

Above Peacock Pool, on the flanks of Mt. Meeker, sits the Chasm Meadows Patrol Cabin, which the National Park Service (NPS) uses to store rescue gear and as an operations base for rescues. The original stone cabin was built in 1931 at the bottom of the gully called The Loft, between Longs and Meeker. Initially it was open to climbers who wanted to try their luck scaling the East Face of Longs Peak. Not all succeeded, and the little cabin sheltered rescue teams. According to a Denver Post article dated April 9, 2003, "It [Chasm Lake Patrol Cabin] once even served as a medical emergency room, when Dr. Sam Luce performed lifesaving brain surgery on a fallen climber who suffered a depressed skull fracture."

The NPS closed the hut to the public in the fall of 1972, but still housed vital rescue gear there. During a mid-March snowstorm in 2003, up to 8 feet of snow fell in about 4 days, the perfect recipe for an avalanche. The white death roared down The Loft, shearing the cabin off its foundation. One official reportedly described the structure's debris as a cabin being 6 inches high and a half-mile long. A temporary cabin was built on the foundation of the old one after the avalanche. The NPS built a permanent structure in the current location in 2008.

Caribou Ranch Loop

The trails of Caribou Ranch Open Space not only wind through excellent wildlife habitat, but also take you on a historic journey into the mining era of the 1870s, past an old homestead, and along a scenic railroad route of the early 1900s. This moderate trail starts in a ponderosa pine and Douglas fir forest. During your hike, you'll circle a beautiful meadow and learn about willow carrs and wetlands from interpretive signs at different overlooks. About 1.2 miles of the trail follow the gentle old railroad bed of the Switzerland Trail of America (the Denver, Boulder & Western Railroad).

Start: Caribou Ranch Open Space bulletin board

Distance: 4.6-mile lollipop with two spurs

Hiking time: 1.5 to 2.5 hours

Difficulty: Moderate due to distance

Elevation gain: 180 feet, plus some undulations

Trail surface: Natural surface trail and old railroad bed

Seasons: Best July through Oct

Other trail users: Equestrians

Canine compatibility: Dogs not allowed at Caribou Ranch

Land status: Boulder County Open Space

Fees and permits: None required

Schedule: This entire property is closed Apr 1 through June 30 to protect migratory birds and elk. The rest of the year Caribou Ranch Open Space is open from sunrise to sunset. The trail system is open to snowshoers and cross-country skiers in winter.

Maps: USGS Nederland; National Geographic Trails Illustrated 102, Indian Peaks/Gold Hill

Trail contact: Boulder County Parks & Open Space, 5201 Saint Vrain Road, Longmont; 303-678-6200; bouldercountyopen space.org

Other: Smoking is prohibited within any Boulder County Parks and Open Space areas. Park visitors are required to stay on trail. Cars parked after hours will be ticketed or towed.

Special considerations: No potable water is available along the trail.

Finding the trailhead: In Boulder, from 28th Street (US 36) and Canyon Boulevard (SH 119), head west on SH 119 South for 18.0 miles to Nederland. Drive partway around the Nederland roundabout and turn right onto SH 72 West (toward Estes Park). Drive another 1.9 miles to Boulder County Road 126. There is a big sign for Caribou Ranch Open Space on SH 72. Turn left onto BCR 126. In 0.3 mile, go straight on BCR 126 past the left turnoff to Mud Lake Open Space. In another 0.3 mile, stay to the right when the road forks. In 0.2 mile, stay left when the road forks. In 0.1 mile, turn right into the parking loop for Caribou Ranch Open Space Park. Picnic tables and vault toilets are available, but no water.

THE HIKE

The beautiful Caribou Ranch has an interesting history starting in the late 1870s. Miners discovered gold and silver all over the hills to the west of Boulder. Getting ore out of the hills and supplies to the mines took time and a lot of energy via cart and horse. Building railroads became the solution.

In 1873, the Colorado Central and the Denver & Boulder Valley railroads (standard gauge) reached Boulder. By 1883, Union Pacific's Greeley Salt Lake & Pacific narrow-gauge railway wound its way up Boulder Canyon, then Fourmile Canyon, to the tiny hamlet of Sunset. A massive flood washed out the tracks in 1894. Undaunted, Boulder citizens formed the Inter-Mountain Railway. Work began in 1897 to connect Boulder with Ward. The new tracks of the Colorado & Northwestern (C&NW) Railroad reached Sunset in February 1898. The first train arrived in Ward in June that year via a 26.1-mile route that climbed some 4,000 feet, with one grade of 7 percent. By December 1904, a southern branch of the C&NW snaked from Sunset to Glacier Lake, past the Blue Bird Mine, and south to Eldora.

Besides hauling ore and supplies, the owners touted this route as the Switzerland Trail of America to attract tourists from all over the country. Just past Sunset, the Mount Alto picnic resort was built under big ponderosa pines, complete with picnic tables, fountains, and a dancing pavilion. The views of the lofty, snowy peaks of the Continental Divide to the west were advertised as rivaling the scenery in Switzerland or Italy. In 1900, the round-trip to Ward from Denver cost $2.25.

In April 1909, the Denver, Boulder & Western (DB&W) Railroad Company purchased the foreclosed C&NW. Tungsten became the king of ores around Nederland during this time, with 80 percent of the tungsten produced in the United States in 1915 coming from Boulder City (Boulder's original name). Two years later the DB&W filed an abandonment application because of declining revenues. Perhaps the rain gods smiled favorably on their plight by sending a

Autumn at the DeLonde Homestead, from the DeLonde Trail.

huge storm and flood that washed out the tracks in Fourmile Canyon and Boulder Canyon. The Public Utilities Commission granted permission to end service. By October 1920, 46.2 miles of track had been torn up and the Switzerland Trail was no more.

In 1936, Lynn W. Van Vleet of Denver purchased a 13,000-acre ranch (the area of Caribou Ranch today). Arabian horses replaced miners and tourists in the lush fields near the abandoned Blue Bird Mine. Horse shows at the Lazy VV Ranch drew visitors from miles around each summer Sunday morning. Horse handlers wore flowing, multicolored robes and rode beautiful, sleek Arabian stallions, entertaining the eager observers with a pageant from the Sahara Desert. On one Sunday in August 1950, a record 3,100 visitors attended the show.

Van Vleet sold the ranch in 1951. Twenty years later, a young record producer purchased 3,000 acres, saving the land from development. A developer had envisioned two golf courses, condominiums, and a hotel. The producer built a twenty-four-track recording studio in an old barn, and produced albums for music greats such as John Lennon, Joe Walsh, Chicago, Elton John, Michael Jackson, Rod Stewart, Dan Fogelberg, Stephen Stills, U2, and more. A fire destroyed the recording studio's control room in March 1985, and the studio never reopened. Don't expect to see the place where so many famous entertainers created their albums—it is located on private property east of Caribou Ranch Open Space.

Today you can listen to the wind through the trees and learn more about the past and present from interpretive signs along the trail.

The DeLonde Homestead from the spur trail.

MILES AND DIRECTIONS

0.0   Start from the Caribou Ranch Open Space trailhead bulletin board. Hike west on the DeLonde Trail. Elevation: 8,560 feet. GPS: N39 58.95' / W105 31.15'.

0.8   Trail junction with the old Switzerland Trail railroad bed. Turn right (north) here. An interpretive sign about the Switzerland Trail of America is a few paces down the road on the left side.

1.2   Junction of the DeLonde Trail and Blue Bird Loop Trail. Turn right (north) onto Blue Bird.

1.4   Junction with the Willow Carr Overlook Trail, which also goes to the DeLonde Homestead. Turn right (southeast) here to look around the homestead and read about willow carrs (a wooded, wetland ecosystem). A picnic table awaits you at the overlook. This spur is 0.2 mile out and back. Return the way you came, back to Blue Bird Loop Trail.

1.6   Turn right (north) to continue on Blue Bird Loop Trail.

1.8   An interpretive sign is on the right. The trail curves to the left here and becomes a single-track. Elevation: 8,540 feet (lowest spot). GPS: N39 59.44' / W105 31.78'.

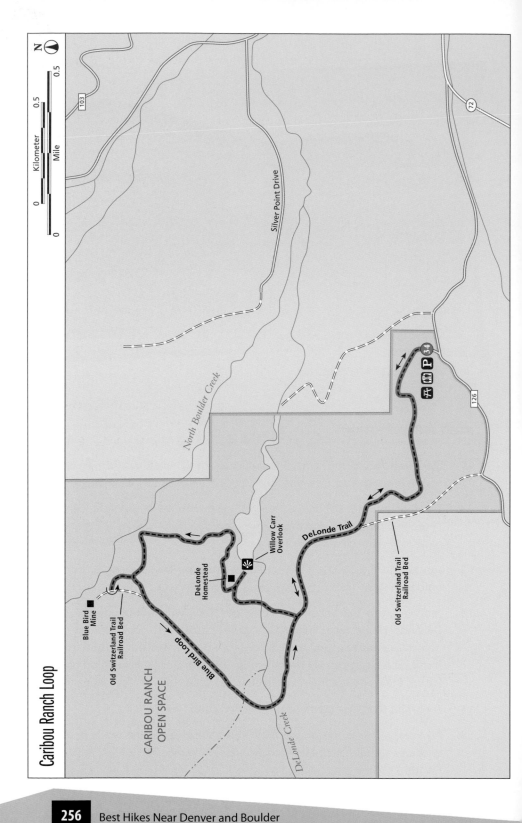

Caribou Ranch Loop

North Boulder Creek

Silver Point Drive

103

72

126

Blue Bird
Mine

Old Switzerland Trail
Railroad Bed

CARIBOU RANCH
OPEN SPACE

Blue Bird Loop

DeLonde Creek

DeLonde
Homestead

Willow Carr
Overlook

DeLonde Trail

Old Switzerland Trail
Railroad Bed

N

Kilometer
0   0.5
Mile
0   0.5

3.4
P

2.1 A very short spur trail on the right leads down to the banks of North Boulder Creek.

2.3 Junction with the spur trail to the Blue Bird Mine and interpretive signs. Turn right (north) to check out the old mining complex. Elevation: 8,720 feet. GPS: N39 59.76′ / W105 31.98′. This spur trail is 0.2 mile out and back. Return the way you came, back to Blue Bird Loop Trail.

2.5 Junction with Blue Bird Loop Trail. Turn right (southwest) to continue the loop.

2.6 The single-track trail rejoins the double-track Switzerland Trail railroad bed that comes in from the right here at a gate. Continue to the left.

3.4 Junction of DeLonde Trail and Blue Bird Loop Trail. Go straight ahead (east) onto DeLonde Trail.

3.8 DeLonde Trail turns left (east) and becomes a single-track trail back to the trailhead.

4.6 Arrive back at the trailhead.

Options

1. Hike to the Blue Bird Mine by turning left (west) at mile 1.2 above. Out and back to the mine is 4.4 miles, including the spur to the mine.
2. Hike to the DeLonde Homestead and Willow Carr Overlook only for a 3.0-mile out-and-back hike.

HIKE INFORMATION

Local Information: Town of Nederland; 303-258-3266; nederlandco.org
Local Events/Attractions: Carousel of Happiness, Nederland; 303-258-3457; carouselofhappiness.org
Frozen Dead Guy Days, Nederland; 303-763-0270, frozendeadguydays.org
Nederland High Peaks Art Festival; highpeaksartfestival.com
Peak to Peak Scenic Byway; codot.gov/travel/scenic-byways/north-central/peak-to-peak
Hike Tours: Boulder County Parks and Open Space, Longmont; 303-678-6214; bouldercountyopenspace.org
Organizations: Volunteer for Boulder County Parks and Open Space, Longmont; 303-678-6216; bouldercountyopenspace.org

Arapaho Glacier Trail 905

As you walk up the Arapaho Glacier Trail past treeline, a spectacular sight unfolds before your eyes. Jagged peaks on the spine of the Continental Divide suddenly appear above the rounded curve of the alpine tundra. Far below to the right is Boulder's beautiful Silver Lake Watershed, with its string of pristine lakes. The alpine tundra, rich with colorful wildflowers, stretches to the horizon. At the 2.5-mile viewpoint turnaround, you catch a glimpse of the remains of the Arapaho Glacier. Two additional options are offered here, depending on the weather and your preference.

Start: Rainbow Lakes Trailhead

Distance: 5.6 miles out and back

Hiking time: 2.5 to 3.5 hours

Difficulty: Difficult due to high elevation and steep sections of trail.

Elevation gain: 1,150 feet

Trail surface: Natural surface and rocky trail with some tree roots

Seasons: Late June through early Oct

Other trail users: Equestrians

Canine compatibility: Dogs must be on leash at all times.

Land status: National forest wilderness

Fees and permits: None required for day hikes. Permits required for overnight stays in Indian Peaks Wilderness June 1 to Sept 15. Permits are available from the Boulder Ranger District office in Boulder and the Sulphur Ranger District office in Granby. A permit form is downloadable at www.fs.usda.gov/recmain/arp/recreation, but it must be mailed in or brought in person to either ranger district office. This trail is in the Glacier Backcountry Zone.

Schedule: Open year-round, but the access road is closed about 4.3 miles from the trailhead around mid-Nov. The trail is neither marked nor maintained for winter use.

Maps: USGS Ward and Monarch Lake; National Geographic Trails Illustrated 102 Indian Peaks/Gold Hill; Latitude 40°: Boulder County Trails

Trail contact: Roosevelt National Forest, Boulder Ranger District, 2140 Yarmouth Avenue, Boulder; 303-541-2500; www.fs.usda.gov/recmain/arp/recreation

Other: Please observe Wilderness Regulations on this trail. Group size limited to twelve people and pack stock combined. No campfires allowed. The trail goes in and out of the watershed above treeline; the boundary is marked. Please stay on the trail. The City of Boulder patrols the Silver Lake Watershed and will ticket and fine trespassers.

Special considerations: This trail takes you above treeline, with danger of lightning from thunderstorms. Bring extra warm clothes, including gloves. The ever-present wind gets mighty chilly above treeline, even in summer. The road is closed in winter about 4.3 miles from the trailhead. Please observe all Wilderness Regulations. Bring plenty of water, as little to none is found on this trail.

Finding the trailhead: In Boulder, from 28th Street (US 36) and Canyon Boulevard (SH 119), head west on SH 119 for 18 miles to Nederland. Drive partway around the Nederland roundabout and turn right onto SH 72 West (toward Estes Park). Drive another 1.1 miles just north of mile marker 39 to the signed turnoff to Rainbow Lakes and the University of Colorado Mountain Research Station. Turn west (left) here onto Boulder County Road 116, a dirt road. Drive past the Sourdough Trailhead. In 0.8 mile the road forks—take the left branch, Forest Road 298. The winter closure gate is at this junction. At 4.3 miles the road forks with a four-wheel drive road—stay on the main road to the right. At 4.9 miles you'll enter Rainbow Lakes Campground. Drive through the campground and turn right into the semi-circular parking lot for the Rainbow Lakes Trailhead, before the west end of the campground. Do not park anywhere in the campground unless you are camping in one of the campsites. Day-hikers must use the trailhead parking lot. Vault toilets are near the trailhead, but bring your own water.

THE HIKE

About 0.3 mile up the Arapaho Glacier Trail, you'll enter the Indian Peaks Wilderness. The trail slowly climbs through a spruce/fir forest dotted with limber pines. As the trail curves north, notice the fence and signs about the Boulder Watershed on your right. After about 1.7 miles of fairly gentle hiking, the trail climbs more steeply through nine switchbacks into the ecotone between the subalpine and alpine life zones. Limber pines and Englemann spruces grow smaller, twisted and stunted by wicked winter winds. You're soon above treeline, with a broad expanse of tundra and a trail climbing before you.

At the first tundra switchback to the left, with a City of Boulder Watershed sign on the right, the featured hike ends with a view of Boulder's Silver Lake Watershed and the remains of the Arapaho Glacier, once the largest in Colorado. The amount of water that's available from this watershed depends on the level of snowpack in the nearby mountains and varies from one year to the next.

Three years after Boulder incorporated in 1871, citizens approved a bond issue to build a water-storage facility near the mouth of Boulder Canyon. As Boulder grew, so did its need for water. One real estate tycoon, James Maxwell,

35

The Indian Peaks above the Arapaho Glacier Trail.

held considerable land investments in Boulder and needed more water for his envisioned developments than the municipal water system could supply. He and George Oliver formed the Silver Lake Ditch and Reservoir Company (SLD&RC) in the 1880s. The company obtained land that included several natural lakes below the Arapaho Glacier, many miles from Boulder. They built small dams on the lower two lakes, Island Lake and Silver Lake, to increase their capacity. Water from these reservoirs flowed to Boulder in the Silver Lake Ditch.

Over the years, Boulder Creek carried increasing amounts of contaminants from growing human activity and mining operations into the town's municipal water system. Citizens demanded that the town leaders do something about the polluted water supply, and in 1902 the town council decided to move the intake for the water system farther upstream. By 1906, the SLD&RC had sold to Boulder the land below Arapaho Glacier that contained not only Silver Lake and Island Lake reservoirs, but also the higher lakes, Oval Lake (renamed Goose Lake) and Triple Lakes. The area became known as the Silver Lake Watershed.

Because of the previous pollution problems with its water supply, Boulder City Council wanted to protect the water quality in their watershed. After years of discussion, two congressional acts in 1919 and 1927 allowed Boulder to purchase federal lands in the Colorado National Forest in the Silver Lake Watershed, including the Arapaho Glacier. The City also purchased land from other owners, and now owns 8,500 acres in the area.

In the early 1900s, people loved to recreate in the watershed, skiing in winter and picnicking, fishing, and climbing in summer. To prevent water pollution by visitors, in 1911 Boulder hired a watershed caretaker. By 1920, after a cholera outbreak, the City closed the area to public use to protect not only water quality, but also wildlife habitat and the fragile alpine environment.

The Arapaho Glacier Trail skirts the southern boundary of the Silver Lake Watershed in the Roosevelt National Forest. Please stay on the trail to avoid trespassing in the watershed and a possible ticket and fine.

When the Indian Peaks Wilderness area was designated by Congress in 1978, the Silver Lake Watershed became a private thumb of land bordered by wilderness to the west and south. The Niwot Ridge Biosphere Reserve, established by the United Nations in 1979, is located to the north.

MILES AND DIRECTIONS

0.0   Start from the Rainbow Lakes Trailhead bulletin board. Elevation: 9,960 feet. GPS: N40 00.59' / W105 34.13'. Be sure to read and follow the regulations listed on the bulletin board. You'll start on the Rainbow Lakes Trail No. 918, heading right just after the bulletin board.

Looking east to the Foothills above Boulder.

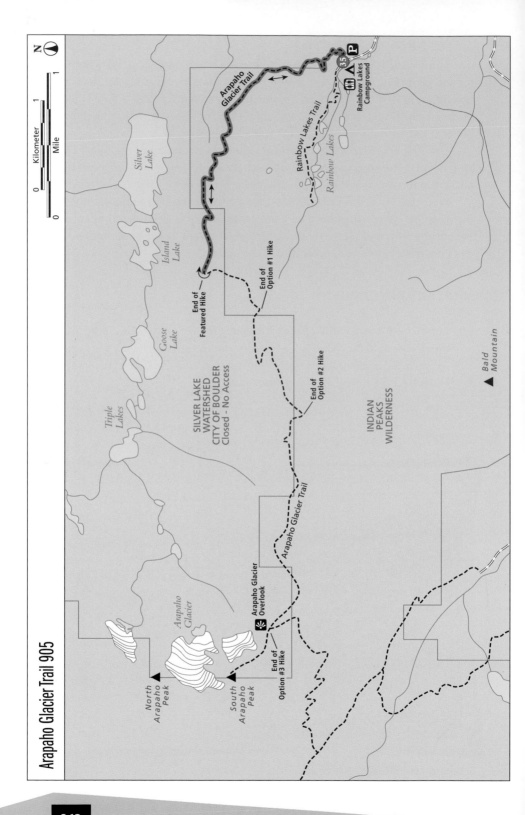

Arapaho Glacier Trail 905

Silver
Lake

Island
Lake

Triple
Lakes

Goose
Lake

North
Arapaho
Peak

Arapaho
Glacier

South
Arapaho
Peak

SILVER LAKE
WATERSHED
CITY OF BOULDER
Closed - No Access

INDIAN
PEAKS
WILDERNESS

Bald
Mountain

Arapaho Glacier
Overlook

End of
Option #3 Hike

Arapaho Glacier Trail

End of
Option #2 Hike

End of
Featured Hike

End of
Option #1 Hike

Arapaho
Glacier Trail

Rainbow Lakes Trail

Rainbow Lakes

Rainbow Lakes
Campground

N

Kilometer

0   1

Mile

0   1

0.3 Junction with the Arapaho Glacier Trail. Turn right onto this trail and soon enter the Indian Peaks Wilderness. GPS: N40 00.69' / W105 34.23'. The trail climbs up to the right of the rocky drainage.

1.7 After this left switchback, the trail climbs more steeply, with eight more switchbacks.

2.5 The trail climbs above treeline. Keep an eye and ear out for thunderstorms!

2.8 Viewpoint of the Silver Lake Watershed at the left switchback near the sign denoting the City of Boulder Watershed boundary. This is the turnaround point for the featured hike. Elevation: 11,120 feet. GPS: N40 01.37' / W105 35.92'. Return the way you came.

5.6 Arrive back at the trailhead.

Options

1. If the weather is fine, hike another 0.5 mile from the turnaround at mile 2.8 above for a nice view south to Pikes Peak and east to the plains. This option adds 1.0 mile to your hike.

2. For a Most-Difficult 8.5-mile out-and-back hike with a 2,350-foot gain, from the turnaround at mile 2.8, continue up the trail another 1.75 miles to where the trail crosses a saddle and starts to traverse onto the southern side of the ridge. Turn around at a right switchback where the trail starts to climb up the next ridge. Elevation: 12,320 feet. GPS: N40 00.79' / W105 36.95'.

3. For a strenuous 12.0-mile out-and-back hike with a 2,750-foot gain, from the turnaround at mile 2.8, continue another 3.5 miles and 1,600 feet to the Arapaho Glacier overlook at 12,720 feet.

HIKE INFORMATION

Local Information: Boulder Convention and Visitors Bureau; 303-442-2911; bouldercoloradousa.com
Boulder Chamber of Commerce; 303-442-1044; boulderchamber.com
Local Events/Attractions: Peak to Peak Scenic Byway; codot.gov/travel/scenic-byways/north-central/peak-to-peak
Organizations: Indian Peaks Wilderness Alliance, Boulder; indianpeakswilderness.org
Colorado Mountain Club Boulder Group, Boulder; 303-554-7688; cmcboulder.org
University of Colorado Mountain Research Station, Nederland; 303-492-8842; colorado.edu/mrs

The North American record for the most snowfall in a 24-hour period—76 inches—was set at Silver Lake on April 14–15, 1921. The snowstorm lasted 28 hours, dumping a total of 86 inches of snow.

No Longer a Glacier

A glacier is by definition a slowly moving mass or river of ice. Over the past 10,000 years since the last period of glaciation, the Arapaho Glacier has been slowly shrinking, except during the Little Ice Age, which occurred from the fourteenth to the mid-nineteenth century.

"Over the last couple of decades, and especially over the last 10 years, we have entered a period of warming and retreat that is as great, or greater, than any we know of since the end of the last ice age [10,000 years ago]," said glaciologist Tad Pfeffer of the University of Colorado's Institute of Arctic and Alpine Research (INSTAAR) in "Front Range glaciers are melting," by Jim Erickson, Scripps Howard News Service (November 7, 2004).

According to an article in the *Boulder Daily Camera* on December 2, 2007, the Arapaho Glacier was downgraded to a permanent snowfield status (no longer sliding downhill) in 1998.

Black Bear/Horseshoe Loop—Golden Gate Canyon State Park

Constant surprises and interesting twists occur along this trail as it climbs up toward Ralston Roost and then drops through an aspen forest and flower-filled meadows. Back-country sites offer a close-to-home camping opportunity in this area. A side spur takes you to the remains of John Frazer's barn and the beautiful meadow where he grew vegetables. This area is close to Denver, yet seems so remote while you are hiking here. The rocky ridges around Ralston Roost provide views of the Continental Divide and fun hiking. Different seasons bring new varieties of flowers and colors to the meadows.

Start: Black Bear/Ralston Roost Trailhead
Distance: 5.4-mile loop
Hiking time: 2.5 to 3.5 hours
Difficulty: Difficult due to elevation gain and the rockiness of Black Bear Trail
Elevation gain: 1,370 feet total
Trail surface: Natural surface and rocky trail
Seasons: Best late May through Oct
Other trail users: Hikers only, except for multiple use on Mule Deer Trail
Canine compatibility: Dogs must be on a 6-foot leash at all times.
Land status: Colorado state park
Fees and permits: Daily fee or annual state parks pass required.

Backcountry camping permit (fee charged) required for overnight camping.
Schedule: Open year-round
Maps: USGS Black Hawk; National Geographic Trails Illustrated 100 Boulder/Golden; Latitude 40°: Colorado Front Range
Trail contact: Golden Gate Canyon State Park, 92 Crawford Gulch Road, Golden; 303-582-3707; cpw.state.co.us/placestogo/parks/goldengatecanyon
Special considerations: No fires are allowed in the backcountry. Bring your own water, as little to none is available along the trail.

Finding the trailhead: In Golden, from the mouth of Clear Creek Canyon at the junction of SH 93, SH 58, and US 6, drive north on SH 93 heading toward Boulder. In 1.3 miles turn left onto Golden Gate Canyon Road. Drive 12.5 miles up Golden Gate Canyon Road (ignore all side roads) to the entrance fee station on the right and pay the daily fee. In 0.1 mile turn right onto Crawford Gulch Road. The Golden Gate State Park Visitor Center is 0.1 mile on the right and has restrooms and water. The Black Bear/Ralston Roost Trailhead is 0.2 mile past the Visitor Center on Crawford Gulch Road. Parking lots are on both the left and right sides of the road. No facilities are available at the trailhead.

THE HIKE

In 1850, Lewis Ralston headed through Kansas Territory to the California goldfields. At a campsite in present-day Arvada, he found gold flakes in his pan in a creek that now bears his name. Some miners, disappointed by their luck in California, returned to Kansas Territory, remembering Ralston's discovery. One group found gold near the confluence of Cherry Creek and the South Platte, and some group members then headed west.

In 1859, John H. Gregory started systematically panning for gold in Clear Creek and its tributaries. In a gulch west of North Clear Creek he found a lode of gold, not just flakes in a creek. Gregory's Diggings were located on the border between today's Central City and Black Hawk. In those days, roads were few and far between. The Gregory Toll Road was built from Golden to Gregory's Diggings. Much of Golden Gate Canyon Road follows this old route.

Not everyone liked the rough mining life. A few people realized that miners needed food and wood, and around Ralston Creek they found suitable land to raise vegetables and cut lumber to sell to the miners. One such person was John Frazer; you'll see what remains of his barn on this hike. An interpretive sign describes his life from 1868 to 1896.

In 1920, Charles Greenfield moved his family to a 320-acre homestead near a spring and an intermittent brook east and downstream of Frazer's homestead. He built a three-room log cabin near the spring for his wife and three children, and later a cow barn with hayloft, a horse barn, a chicken coop, and an icehouse.

Looking back across the canyon to the south from the Black Bear Trail.

The forested acreage became pasture and a firewood source. The family cleared about 20 acres for crops on soil Greenfield thought would best produce, but the short summers at 9,000 feet limited what could be grown. Area farmers typically grew potatoes, rutabagas, turnips, lettuce, peas, hay, barley, and oats. The Greenfields raised a few cows, horses, a pig, and some chickens. Rabbits and grouse often ended up on the dinner table accompanied by potatoes. Deer and elk were seldom seen, their population decimated for food for the mining camps. The farm animals provided eggs, cream, and milk.

Any produce that the family didn't need was taken to a neighboring house 2 miles away on Golden Gate Canyon Road. These neighbors, the Bohees, then drove to Golden and Denver to sell the local produce. Money earned purchased flour, kerosene, and other necessities. Greenfield's wife, Clara, also made cottage cheese and cream puffs, which she sold to restaurants in Central City.

This hike starts on the Black Bear Trail, which provides a surprise at every curve as it winds its way up a ridge of rock outcroppings toward Ralston Roost. Occasionally, the Continental Divide comes into view between lodgepole pines. In places, the trail takes you up rock slabs or ledges with good places for feet and hands. Watch for trail posts that show the way. Stickers on the Black Bear Trail posts have a black bear paw on them with BLACK BEAR printed below.

Heading down from the top viewpoint, you'll walk along a narrow rocky ridge reminiscent of a stegosaurus's back. Along the Mule Deer Trail and Horseshoe Trail, colorful wildflowers bloom profusely in the meadows and aspen

View of Mount Bancroft and James Peak from a rocky outcrop on the Black Bear Trail.

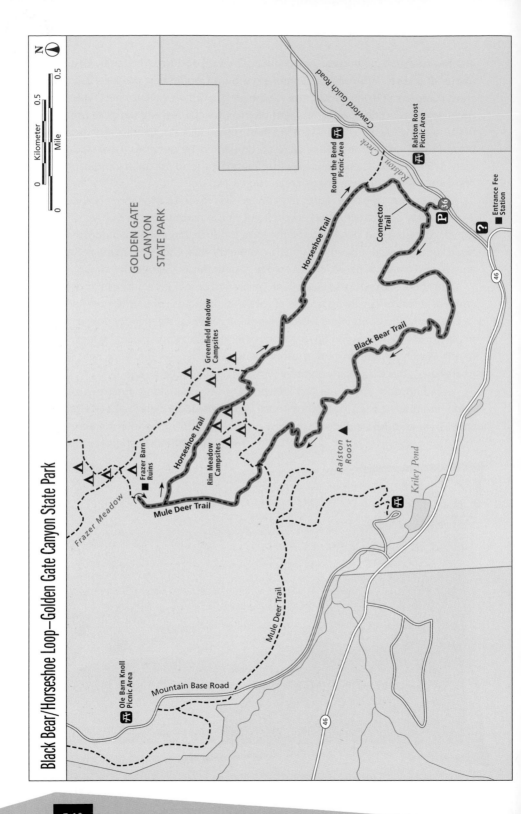

Black Bear/Horseshoe Loop–Golden Gate Canyon State Park

GOLDEN GATE
CANYON
STATE PARK

Frazer Meadow

Ole Barn Knoll
Picnic Area

Mountain Base Road

Mule Deer Trail

Frazer Barn
Ruins

Horseshoe Trail

Greenfield Meadow
Campsites

Rim Meadow
Campsites

Mule Deer Trail

Ralston
Roost

Kriley Pond

Horseshoe Trail

Round the Bend
Picnic Area

Ralston Creek

Crawford Gulch Road

Ralston Roost
Picnic Area

Connector
Trail

Black Bear Trail

Entrance Fee
Station

46

36

N

Kilometer
0   0.5

Mile
0   0.5

groves glow brilliant gold in fall. The Horseshoe Trail occasionally crosses the old road that accessed the Greenfield homestead. Not far off the Horseshoe Trail, you can camp overnight at Rim Meadow or Greenfield Meadow campsites. A perfect way to experience the beauty of this land is to hike during different seasons.

MILES AND DIRECTIONS

0.0   Start from the Black Bear/Ralston Roost Trailhead. Hike up the Black Bear Trail. Elevation: 8,200 feet. GPS: N39 49.98′ / W105 24.52′.

0.1   Junction of Black Bear Trail with the connecting trail to Horseshoe Trail. Continue left up the Black Bear Trail.

0.75   Trail sign says to follow trail markers through rock outcroppings ahead. The trail is well-marked and does cross a number of rocky stretches. The craggy rocks of Ralston Roost appear as you twist and turn up the trail.

2.0   The trail climbs through some slanting rock faces, so keep an eye open for the trail markers. At the top of the rocky trail, look a few feet off the trail to the left for a good view of the Continental Divide and Ralston Roost from a rocky outcropping. Elevation: 9,480 feet. GPS: N39 50.38′ / W105 25.45′.

2.1   The trail follows a narrow ridge with upstanding rocks, like the plates on a stegosaurus's back. From here the trail drops steadily through some rocky sections, then through a lodgepole pine, Douglas fir, and aspen forest.

2.5   Junction with the trail to Rim Meadow campsites. Stay on the trail to the left and you'll intersect the Mule Deer Trail in about 50 feet. Turn right onto Mule Deer. GPS: N39 50.56′ / W105 25.59′. This section of trail is open to mountain bikers, equestrians, and hikers.

3.0   Junction of the Mule Deer and Horseshoe Trails. Continue straight ahead on Mule Deer to Frazer Meadow and remains of the Frazer barn.

3.1   Interpretive sign by the remains of the old barn in Frazer Meadow. Elevation: 9,040 feet. GPS: N39 50.95′ / W105 25.72′. Once you've finished reading and exploring, return the way you came to the junction with Horseshoe Trail (mile 3.0).

3.2   Junction of the Mule Deer and Horseshoe Trails. Turn left onto Horseshoe and head downhill through aspens and flower-filled meadows. The Horseshoe Trail is hikers-only.

3.8   Junction with a trail to the Rim Meadow campsites. Continue straight ahead on Horseshoe Trail.

3.95   Junction with a trail to the Greenfield Meadow campsites. Continue straight ahead on Horseshoe Trail.

5.0   Junction of Horseshoe Trail and the connecting trail to Black Bear Trail. Turn right here and cross the little creek, then head up the ridge. GPS: N39 50.22' / W105 24.42'.

5.3   Junction with Black Bear Trail and the connecting trail to Horseshoe Trail. Turn left and head downhill on the Black Bear Trail.

5.4   Arrive back at the trailhead.

Option
For a shorter, moderate, 4.6-mile out-and-back hike to Frazer Meadow, turn right at mile 0.1 and hike over to the Horseshoe Trail. Turn left onto Horseshoe and hike to the Mule Deer Trail. Turn right to the interpretive sign by the Frazer barn. This hike is mile 3.1 to mile 5.4 above in reverse. Return the way you came.

HIKE INFORMATION

Local Information: Greater Golden Chamber of Commerce, Golden; 303-279-3113; goldencochamber.org
Gilpin Historical Society, Central City; 303-582-5283; gilpinhistory.org
Local Events/Attractions: Colorado Railroad Museum, Golden; 800-365-6263, 303-279-4591; coloradorailroadmuseum.org
Central City Opera House, Central City; 303-292-6700; centralcityopera.org
Organizations: Friends of Golden Gate Canyon State Park, Golden; friendsofcoloradostateparks.com
The Colorado Parks Foundation, Denver; 303-818-8078; coloradoparksfoundation.org

> **Green Tip:**
> *Never let your dog chase wildlife. It is illegal in Colorado for dogs to chase or harass wildlife, including chipmunks and squirrels.*

Friends of Golden Gate Canyon State Park

The Friends of Golden Gate Canyon State Park help the park by providing volunteer and financial assistance. They aid in the purchase of land and conservation easements around the park, which increases recreation opportunities. The group also helps provide financial support for State Historical Fund restoration projects. Development and maintenance of trails keep volunteers busy, as do interpretive and environmental education programs. The Friends group also advocates for Golden Gate State Park and all state parks with legislators, agencies, and boards at both the state and county levels. To find out more information about Friends of Golden Gate Canyon State, contact the Visitor Center at 303-582-3707.

A variety of Colorado blue columbine.

Mount Goliath Natural Area contains subalpine and alpine ecosystems along Mount Evans Road. The M. Walter Pesman Trail winds and climbs through an ancient bristlecone pine forest (some trees are over 1,500 years old) in the Natural Area. It crosses alpine tundra with fantastic tiny wildflowers (peak bloom is in mid-July) to the upper trailhead. To return, hike a little higher on the Alpine Garden Loop 49 for spectacular 360-degree views, then rejoin the Pesman Trail. End your hike by exploring the Bristlecone Loop Trail and Interpretive Gardens by the Dos Chappell Nature Center.

Start: Lower Mount Goliath Trailhead interpretive poster behind the Dos Chappell Nature Center

Distance: 2.5 miles out and back, with two little half-loops

Hiking time: 1.5 to 3 hours

Difficulty: Difficult due to altitude

Elevation gain: 680 feet

Trail surface: Natural surface and rocky trail

Seasons: Best late June through Sept (Mount Evans Road must be open)

Other trail users: Hikers only

Canine compatibility: Dogs must be on leash

Land status: National forest

Fees and permits: A daily Recreation Amenity fee, a valid season pass, "America the Beautiful" National Parks and Federal Recreation Pass, Access pass, or Senior pass required if stopping at the Mount Goliath Natural Area, Summit Lake, or the Mount Evans summit.

Schedule: Mount Evans Road is closed for the winter starting the first Monday in Oct or after the first major snowfall.

Maps: USGS Idaho Springs; National Geographic Trails Illustrated 104 Idaho Springs/Loveland Pass; Latitude 40°: Colorado Front Range Trails

Trail contact: Arapaho National Forest, Clear Creek Ranger District, Idaho Springs Visitor Center, 2060 Miner Street, Idaho Springs; 303-567-4382; www.fs.usda.gov/detail/arp

Special considerations: Much of this hike is above treeline, so plan your trip to avoid thunderstorms and lightning. Bring extra warm clothes, including gloves. The ever-present wind gets mighty chilly above treeline, even in summer. No water is available along the trail.

Finding the trailhead: From I-70, take exit 240, Mt Evans/SH 103. Drive on SH 103 about 13.0 miles to SH 5, Mount Evans Road (Mount Evans Scenic Byway), by Echo Lake Lodge. Turn right onto Mount Evans Road, drive to the entrance station, and pay the fee. Continue driving up the twisty road 2.9 miles to the Lower Mount Goliath Trailhead and the Dos Chappell Nature Center. Vault toilets, but no water, are available at the nature center. For the optional point-to-point hike with a car shuttle, drive to the Upper Mount Goliath trailhead, another 1.8 miles up Mount Evans Road. Trailhead parking is on the left side of the road. No facilities are available.

THE HIKE

The Mount Evans area harbors a very large stand of bristlecone pine trees, which grow where the weather is harsh and the soil is rocky. Some of these twisted and contorted trees are over 1,500 years old! The USDA Forest Service (USFS) set aside 160 acres of this ancient forest as a Research Natural Area (RNA) many years ago. The RNA is protected from development and most human use, so scientists are able to study an "untouched" area.

In the 1950s, the Denver Botanic Gardens (DBG) developed a program of "planned altitude units" and surveyed potential areas. The area near Mount Goliath RNA appeared to be a perfect match. DBG approached the USFS, and they formed a partnership for the Alpine Unit. They built a trail along the flank of Goliath Peak, allowing people to see the bristlecone pines and the abundant subalpine and alpine tundra flowers along the route. About 0.5 mile of the trail is in the RNA. In August 1962, DBG and the USFS dedicated the M. Walter Pesman Alpine Trail. Mount Goliath was designated a Colorado Natural Area in 1980.

M. Walter Pesman arrived in Fort Collins, Colorado, in 1908. A native of the Netherlands, he earned his BS degree in horticulture from Colorado State College (now University) in 1910. Although his career revolved around landscape architecture, he loved the native flora of Colorado. He wrote the first Colorado wildflower identification book geared to laypeople instead of botanists. In *Meet the Natives*, he separated flowers by colors and by the life zones in which they were usually found. DBG's board of trustees named the trail at Mount Goliath in Pesman's honor in appreciation of his many years teaching the general public about plants and his love of natural landscapes and native plants.

Over the years, the Pesman Trail deteriorated as a result of the elements and general use, but in 1996 the Garden Club of Denver made a three-year commitment to repair the trail and to develop guided tours. Volunteers for Outdoor Colorado (VOC) pitched in with manual labor to fix the trail. The USFS trail crew worked on the more difficult sections. A new trail was built

Bristlecone forest on the Bristlecone Loop Trail.

through the first part of the bristlecone forest—a fairly level and easy trail, semi-friendly to wheelchairs, so people unable to hike the Pesman Trail can still see and enjoy the ancient trees. Money from the Mount Evans fee demo project was combined with funds raised by DBG and the Garden Club to pay for these projects.

Before starting your hike, stop in the nature center and look at the interpretive displays and exhibits. As you hike the Pesman Trail, notice that Engelmann spruce also live here with colorful yellow cinquefoil, bright red Indian paintbrush, fuzzy purple fringe, white chickweed, and blue Jacob's ladder. As you climb toward treeline, small bristlecones next to the trail provide a closer glimpse of needles and cones. The flowers grow smaller, too. Please stay on the trail, because the tundra is very fragile. Plants may grow only a ¼ inch in one year and are easily damaged by hikers' shoes! The "big" yellow sunflowers are old-man-of-the-mountain. Purple sky pilot, yellow cinquefoil, white American bistort, alpine phlox, and little sage line the trail. Occasionally look behind you for a view of the eastern plains south of Denver.

Once above treeline, you're exposed to the ever-present wind. Be sure to bring extra layers with you, as it's mighty chilly at 12,000 feet. Come often to this trail and the bristlecones. Various weather conditions change the feel of the area—get to know it in all its different moods.

Approaching the Alpine Garden Loop from the M. Walter Pesman Trail.

MILES AND DIRECTIONS

0.0   Start at the LOWER MOUNT GOLIATH TRAILHEAD interpretive sign behind the Dos Chappell Nature Center. Start hiking on the M. Walter Pesman Trail, which goes straight ahead through the interpretive gardens. Elevation: 11,540 feet. GPS: N39 38.56' / W105 35.56'.

0.1   Intersection with Bristlecone Loop Trail. Continue straight ahead and head uphill on the Pesman Trail.

0.3   What looks like a trail comes in from the right (it goes to a little overlook). Continue to the left around the switchback.

0.75   The trail makes a short right switchback and seems to disappear. It then makes an immediate left switchback.

0.9   You're basically above treeline.

1.0   Trail junction with the Alpine Garden Loop 49. Continue to the left to the upper trailhead.

1.2   Arrive at the Upper Mount Goliath Trailhead. On your return, hike up the Alpine Garden Trail 49 to the left of the interpretive sign. Elevation: 12,152 feet. GPS: N39 37.98' / W105 36.24'.

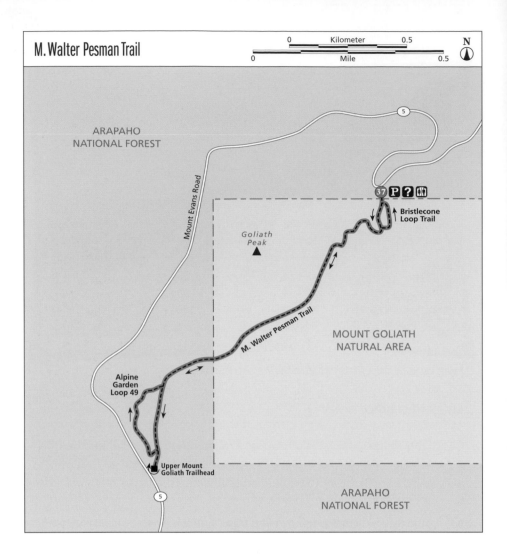

1.4 Reach the top of the ridge and enjoy the great 360-degree view. Elevation: 12,220 feet. GPS: N39 38.12' / W105 36.26'.

1.5 Junction with the M. Walter Pesman Trail. Turn left onto the Pesman Trail and head downhill the way you came.

2.4 Junction with the Bristlecone Loop. Turn right onto Bristlecone.

2.5 Arrive back at the trailhead.

Option

For a shorter, moderate, 1.2-mile point-to-point hike going downhill, start at the Upper Mount Goliath Trailhead. Elevation loss is 612 feet. Start your hike at mile 1.2 above and follow the directions in reverse.

HIKE INFORMATION

Local Information: Clear Creek County Tourism Bureau, Idaho Springs; 303-567-4660, 866-674-9237; clearcreekcounty.org

Local Events/Attractions: Mount Evans Scenic Byway, Clear Creek County Tourism Bureau, Idaho Springs; 303-567-4660, 866-674-9237; clearcreekcounty.org/scenic-drives

Argo Gold Mine & Mill, Idaho Springs; 303-567-2421; historicargotours.com

Phoenix Gold Mine, Idaho Springs; 303-567-0422; phoenixmine.com

Indian Hot Springs, Idaho Springs; 303-989-6666; indianhotsprings.com

Hike Tours: Free interpretive wildflower hikes are offered by the Denver Botanic Gardens from the end of June through early Aug on certain days. Call 720-865-3501 for details and to make a required reservation; botanicgardens.org/outreach/mount-goliath-wildflower-hikes

Organizations: Denver Botanic Gardens; 720-865-3500; botanicgardens.org

Mount Evans Volunteers, Arapaho National Forest, Clear Creek Ranger District, Idaho Springs; 303-567-4382; www.fs.usda.gov/detail/arp

Bristlecone Pines

Pinus aristata, bristlecone pines, have witnessed many happenings in their 1,500- to 2,000-year life spans. Contorted by wind, often polished on one side by ice crystals and blowing dirt, it's hard to imagine how they survive. Bristlecones grow in windy areas in coarse, rocky soils where the slope is sunny, dry, well-drained, and prone to cold temperatures and frost. Reasonably easy to spot, they sport fairly dense needles that come in packets of five and produce a brushlike effect, thus the name "bristle." The needles are no longer than 2 inches and usually have sticky resin drops on them.

During tough years, bristlecones may shut off nutrients to a branch or two, killing the branch to save the rest of the tree. Another survival secret is slow growth, which produces very dense wood that protects the tree from fire, insects, and diseases. Even after death, the twisted, contorted ghost trees attract photographers and artists with their interesting shapes and gray-to-brown-to-black hues. Take a moment to be quiet with these trees that have seen so many changes in their lives. Be kind and don't damage them—let them continue to live, much longer than any human ever will.

The relatively gentle "climb" of 13,132-foot Mount Flora along the Mount Flora Trail section of the Continental Divide National Scenic Trail passes through the old Berthoud Pass Ski Area then into the "Land Above the Trees." The trail wanders in and out of the James Peak Wilderness. The miniature world of the alpine tundra will dazzle you with a carpet of tiny, colorful wildflowers surviving in a harsh place. The 360-degree views from Mount Flora's summit range from the expansive flatness of the eastern plains, to valleys with beautiful alpine lakes, to peaks as far as you can see.

Start: Big Continental Divide Trail kiosk in the parking lot at the east side of Berthoud Pass summit
Distance: 6.4 miles out and back
Hiking time: 2.5 to 3.5 hours
Difficulty: Most Difficult due to elevation gain and altitude
Elevation gain: 1,817 feet
Trail surface: Dirt road (closed to the motorized public), and natural surface and rocky trail
Seasons: Late June through early Oct
Other trail users: Equestrians; mountain bikers on road only
Canine compatibility: Dogs must be on leash
Land status: National forest wilderness
Fees and permits: None required
Schedule: Open year-round
Maps: USGS Berthoud Pass and Empire; National Geographic Trails Illustrated 104 Idaho Springs/ Loveland Pass; Latitude 40°: Colorado Front Range Trails
Trail contacts: Arapaho National Forest, Clear Creek Ranger District, Idaho Springs Visitor Center, 2060 Miner Street, Idaho Springs; 303-567-4382; www.fs.usda.gov/ detail/arp. James Peak Wilderness Fact Sheet available at wilderness. net; click on Find a Wilderness, and List by Name to select "J" then James Peak Wilderness.
Other: Please stay on Mines Peak Road and do not bushwhack up the open ski slopes. Be careful when walking on the trail across the alpine tundra—the plants are very fragile. They must grow, bloom, and reproduce in about six short weeks of summer. When the same plant is trampled by many boots, it dies.
Special considerations: This trail takes you above treeline, with danger of lightning from thunderstorms. Bring extra warm clothes, including gloves. The ever-present wind gets mighty chilly above treeline, even in summer. This area is prone to avalanches in winter. The trail is neither marked nor maintained for winter use. The James Peak Wilderness limits

group size to twelve people and stock combined; campfires are prohibited. Follow Leave No Trace

techniques on this trail. Bring plenty of water, as little to none is found on the trail.

Finding the trailhead: From I-70, exit 232, US 40 / West Empire and Granby, drive 14.4 miles west on US 40 to the top of Berthoud Pass and the Berthoud Pass Trailhead. You'll pass through Empire on the way. Turn right (east) and park in the parking lot. A warming hut with vault restrooms is located at the north end of the parking lot. The trail starts at the Continental Divide Trail kiosk near the warming hut and behind the BERTHOUD PASS sign.

THE HIKE

Heading up Mount Flora Trail on Mines Peak Road (FR 239) gives you a chance to chat with your buddies and wake up. The road leads to the communications complex at the top of Colorado Mines Peak (12,493 feet). On the north side of Mines Peak Road is part of the old Berthoud Pass Ski Area, which opened in 1937. One of the first major ski areas in Colorado, an 848-foot rope tow powered by a V-8 engine moved skiers uphill. In 1947, the area boasted the first double chairlift in the state. The base lodge at the top of the pass contained a ski shop, restaurant, and cafeteria, and it remained open during the summer for tourists.

A series of misfortunes befell the ski area in 1988 and 1991, resulting in the owners filing for bankruptcy. The area reopened in January 1998, but by 2001 it could no longer compete with the larger resorts. It remained open as a powder cat operation for a couple of years, but in 2003 the owners decided to end operations and removed the ski lifts that summer. They demolished the base lodge and rehabilitated the site in 2005.

This section of the Continental Divide National Scenic Trail (CDNST) is named Mount Flora Trail. When you come to the fourth switchback on the road going up Colorado Mines Peak, look straight ahead to see the trail sign at the lip of the road. Once on the single-track CDNST, you'll contour around the peak through spruce-fir forest. Near the trail sign are some of the old concrete footings for a chairlift. As the trail curves to the east, it climbs steadily through the ecotone where subalpine forest and alpine tundra meet. The trees grow sparser and smaller in this exposed land where the winds blow harder, creating lower temperatures. The mean summer temperature is usually less than 50°F. Speaking of wind, a chilly breeze often blows over these high spaces, and rare is the day when you can sit on the summit without wearing a jacket.

Mount Flora.

Finally, you are in the land above the trees, with its miniature plants and flowers that somehow survive a summer that may only last for six weeks. The flowers bloom brilliantly after the Fourth of July. Perhaps the carpet of teeny flowers gave Mount Flora its name. Patches of blue forget-me-nots grow along the trail, accompanied by grayish-green stalks of alpine sage, the bright yellow of alpine avens and cinquefoil, pink moss campion, white alpine phlox, yellow paintbrush, and bistort. Plants such as the moss campion grow in cushions for protection against wind and ice particles. Their taproots may reach 4 to 5 feet underground to find moisture and anchor against the winds. The moss campion grows slowly—about a quarter inch a year. The big golden sunflowers that tower over the smaller plants are old-man-of-the-mountain. These "giants" take several years to gather and store enough energy to bloom. Once the flower fades away, the plant dies.

For all their apparent toughness, alpine plants are quite fragile. Frequent trampling by boots can destroy them. A piece of paper covering a small cushion plant may deny it the energy needed to make it through the winter. Please stay on the trail. If you do need to walk across alpine tundra, do so on rocks as much as possible, and spread your group out so no two footsteps land on the same plant.

Past the saddle at mile 1.6, the trail meanders in and out of the James Peak Wilderness. Mount Flora's summit is in this wilderness area.

MILES AND DIRECTIONS

0.0   Start from the Continental Divide Trail kiosk near the warming hut at the northeast end of the parking lot at the east side of Berthoud Pass summit. The trail starts here and traverses the slope above the parking lot. Elevation: 11,315 feet. GPS: N39 47.90' / W105 46.56'.

380 feet   The trail merges with Mines Peak Road (Forest Road 239). Turn left and walk up the dirt road.

0.85   As you approach the fourth switchback (curves to the right), look straight ahead to find the CDNST sign. The hike continues on the single-track trail. GPS: N39 47.80' / W105 46.32'.

1.6   The trail reaches a saddle, then starts climbing the ridge of the Continental Divide.

2.7   The trail climbs a little boulder bump. Look to the right for stone steps and a cairn as you head up the boulders.

3.2   The summit of Mount Flora, which is flat enough that it's hard to determine the top. Look to your left for a rock-wall shelter, especially if it's windy. You are in the James Peak Wilderness. Elevation: 13,132 feet. Rock shelter at N39 48.29' / W105 44.13'. Return the way you came.

6.4   Arrive back at the trailhead

Ascending the Continental Divide from the saddle on the Mount Flora Trail.

Mount Flora Trail

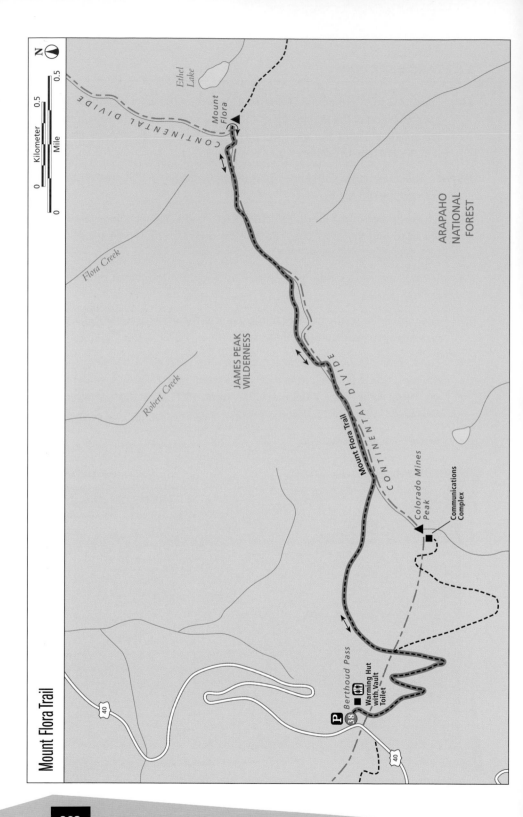

N

| 0 | Kilometer | 0.5 |
| 0 | Mile | 0.5 |

CONTINENTAL DIVIDE

Ethel Lake

Mount Flora

Flora Creek

Robert Creek

JAMES PEAK WILDERNESS

Mount Flora Trail

CONTINENTAL DIVIDE

Colorado Mines Peak

Communications Complex

ARAPAHO NATIONAL FOREST

Berthoud Pass

Warming Hut with Vault Toilet

P
38

40

40

HIKE INFORMATION

Local Information: Clear Creek County Chamber Bureau, Idaho Springs; 303-567-4660, 866-674-9237; clearcreekcounty.org

Local Events/Attractions: Argo Gold Mine & Mill, Idaho Springs; 303-567-2421; historicargotours.com

Indian Hot Springs, Idaho Springs; 303-989-6666; indianhotsprings.com

Organizations: Continental Divide Trail Coalition, Pine; 303-996-2759; continentaldividetrail.org

Continental Divide Trail Society, Baltimore, MD; 410-235-9610; cdtsociety.org

Indian Peaks Wilderness Alliance, Boulder; indianpeakswilderness.org

Charles Christopher Parry, an eminent botanist in the late 1800s, named Mount Flora—perhaps for the alpine wildflowers, his favorite. In summer 1861, he collected over 417 species of plants in Colorado. He also named Grays Peak and Torreys Peak after his contemporaries, botanists Asa Gray and John Torrey.

Arctic gentian on the slopes of Mount Flora.

The Continental Divide National Scenic Trail

Benton Mackaye, founder of the Appalachian Trail, first proposed the Continental Divide National Scenic Trail (CDNST) in 1966. A congressionally authorized study reported that trail users would access great scenery, various ecosystems and life zones, and historical areas while crossing twenty-five national forests and three national parks (Glacier, Yellowstone, and Rocky Mountain).

In 1978, Congress designated a National Scenic Trail along the Continental Divide, snaking from the Canadian border across Montana, Wyoming, Colorado, and New Mexico to the Mexican border. Because some ridges on the actual Divide might be difficult and/or dangerous, a 50-mile wide corridor on either side could be used for the trail. Approximately 1,900 miles of trails and seldom-used roads shaped the initial configuration of the 3,100-mile trail. Most of the trail was designated as closed to motor vehicles.

Congress gave the USDA Forest Service responsibility for coordinating the completion of the trail. Even though existing trails would be used in places, many miles needed maintenance or improvement. Proposed routes crossed private property in some areas, requiring negotiations with landowners for either purchase or access of the trail corridor.

About 72 percent of the CDNST has been completed, but many miles of existing trail needs repair, rerouting for environmental protection, or removal from roads.

Griffin Monument

The old wagon road (nonmotorized) to the 7:30 Mine climbs steadily above Silver Plume, past relics of the silver boom of the 1880s. Bristlecone pines, lodgepole pines, and aspens line the trail. After 1.5 miles, the trail becomes narrower, and occasionally you'll have to negotiate a side-sloping, slippery route. Local residents have been working hard to improve and maintain the trail, which is not easy at this altitude on steep terrain. The Griffin Monument obelisk stands on a rock outcropping below the 7:30 Mine Road near the upper mouth of Brown Gulch. A little farther up the narrow trail are two rusting boilers from the 7:30 Mine, the remains of which lie across the creek.

Start: Trailhead at the top of Silver Street on the north side of Silver Plume

Distance: 3.7 miles out and back

Hiking time: 1.5 to 2.5 hours

Difficulty: Most Difficult due to elevation gain in short distance, steepness, and exposure.

Elevation gain: 1,110 feet

Seasons: Best mid-June through mid-Oct

Trail surface: Natural surface trail and old road (closed to the motorized public)

Other trail users: Mountain bikers and equestrians

Canine compatibility: Dogs must be on leash

Land status: County right-of-way, Historic District public lands

Fees and permits: None required

Maps: USGS Georgetown; National Geographic Trails Illustrated 104 Idaho Springs/Loveland Pass

Trail contact: George Rowe Museum, 315 Main Street, Silver Plume; 303-569-2562 (summer season)

Other: Be sure to bring water with you. The trail is a County right-of-way and crosses numerous private mining claims, so please stay on it.

Special considerations: The trail crosses at least one avalanche path (Cherokee Creek). Hunters use this area during hunting season.

Finding the trailhead: From I-70 exit 226, Silver Plume, turn right (north) and drive about 0.1 mile to Main Street. Turn right (east) on Main Street and drive about 0.1 mile, where you can park between Silver Street and Jefferson Street. The trailhead is 0.1 mile uphill (north) on Silver Street from Main Street. Look for the 7:30 MINE ROAD HISTORIC DISTRICT PUBLIC LANDS sign, which marks the trailhead. Additional parking is available at the I-70 exit.

THE HIKE

Some people say you can still hear the sounds of his violin from the lofty rock outcrop 1,250 feet above Silver Plume. While hiking up the 7:30 Mine Road to the Griffin Monument, listen closely. Do you hear the sweet violin playing of Clifford Griffin's ghost, or is it just the wind?

Several legends surround Clifford Griffin and his obelisk-shaped memorial. One tells the sad tale of the Englishman whose fiancée died the night before their wedding. Heartbroken, he traveled west to work in Colorado's mines, where he became the manager of the 7:30 Mine. Another version says he discovered the 7:30 Mine and became the wealthiest mine owner in the area. At night he played his violin from a rock outcrop above Brownville, just west of Silver Plume. One night the music stopped, and a gunshot rang out. Miners rushed to see what had happened and found Clifford dead with a bullet through his heart, suicide note in his hand.

Another report claims that Heneage (Henry) M. Griffin owned the 7:30 Mine. He summoned his alcoholic brother, Clifford, to manage his mine in hopes that a responsible position would temper Clifford's drinking problem. Still another tale reports that the brothers co-owned the mine and Henry shot Clifford to gain full ownership.

The trail to the Griffin Monument switchbacks up past various mines and tailings. When miners swarmed to Colorado in 1859 after hearing about gold discoveries in the Pikes Peak area, they spread out across the state in search of

Looking down into the town of Silver Plume from the 7:30 Mine Trail.

their fortunes. The mountains north of Silver Plume contained rich veins of silver. The first vein discovered was reportedly so rich that silver flakes broke off in the shape of feathers. The Silver Plume Mine started in 1863 and produced $500,000 in silver ore. The town, incorporated in 1880, probably took its name from the mine. The remains of the old Silver Plume Mine are about 800 feet above the first switchback in the trail. The 7:30 Mine, an optional short walk past the turnoff to the Griffin Monument, produced $2 million and employed a hundred men.

With mines dotting Sherman and Republican Mountains, trees quickly disappeared for use in mine tunnels, houses, and heating. Mud and snow slides became a major problem for Silver Plume and its neighbor Brownville. Newspapers of the time reported five to ten avalanches each year—one in February 1899 destroyed miners' cabins and killed ten Italians. A granite memorial in their honor is located in the Silver Plume cemetery. Spring brought rock and mud slides, loosened by snowmelt and rain. A series of slides from the tailings of the 7:30 Mine literally wiped out Brownville.

Peak mine production in the Silver Plume area came in 1894. By 1904, the seventy-two working mines had produced over $60 million in silver ore. Silver had lost value by 1907, but tourism became popular. Between 1907 and 1914, the Sunrise Peak Aerial Tram took people from Silver Plume to the top of Pendleton Mountain. From the Griffin Monument, you can see the remaining buildings on the peak on the other side of I-70. In the early 1900s, a train trip from Denver

Griffin Monument.

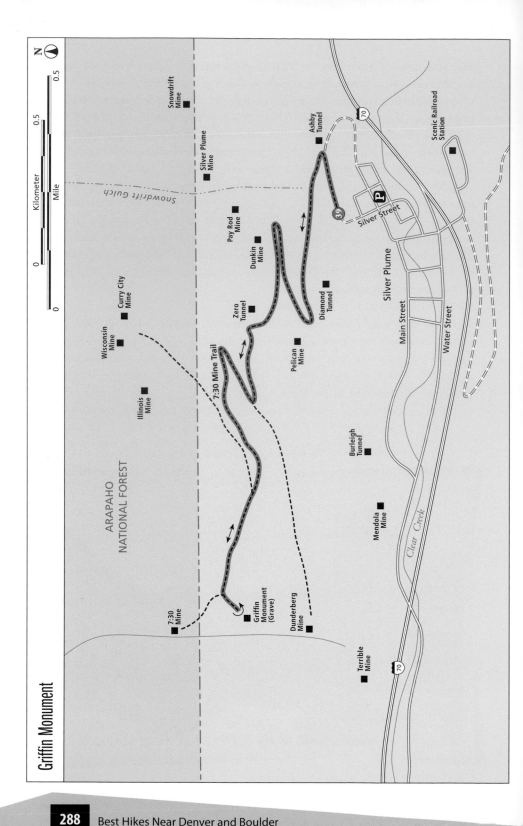

Griffin Monument

up Clear Creek Canyon and over the Georgetown Loop, including the tram ride, cost $3 on weekends and $4 on weekdays.

While hiking up the trail, notice the pine trees with five needles grouped together covered with droplets of "sap." These bristlecone pines can live over 1,500 years in Colorado. As you walk by these long-lived trees, think of all that they have seen during the mining boom and bust, and today's world. Maybe they know the true tale of Clifford Griffin.

The Sunrise Peak Aerial Tramway had twenty-six four-passenger cars weighing 300 pounds each that were carried on a 1.5-inch cable. Round-trip time from Silver Plume to Sunrise Peak was forty-six minutes.

MILES AND DIRECTIONS

0.0 Walk up Silver Street from Main Street and head right to the 7:30 Mine Trailhead at the top of Silver Street. Elevation: 9,175 feet. GPS: N39 41.88' / W105 43.53'.

300 feet A trail comes in from the left (west). Do not turn here. Continue straight ahead (east) and uphill on the trail.

0.5 The trail switchbacks by the tailings of the old Pelican Mine.

0.7 The third switchback. To the right is a nice view down into town and the train station for the Georgetown Loop railroad. Check out the bristlecone pine trees, with five needles in a packet, along the trail. GPS: N39 41.99' / W105 43.55'.

0.9 The trail crosses Cherokee Gulch. Note the avalanche debris on both sides of the trail.

1.1 The fourth switchback and an old mine building.

1.2 Cross the downed cables from an old mine tram. The fifth (last) switchback is soon after.

1.6 The trail becomes narrower beyond this point. Watch for low tree branches across the trail! Grates cover several old mine shafts.

1.8 A large cairn (pile of rocks) on the left (south), across from a metal grate to the right of the trail, marks the trail to the Griffin Monument. GPS: N39 42.10' / W105 44.43'. Follow the left trail downhill. Where the trail splits around a large boulder, take your pick—both trails lead to the monument.

1.85 Griffin Monument. Elevation: 10,285 feet. GPS: N39 42.08' / W105 44.46'. Return the way you came to the 7:30 Mine Trail.

1.9 Back on the 7:30 Mine Trail. Return the way you came.

3.7 Arrive back at the trailhead.

Option
Back on the 7:30 Mine Road, turn left (west) at the turnoff for the Griffin Monument and walk a little over 0.1 mile one-way to where the trail crosses Brown Creek. Two old boilers from the 7:30 Mine lie in the creek bed. Elevation: 10,500 feet.

HIKE INFORMATION

Local Information: George Rowe Museum, Silver Plume; 303-569-2562 (summer season)
Gateway Visitor Center, I-70 exit 228, Georgetown; 303-569-2405; georgetowntrust.org/gateway-visitor-center.html
Clear Creek County Tourism Bureau, Idaho Springs; 303-567-4660, 866-674-9237; clearcreekcounty.org
Local Events/Attractions: George Rowe Museum, Silver Plume; 303-569-2562 (summer season)
Georgetown Loop Railroad, Georgetown; 888-456-6777; georgetownlooprr.com

> 🌿 **Green Tip:**
> *Before you start for home, have you left the wilderness as you'd like to find it?*

Avalanches still occur in this area, although the hillsides are mostly forested. On March 23, 2003, after several days of heavy snows, an avalanche roared down Pendleton Mountain, destroying Silver Plume's water-treatment plant and reaching the edge of I-70.

Herman Lake

The popular hike to Herman Lake starts on an old sawmill road through thick forest. The trail then wanders through fields of colorful wildflowers, with spectacular views of the Continental Divide. Most of the trail doubles as a section of the Continental Divide National Scenic Trail. A last steep pitch takes you to treeline, where the trail mellows on the final stretch to Herman Lake, nestled in a bowl at 12,000 feet with Pettingell Peak towering above.

Start: Herman Gulch Trail 98 trailhead

Distance: 6.7 miles out and back

Hiking time: 2.7 to 4.5 hours

Difficulty: Difficult due to elevation gain and high altitude

Elevation gain: 1,710 feet

Trail surface: Natural surface trail

Seasons: Best July through early Oct

Other trail users: Mountain bikers and equestrians

Canine compatibility: Dogs must be on leash

Land status: National forest

Fees and permits: None required

Schedule: Open-year round but prone to avalanches in winter

Maps: USGS Loveland Pass, Grays Peak; National Geographic Trails Illustrated 104 Idaho Springs/ Loveland Pass; Latitude 40°: Colorado Front Range Trails

Trail contact: Arapaho National Forest, Clear Creek Ranger District, Idaho Springs Visitor Center, 2060 Miner Street, Idaho Springs; 303-567-4382; www.fs.usda.gov/detail/arp

Special considerations: Herman Lake is above treeline, with danger of lightning from thunderstorms. The bark beetle has killed many trees along the trail, so use caution when hiking in windy weather because dead trees may blow over. Bring extra warm clothes, including gloves. The ever-present wind gets mighty chilly above treeline, even in summer. Several avalanche paths cross the trail. Be aware of avalanche danger if skiing or snowshoeing this trail during winter. The trail is neither marked nor maintained for winter use.

Finding the trailhead: Take I-70 to exit 218 (the exit has no name). Turn right, then make a sharp right turn onto the dirt frontage road. Drive about 0.2 mile into the big parking lot. A port-a-potty is available, but no water.

THE HIKE

Herman Hassell, an early timber operator in the area, supposedly named Herman Gulch after himself. While timber may have been Herman's ambition, today wildflower aficionados consider this trail a "100 wildflower" hike because of the possibility of seeing around a hundred different flower species during peak bloom in late July.

After the junction at mile 0.2 with Watrous Gulch Trail, the Herman Gulch Trail climbs through a lodgepole pine, spruce, and fir forest above the creek in Herman Gulch. Willows, common junipers, fireweed, dandelions, strawberries, buffaloberries, and various other berry bushes line the trail. After about 0.6 mile, the trail levels a little, with white geraniums, arrowleaf senecio, monkshood, little red elephants, and cinquefoil blooming in the moist area by a creek. The trail crosses several avalanche paths that descend from unnamed peaks to the northeast.

As the summer sun rises higher in the sky and warms the ground, more wildflowers appear. In late June, blue Colorado columbines burst forth in the meadows. Various members of the gentian family; purple fringe; paintbrush in different hues of yellow, magenta, and red; daisies; Jacob's ladder; lousewort; clover; Parry's primrose; sky pilot; chickweed; sage; and chiming bells are among the other flowers gracing the trail. The path is generally well-maintained, with stone steps in places, although an occasional boggy area makes for mucky walking. Please walk through any mud on the trail, instead of going around it, to avoid trampling trailside vegetation, which widens the bog. A nice feature of Herman Gulch is that the trail climbs then levels out, so you can catch your breath before the next climb.

Ascending the Herman Gulch Trail through a rocky meadow below Pettingell Peak.

View of The Citadel to the west.

After about 2.5 miles, the trail climbs steeply for the next 0.5 mile. The trail splits, with the Jones Pass Trail and the Continental Divide National Scenic Trail (CDNST) climbing to the right to a saddle on the Continental Divide. The CDNST was designated by Congress in 1978 and travels 3,100 miles from the Canadian border to the Mexican border through challenging and primitive areas of Montana, Wyoming, Colorado, and New Mexico. The scenic route uses existing trails, like the Jones Pass Trail, whenever possible. Although many sections of the trail are completed, others need to be maintained, created, or rerouted.

The trail to Herman Lake heads northwest and continues steeply before it turns west on a bench and passes a little pond. You may find a snowbank still covering the trail in early July. The trees are small and twisted up here, and they tend to grow in a row in the direction of the prevailing winds. Known as *krummholz*, German for "crooked wood," they survive strong winds, blasts of ice crystals, and about a two-month growing season. The windward side of the organism protects the rest of the tree from the elements. *Krummholz* generally sprouts via roots from existing branches, the summers being too short to produce many seeds. Because any dead branches protect the rest of the tree, please do not use any wood from *krummholz* for campfires.

Plants and flowers are smaller at this elevation, too. Miniature willows, blue forget-me-nots, pink moss campion, bright yellow alpine avens, grayish-green sage, alpine phlox, and white death camas bloom in the rocky soil.

Herman Lake finally appears, nestled in a bowl beneath 13,553-foot Pettingell Peak. The Continental Divide rises over 1,000 feet above the lake. Water from melting snow cascades down to the lake in shimmering ribbons between willows and rocks. A few trails wander down to the right, but one in particular heads to a large rock slab, a great place to sit in the sun and enjoy a picnic.

MILES AND DIRECTIONS

0.0   Start at Herman Gulch Trailhead. Elevation: 10,300 feet. GPS: N39 42.15' / W105 51.26'.

0.2   The trail reaches a T. Turn left (northwest) onto Herman Gulch Trail 98. GPS: N39 42.19' / W105 51.08'.

0.8   The trail crosses the first of several avalanche paths. GPS: N39 42.53' / W105 51.48'.

1.1   The trail crosses a meadow. Look ahead for a view of Pettingell Peak and the trail above the trees. GPS: N39 42.73' / W105 51.66'.

2.5   The trail crosses a little creek. A nice log provides a rest stop before the trail starts climbing steeply. GPS: N39 43.26' / W105 52.95'.

2.9   Arrive at a trail junction. Turn left (northwest) to climb to Herman Lake. Jones Pass Trail and the Continental Divide National Scenic Trail (CDNST) head to the right (northeast). GPS: N39 43.37' / W105 53.28'.

3.3   Arrive at a trail junction. Turn right (northwest) down the trail to the lake. Elevation: 12,010 feet.

Herman Lake.

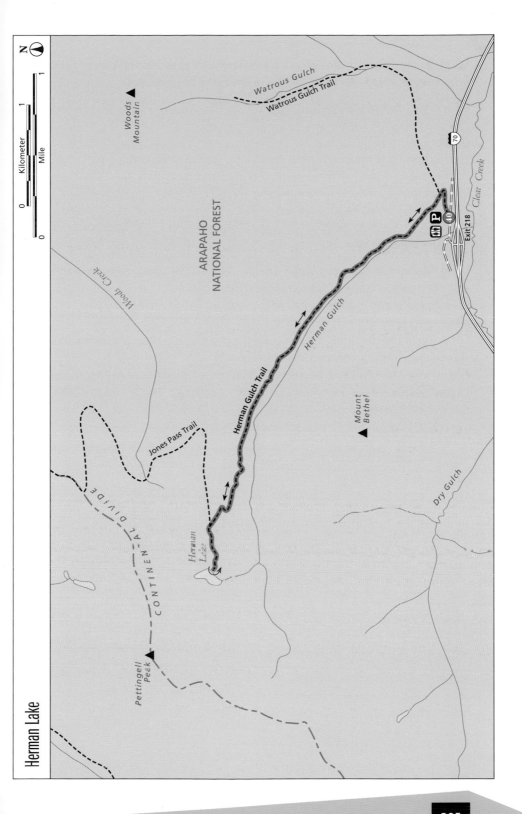

Herman Lake

3.35 Herman Lake. The big flat rock is a great place for a picnic. Elevation: 11,990 feet. GPS: N39 43.40' / W105 53.67'. Return the way you came.

6.7 Arrive back at the trailhead.

Option

You can take a side trip on the Jones Pass Trail to the top of the Continental Divide. Turn northeast at the junction of Herman Gulch and Jones Pass Trail/CDNST and hike for about 1.9 miles one-way, gaining about 1,065 feet in elevation to a saddle. The trail may not be well defined.

HIKE INFORMATION

Local Information: Gateway Visitor Center, I-70 exit 228, Georgetown; 303-569-2405; georgetowntrust.org/gateway-visitor-center.html

Clear Creek County Tourism Bureau, Idaho Springs; 303-567-4660, 866-674-9237; clearcreekcounty.org

Local Events/Attractions: Clear Creek County historic sites and museums; clearcreekcounty.org/historic-clear-creek-county

Georgetown Loop Railroad, Georgetown; 888-456-6777; georgetownlooprr.com

Organizations: Continental Divide Trail Coalition, Pine; 303-996-2759; continentaldividetrail.org

Continental Divide Trail Society, Baltimore, MD; 410-235-9610; cdtsociety.org

Honorable Mentions

E. Kruger Rock Trail

After an easy scramble up the rocky top of Kruger Rock, you'll get a fantastic view of peaks in Rocky Mountain National Park, the eastern plains, and points south along the Front Range. This well-designed and well-built trail opened in 2008. It winds up a grassy hillside, over some granitic rocks, and curves around, providing excellent views of the Estes Park area. The trail continues to climb, its switchbacks making for ease of elevation gain. Stone steps take you up a few steep sections. The final scramble is up a wide crack with good handholds and footholds. The top is rocky but broad—a pleasant place for lunch if the wind's not blowing.

Start at the Kruger Rock Trail parking area near the group-use area. Walk past the vault toilets and the picnic pavilion, then cross the road to the signed trail near the winter closure gate. Elevation: 8,430 feet. N40 20.46' / W105 28.39'. The top of Kruger Rock is at 2.0 miles, for a difficult 4-mile out-and-back hike with a 925-foot elevation gain.

Finding the trailhead: In Boulder, from 28th Street (US 36) and Canyon Boulevard (SH 119), head north on US 36 to its junction with SH 66. Turn left on SH 66 and drive through Lyons to the yield sign at the T-intersection (US 36 and SH 7). Turn right onto US 36 and drive 17.2 miles to the Hermit Park Open Space just past mile marker 4. Turn left onto the access road. The entrance station is in 0.2 mile; stop and pay the fee. Continue on the park road for 2.9 miles, passing various turns to different camping and picnic areas, until you reach the first turnoff to the group-use area and the Kruger Rock Trailhead parking lot. Turn left to the parking lot, which is down on the right. A short trail at the north edge of the parking lot takes you past the toilets and picnic pavilion. Cross the main park road and head up the trail. Bring water, as none is available along the trail. Dogs must be on leash.

F. Burro Trail to Windy Peak

Winding through ponderosa pine forest, the Burro Trail slowly and steadily climbs to Windy Peak, a rock promontory at 9,141 feet. You can return the way you came for a 6.7-mile out-and-back hike or make the complete Burro Trail Loop, which is also 6.7 miles out and back. Completing the loop takes you through some grassy meadows for a nice variety. A short section of trail wanders along lush Nott Creek.

Start at the Bridge Creek Trailhead bulletin board. Elevation: 7,800 feet. GPS: N39 50.79' / W105 22.68'. Go right from the bulletin board and cross the bridge over Ralston Creek. Follow the trail markers with burro hoofprints. The trail climbs a ridge, then drops down into Nott Creek. This part of the trail is multiuse. The loop part of the Burro Trail heads left uphill and is hikers-only. At the top of the loop, a spur trail heads left to Windy Point. After the junction with the

Mountain Lion Trail, which comes in from the right, continue to the left, climbing to Windy Peak. Elevation: 9,141 feet. GPS: N39 51.70' / W105 22.81'. Return the way you came past Mountain Lion Trail at the top of the loop, and continue straight ahead (a tad left) to continue the loop. At another junction, turn left on Burro Trail, which is once again multiuse. Return along Nott Creek, then climb the little ridge before dropping down to the trailhead.

Finding the trailhead: In Golden, from the mouth of Clear Creek Canyon at the junction of SH 93, SH 58, and US 6, drive north onto SH 93 heading toward Boulder. In 1.3 miles turn left onto Golden Gate Canyon Road. Drive 12.5 miles up Golden Gate Canyon Road (ignore all side roads) to the entrance fee station on the right and pay the daily fee. In 0.1 mile turn right onto Crawford Gulch Road. The Golden Gate State Park Visitor Center is 0.1 mile on the right and has restrooms and water. The Bridge Creek Trailhead is 2.2 miles past the Visitor Center on Crawford Gulch Road—the third parking lot on the left side of the road. An outhouse and picnic tables are available at the trailhead.

Looking across the Estes Valley from the Kruger Rock Trail to the peaks of Rocky Mountain National Park.

Clubs and Trail Groups

Action Committee for Eldorado, PO Box 337, Eldorado Springs, CO 80025; aceeldo.org

Colorado Mountain Club, 710 10th Street, Suite 200, Golden, CO 80401; 303-279-3080; cmc.org

Continental Divide Trail Alliance, PO Box, Pine, CO 80470; 303-996-2759; continentaldividetrail.org

Continental Divide Trail Society, 3704 North Charles Street #601, Baltimore, MD 21218; 410 235 9610; cdtsociety.org

Friends of Castlewood Canyon State Park, PO Box 403, Franktown, CO 80116; castlewoodfriends.org

Friends of Cheyenne Mountain State Park, Cheyenne Mountain State Park, 410 JL Ranch Heights Road, Colorado Springs, CO 80926; friendsofcmsp.org

Friends of Dinosaur Ridge, 16831 West Alameda Parkway, Morrison, CO 80465; 303-697-3466; dinoridge.org

Friends of Golden Gate Canyon State Park, Golden Gate Canyon State Park, 92 Crawford Gulch Road, Golden, CO 80403; friendsofcoloradostateparks.com

Friends of Larimer County Parks and Open Lands, c/o Bison Visitor Center, 1800 South County Road 31, Loveland, CO 80537; 970-619-4570; larimer.org/naturalresources/friends

Friends of Roxborough, Volunteer Naturalists, Trail Stewards, Roxborough State Park, 4751 North Roxborough Dr., Littleton, CO 80125; 303-973-3959; cpw.state.co.us/placestogo/Parks/Roxborough/pages/friendsofroxborough.aspx

Friends of the Front Range Wildlife Refuges; 303-287-0210; ffrwr.org

Indian Peaks Wilderness Alliance, PO Box 17382, Boulder, CO 80308; indianpeakswilderness.org

Rocky Mountain Conservancy, PO Box 3100, Estes Park, CO 80517; 970-586-0108; rmconservancy.org

Volunteers for Outdoor Colorado, 600 South Marion Parkway, Denver, CO 80209; 303-715-1010; voc.org

Further Reading

History

Crum, Sally. *People of the Red Earth: American Indians of Colorado.* Lake City, CO: Western Reflections Publishing Company, 2009.

Pickering, James H. *America's Switzerland: Estes Park and Rocky Mountain National Park, the Growth Years.* Boulder, CO: University Press of Colorado, 2005.

Young, Mary Taylor. *Rocky Mountain National Park: The First 100 Years.* Helena, MT: Farcountry Press, 2014.

Natural History

Benedict, Audrey DeLella. *A Sierra Club Naturalist's Guide: The Southern Rockies.* Golden, CO: Fulcrum Publishing, 2008.

Carter, Jack L. *Trees and Shrubs of Colorado.* Silver City, NM: Mimbres Publishing. Distributed by: Boulder, CO: Johnson Books, 1997.

Chronic, Halka. *Roadside Geology of Colorado.* Missoula, MT: Mountain Press Publishing Company, 1993.

Elmore, Francis H. *Shrubs and Trees of the Southwest Uplands.* Southwest Parks and Monuments Association, 1981.

Guennel, G.K. *Guide to Colorado Wildflowers. Volume 1. Plains & Foothills.* Englewood, CO: Westcliffe Publishers, 2004.

———. *Guide to Colorado Wildflowers. Volume 2. Mountains.* Second Edition. Englewood, CO: Westcliffe Publishers, 2005.

Kershaw, Linda. *Edible & Medicinal Plants of the Rockies.* Edmonton, AL: Lone Pine Publishing, 2000.

MacDonald, Dougald. *Longs Peak, The Story of Colorado's Favorite Fourteener.* Englewood, CO: Westcliffe Publishers, 2004.

Matthews Ph.D., Vincent, Katie KellerLynn, Betty Fox, Eds. *Messages in Stone: Colorado's Colorful Geology.* Denver, CO: Colorado Department of Natural Resources: Colorado Geological Society, 2003. Printed in Canada.

Mutel, Cornelia Fleischer, and John C. Emerick. *From Grassland to Glacier.* Boulder, CO: Johnson Books, 1992.

Nelson, Mike. *The Colorado Weather Book.* Englewood, CO: Westcliffe Publishers, 1999.

Stokes, Donald and Lillian. *Stokes Field Guide to Birds Western Region*. Boston, MA: Little, Brown and Company, 1996.

Zwinger, Ann H. and Willard Beatrice E. *Land Above the Trees*. Boulder, CO: Johnson Books, 1996.

Available at Visitor Centers

Bird, Isabella L. *A Lady's Life in the Rocky Mountains*. New York, NY: Ballantine Books, 1960.

Colorado Division of Parks and Outdoor Recreation, Roxborough State Park, CO: *Hogbacks and History,* booklet, 1999.

Friends of Dinosaur Ridge. *A Guide to Triceratops Trail at Parfet Prehistoric Preserve*. Lockley-Peterson Publishing, 2008.

Howe, Hazel M. *The Story of Silver Plume*. Idaho Springs, CO: Sander Graphics Printing, 1960.

Lockley, Martin. *Fossil Footprints of the Dinosaur Ridge and Fossil Trace Areas*. Friends of Dinosaur Ridge and University of Colorado at Denver Dinosaur Tracker Research Group, 2003.

Randall, Sharon, Tracy Dixon, and Patty Horan. *The Night the Dam Gave Way: A Diary of Personal Accounts*. Castlewood Canyon State Park, CO, 1997.

Sampson, Joanna. A *Glimpse at Eldorado's Colorful Past*. Colorado State Parks, CO, 2007.

Stevenson, Malcolm G. *In the High Country. Settlers on the Land at Golden Gate Canyon State Park*. Black Hawk, CO: Birdwood Press, 2005.

Hike Index